ACTING

In Person and In Style

ACTING
In Person and In Style

Fifth Edition

Jerry L. Crawford
University of Nevada–Las Vegas

Catherine Hurst
St. Michael's College

Michael Lugering
University of Nevada–Las Vegas

Boston, Massachusetts   Burr Ridge, Illinios   Dubuque, Iowa
Madison, Wisconsin   New York, New York   San Francisco, California   St. Louis, Missouri

McGraw·Hill

A Division of The McGraw·Hill Companies

Production Editor *Terry Routley*
Designer *Kristyn A. Kalnes*
Art Processor *Renee Grevas*
Photo Editor *Rose Deluhery*
Visuals/Design Freelance Specialist *Mary L. Christianson*

The credits section for this book begins on page 333, and is considered an extension of the copyright page.

Original cover illustration by Louis Kavouras

Copyedited by Jane DeShaw

Library of Congress Catalog Card Number: 94-72076

http:\\www.mhhe.com

Contents

In an era struggling with new respect for diversity and a heightened aware-ness of multiculturalism, our increasingly technologically-centered and money-driven society has a great need for a strong theatre, peopled with actors who are adventurous enough, courageous enough, committed enough, and gifted enough to remind us, through the practice of their art, what it is to be human.

Acting is a basic human impulse. When we observe children playing ''pretend,'' we can distill that this activity is more than fun and enter-tainment. It provides a very personal means of making sense of the world—a means of figuring out who's who and what's what. Through role-playing, a child explores what it might be like to be a doctor, a fire fighter, an astronaut, a mother, a father, a neighbor. Through a child's ''pretending'' to be sad, angry, or happy, the emotions are explored and a foundation for understanding is laid.

Increasingly in our culture, a child's creative playtime is being re-placed by more and more structured activity produced by adults. Time in front of the television, the playing of violent video games, participation in organized sports activities at even younger and younger ages can negate a child's basic instinct to explore the complexities of his/her humanity. As a child, I explored, imagined, and learned much through playing ''pre-tend.'' In this nonstructured make-believe, there are no stereotypical boundaries with respect to race, creed, religion, gender, or occupation that can be divisive and destructive to our larger identity as human beings. Society continues, by whatever means necessary, to define borders and boundaries, to enforce laws and rules, and to create codes of ''proper conduct.'' Consequently, human beings—both child and adult—who are by nature individualistic in spirit, find an increasing need to make sense of things, to sort through complexities of reality and truth, to explore human nature. As a people, we must find ways and means for as many as possible to live lives that are as fully realized as possible.

The teaching of acting must, at some point, address intrinsic human instincts and impulses. Not unlike the ''pretend'' play of a child, an ac-tor's art provides legitimate and healthy experiences for fun and enter-tainment, but also courageously holds up before human society a full range of varying images of ourselves as individuals, as communities, as cultures, as nations, and as a species. In this view, actors are servants of humanity. (In relation to the courage it takes to carve a meaningful career, considering the odds against that in our society, they indeed become war-riors to protect our humanity.)

Theater provides, allows, and encourages a structured haven for the exploration of the self. Because theatre mirrors our culture, we are often asked to see images of ourselves that are hard to look at, confusing to see, and frightening to consider. Yet, what better way to gain the much needed perspective of ourselves as we struggle to respect our differences and celebrate our commonality. By doing and seeing theatrical performances from or about different cultures, different nations, different points of view in our evolving history on this planet, we are best able to understand others, thereby enriching a larger and specific understanding of ourselves. Whether an actor is on stage, on film, or on television, in plays or musicals, traditional or nontraditional forms, his/her connection must remain grounded in a responsible understanding that he/she is a human being ''playing'' in front of other human beings for the greater welfare of all humanity both on and off the stage. There is a strong need for a more vital articulation of the significance of this experience.

Hopefully, our best actors can find financially sustaining, artistically rewarding careers. But we must not forget that, for many, the onstage experiences of nonprofessionals thrive in many venues in many communities. Ideally, the theater and all its practitioners—both professionals and amateurs—directors, designers, technicians, teachers, literary and business managers, administrative staffs, and at the heart of it all, I believe, the actors and playwrights—can help us as a society increase our perspective so that we can identify with and have empathy for all human beings.

This book, at its heart—because I have glimpsed the hearts of its authors—seeks to provide a basis for young and old actors alike, for teachers as well as the general reader, to dissect the complex and often mysterious art of the actor and the creative components of acting. For the young actor, it opens a huge new world of ideas and approaches to the study of acting, voice, and movement in a carefully organized structure. It also includes a historical perspective of acting throughout the history of humankind, which lays a foundation from which we can better project our future. For the experienced actor, its pages serve as a healthy dose of review, providing new insights and, at the very least, help in putting one's own acting experiences in a different perspective. For the teacher, it can provide the inspiration to unlock the creative instincts of the student who, on some instinctive level, made deliberate decisions to experience the art of acting—whether it be with professional aspirations or simply the exploration of a creative human endeavor. For the general reader, it opens the door to an appreciation and respect for those ''servants and warriors of humanity.''

Kenneth H. Washington
Professor and Director
BFA Actor Training Program
University of Utah
Salt Lake City

It is with considerable gratitude and pride that I expand authorship of this book for the fifth edition. My colleagues, Cathy Hurst and Michael Lugering, specialized in acting, voice, and movement, join me to continue the journey of this book, which began in 1976. I am closing my formal career in education in 1994; retiring to Emeritus status and working playwright.

Acting In Person and In Style approaches acting training at both the fundamental and advanced levels through the concept of personalization. Personalization is a process with its origins in the work of the great Russian director, actor, and mentor, Constantin Stanislavski. In this book, we define the personalization process as one in which the actor discovers and explores in the self, characteristics, qualities, attitudes, and experiences that are legitimate dimensions of the role being created. In this edition, we make a renewed effort to begin each chapter in Part 1 with the personalization factor as a launching point for specific work under investigation.

With this goal in mind, understand personalization is a visceral, primarily physical process rooted in the idea or theory that acting is doing. That is, acting is best described as "felt experience"—not merely a cerebral or an imagined activity. The tools of the actor are all located in the being, or body in action. Action implies movement activity: thinking, feeling, and speaking. Visceral or felt experience—the basis of all personalization—includes autobiographical recall, observation, sensory activity, and imagination, but it is not limited to any one of these things.

In simplest terms, the actors locate the accumulated experiences of life relative to the role being created. Where the person and the role are similar, and direct equations can be associated, the creative acting task is vastly simplified because all the actor must do is be natural—avoiding what is best described as "neon acting," or "forced action/activity." Personalized work is rarely artificial because it is founded on known, visceral, physical, and felt experiences. Such experiences are easily and vividly recalled. The person or actor is obviously well acquainted with his or her own comfortable experience—experience equated to that which is undergone by the character.

Thus, the actor often automatically knows what to do or how to say something because the associative life experience has provided the teaching. What the actor will discover (and frequently, it is a surprising discovery) is that nearly anything a character in a play says or does has a personal life equation to draw upon. In a word, the best personalized acting appears to be nonacting! The actor seems to be the role. In fact, the actor is merely doing what comes naturally from personalized experience in life!

Finally, I would like to say a closing thank you to my family and friends, students, colleagues, and all others who contributed to editions one through four. With that, I close my contribution to this Preface and pass the torch to my coauthors, Cathy and Michael, to comment upon the fifth edition.

Jerry L. Crawford

It is with great pleasure and a genuine sense of honor that we add our names to *Acting In Person and In Style,* Fifth Edition. It is our greatest hope that we will carry the "torch" with the same dignity, respect, knowledge, and uncompromising integrity with which Dr. Jerry L. Crawford has carried it during his tenure as a master teacher, playwright, and scholar. Our heartfelt thanks and best wishes to Dr. Crawford as he assumes an active life outside the halls of academia. He will be greatly missed.

The process of collaborating on a book, like the process of producing a play, is largely give and take. We don't assume to have all the answers, but rather questions about the process that excites, unlocks, and frees an actor. We hope that through the writing of this book, the training of our students, and the creating of theatre we will learn some collective truth about our tentative and fragile humanity. As authors, we agree to disagree—passionately. We encourage our students to question, wonder, dream, and demand new ways, methods, and processes as they take their own journeys and develop a personal aesthetic. We expect no less from you. This book is descriptive of our experience and not prescriptive of set rules and standards for teaching and training the actor. Where it is useful to you, we are naturally delighted and proud. In places, we concede our experience as teachers, students, and human beings may have brought us to different conclusions about the art of acting, its training, and perhaps our perspective on life itself. Again, let's agree to disagree, but continue together to create a type of theatre that demands, questions, teaches, and reveals our commonality as well as our diversity.

Longtime users of *Acting In Person and In Style* will notice the fifth edition differs significantly from previous editions. We are proud of these changes. The majority of the changes occur in Part 1, "Acting in Person," while Part 2, "Acting in Style," remains largely unchanged.

The changes in Part 1 reflect what we as coauthors feel is a more comprehensive and flexible text designed to serve both the serious acting student and the general student. While the book maintains its theoretical base in the importance of "acting in person," with its strong emphasis on felt experience, added importance is placed on the integration of acting, voice, and movement.

These new changes reflect contemporary trends in the training of acting. In particular, you will find innovative and nontraditional approaches to voice and movement training. Whenever possible, voice and movement training is explored in the context of organic human behavior, which is designed to serve the needs of the individual and the actor in the context of the dramatic moment. The process-oriented approach produces an awareness and sensitivity emphasizing posture, gesture, elocution, projection, and external manipulation of the body and voice to produce a desired result.

In many instances a new vocabulary has been adopted to describe more completely the experience of the actor, rather than the spectator. In particular, the "Centering," "Freeing," "Speaking," and "Doing and Feeling" chapters begin with the concept of physical, mental, and psychological release guided by self-discovery and experiential learning. Consequently, we feel the link between the "Acting in Person" section and the "Acting in Style" section is stronger and more coherent.

You will notice there are only nine chapters in Part 1 instead of the ten found in previous editions. While we mourn the loss of balance with ten chapters in both Parts 1 and 2, we rejected symmetry in hopes of what we strongly feel is a more logical and coherent Part 1. From our perspective, it is not less, but more.

In addition, all the scenes for practice study have been removed. As teachers we found we did not use them. The process of searching to find an appropriate scene is an important part of the educational process. We encourage you to send your students to the library or bookstore to seek for playwrights, plays, scenes, monologues, and speeches. We also fear publishing a scene outside the context of the whole play may lead to a process, and a way of working we do not wish to condone or encourage. It is imperative your students have a copy of the whole play in hand during scene study.

You will also find the chapters have been renamed in a manner we feel is more descriptive of "process" rather than "subject." As a result there has been an overall restructuring. Many exercises have been moved from one chapter to another, some have been omitted, and many new ones have been added in their place.

We would like to acknowledge our indebtedness to influential trainers who have preceded us, including F. M. Alexander, Moshe Feldenkrais, Sanford Meisner, H. Wesley Balk, Kristin Linklater, and Constantin Stanislavski. In addition, this book has been influenced by recent studies in psychology, in particular, holistic approaches to mind and body integration, methods of gestalt therapy, and principles of motor learning.

We are especially grateful to the following people, who so generously gave their time, professional ability, and inspiration to *Acting in Person and in Style,* Fifth Edition: Louis Kavouras, for his artistic work on the new graphics and illustrations; Kenneth Washington, for his Foreword to the Fifth Edition; the UNLV faculty, in particular, Linda McCollum, Bob Brewer, and Dr. Jeff Koep; our undergraduate performance students; our

Master students, Jay Duffer, Stacey Plaskett, Elizabeth Brownlee, Paul Truckey, Gerry Schooler, Edward Barker, Kristi Smith, Maura Knowles, Andrea Emerine, and Linda Pierson; and our supportive friends, Rusty Wilson, Ann Baltz, Erika Johnson, Jean-Louis Roderique, Wayne Federman, Jeff Crockett, Michael J. Charron, Christopher Edwards, Don and Joanne Rathgeb, Peter Harrigan, Jim Peterson, Susan Summerfield, John J. McDonald, Paul J. Reiss, and Michael Johnson-Chase. Finally, we would like to thank the two reviewers of the previous edition text, whose comments guided us in the writing and revising of this fifth edition: Dennis Anderson, Mt. San Jacinto College and Dennis Henneman, Youngstown State University.

Cathy Hurst
Saint Michael's College, Vermont

Michael Lugering
University of Nevada, Las Vegas

It is traditional theatre practice to refer to both male and female stage performers as ''actor'' when making general reference to such artists. However, when specific persons or situations arise, we naturally use the term ''actress'' when referring to female performers. Such is the usage applied in books written about acting and the theatre, and such is the usage applied in this fifth edition. Generally, ''actor'' refers to both male and female performers whenever you encounter the term throughout this book. At times you will note specific reference to ''actress.'' The circumstances under description dictate the use. To deviate from this traditional practice would often create a very awkward syntax and, of course, extend the length of this book. Accordingly, I ask for the understanding and acceptance of traditional usage on this point from all of my readers. We must remember that *actor* is a professional term *intended* for its inclusive application to male and female; to constantly separate usage to *actor and actress* would in fact be sexist usage. We no longer say poet/poetess or sculptor/sculptress. The correct nonsexist terminology is *actor,* a fact recently pointed out to me by a leading editor in a leading publishing house who just happened to be female. Further, while the word ''him'' is used more often than ''her'' in reference to an ''actor'' during generic usage, the reference is not necessarily intended as masculine. Again, space and smooth syntax dictates.

A Special Note
to Female
Performers
and Readers

ACTING
In Person and In Style

ACTING: IN PERSON

I

Acting "is forever carving a statue of snow." So stated Lawrence Barrett, nineteenth-century American actor. The actor is at once the piano and the pianist. Acting is being; acting is believing; acting is feeling; acting is doing; acting is becoming; acting is illusion; acting is technique; acting is instinct; acting is craft; acting is creative; acting is reacting; acting is rehearsing; acting is game; and so on.

Traditionally and historically, acting has been associated with mimicry, exhibitionism, and imitation. The eighteenth-century French actor Francois-Joseph Talma declared that acting demanded "unusual sensitivity and extraordinary intelligence." Acting is based on the presentation of "emotion," which is defined as human feeling manifest as impulses toward open action. It follows that the actor must understand the working of the human personality and feeling. The key problem in acting is whether the actor should project the *illusion* of an emotion or genuinely feel that emotion. (Even if a role demands the portrayal of a mechanical robot, that robot will be imitating *human* behavior.) People have always found it difficult to define acting because the appreciation of it is greater than the understanding of it. Despite that difficulty, theorists and practitioners of the art of acting can come to grips with certain skills, processes, and disciplines germane to acting and performance.

What is the reply when the young aspiring actor asks, "What is acting?" Primarily, acting is a person behaving honestly, truthfully, economically, and comfortably in front of other people in a place used for theatrical presentation. Usually an actor performs a role written by a playwright; occasionally the actor performs improvisationally, that is, without a script. No matter what role or character the actor is called upon to create, or what activity he is asked to perform, the actor's person and personality are on public view and frequently exhibit what is typically private behavior. Such work demands physical and vocal dexterity, emotional stability, alert thinking, freedom of behavior, and confidence and trust in one's self and one's fellow actors.

One approach to the study of acting is to progress through theory and exercise work and to go rather quickly into what is popularly called "scene and role creation." Such an approach is designed to train the actor almost exclusively for the performance of roles written in a script by a playwright. While much of contemporary theatre is indeed of this nature, much of it is also improvisational. In improvisational theatre, a play script may evolve out of acting exercises. For example, Megan Terry's *Viet Rock* developed out of improvisational acting. It therefore follows that training in present-day theatre must be broader than it was in the past. Today, the actor must be capable of traditional performance of a written role as well as of improvisational stage behavior that can best be likened to modern dance or even gymnastics and acrobatics—at times with dialogue and at times without it. In improvisational theatre, the actor-performer also uses *himself* as a basis for creation of a performance. In both written and non-written theatre work, the task of the actor should be based upon economical, honest, and truthful use of himself and thereby eliminate much of the artificiality that pervades most acting.

The concept of personalization will be discussed again and again in this book and made specific in terms of its use in training, rehearsal, and performance.

Personalization has always been a feature of acting. Thespis, the acknowledged first actor of Greece in the sixth century B.C., undoubtedly used his entire person to the best of his ability in performing his roles. Dramatic theorists, actors, and directors have usually discussed the problem of how to utilize the actor's person in role creation and performance. Accordingly, it is necessary to review briefly the more important theories of acting to assist the actor in understanding personalization.

One of the earliest and most significant organized statements on the theory of acting was made by an eighteenth-century French theorist, Denis Diderot, in his essay *The Paradox of Acting*. Diderot clarified the famous paradox of acting, namely, that in order to move an audience the actor must remain unmoved. From Thespis to present times, this paradox remains the central problem of acting. How much genuine feeling, if any, must an actor express to move an audience? Diderot knew that at times actors will feel and create believable emotion. However, he also knew that actors could not possibly sustain such creation over long periods of repeated performance. Inevitably, emotion would appear artificial. This fact led Diderot to the realization that actors had to have training and certain skills to create the illusion of believable emotion. While Diderot did not provide a program of training for actors, we are indebted to him for one of the first clearly organized statements of the problem.

A nineteenth-century French teacher, Francois Delsarte, extended the influence of Diderot with respect to training and skills. Delsarte attempted to formulate laws of speech and gesture through diligent observation and study. Valuable and correct though some of his work was, it ultimately led to rigid and mechanical acting techniques.

Near the turn of the nineteenth century, the Russian actor and director Constantin Stanislavski developed a thorough system of actor training. After Stanislavski's death, his protégé, Yvegeny Vakhtangov, refined and completed the system. Stanislavski dedicated himself to the central problem of stimulating the actor's creativity. He based his system on lengthy and careful study of the actor's mind and emotion. He emphasized the use of observation, imagination, intuition, affective memory (sensory and emotional recall), combined with intensive vocal and physical study (these terms are defined in the Glossary). The concept of advanced psychology implicit in Stanislavski's work was heavily influenced by the French psychologist Theodule Ribot who in 1890 described the term *affective memory.*

The post-Stanislavski period has been marked by a variety of refinements of previous theories. Perhaps the most important contributions in this century have been made by Antonin Artaud, Bertolt Brecht, and Jerzy Grotowski. Artaud and Brecht were concerned with aesthetics. Grotowski is concerned with methods.

Artaud, a French actor and director, explained his theories in his essay "Theatre of Cruelty." Artaud believed that actors needed to develop an extreme use of gesture and sensory response in order to communicate psychologically with an audience rather than through words. He believed in assaulting the senses of his audiences through a variety of physical and emotive stage behavior, typified by violence and hysteria. Artaud labeled the actor "an athlete of the heart." He believed there was a kinetic or emotional relationship between the organic life of the actor and his audience. (Later, Grotowski was to refute this point by asserting that Artaud's aesthetics led to stereotyped or caricatured acting.) For further discussion of Artaud, see chapter 18.

Brecht, a German playwright and director, was probably the most influential theorist since Stanislavski. He labeled his plays "epic realism" and published his acting theory under the title "Small Organum for the Theatre." The term *epic realism* relates to both his plays and his acting theory. *Epic* refers to the ancient narrative poem used by Homer. The epic play of Brecht is rambling and episodic in structure. It stresses narration and singing as well as dialogue. Brecht also attempted in his plays to de-emphasize emotional impact for the sake of the intellectual message. He believed in intermingling historic events and persons with modern events and persons. He called this technique "historification." Brecht's acting theories stressed the use of overt theatrical techniques to "alienate" or "make strange" all dramatic activity, thereby reducing emotional impact upon the audience while increasing intellectual reaction. However, with certain characters in his plays Brecht was receptive to the kind of emotion advocated by Stanislavski. For example, the role of Mother Courage in the play of that name by Brecht demands acting that has an emotional effect upon the audience. For a detailed discussion of Brecht, see chapter 17.

Finally, Grotowski, a contemporary Polish director, has made efforts to rediscover the elements of the actor's art. Grotowski rejected Stanislavski because he believed that the Russian permitted natural impulses to dominate the actor. Grotowski rejected Brecht because he thought Brecht was too concerned with the construction of the role for its intellectual impact. To Grotowski, the actor is merely a person working artistically in public with his body. In a sense, the actor publically offers himself to the audience. The Grotowski system involves years of physical, emotional, and vocal training and inordinate concentration for the total commitment necessary to achieve a state of "trance." The actor searches for signs that express the sound and movement impulses between dream and reality. Through these signs the actor develops a special system of psychoanalytic language of gesture. Grotowski's criticism of Artaud concerning acting that leads to stereotype is a criticism that can also be leveled at his work in the Polish Laboratory Theatre. Grotowski's theatre reveals little emotion and as a result has gained little public favor.

As noted, the theories just described will be referred to again and expanded in later sections of this book. All or any of these theories may be used with personalization to assist an actor in successful performance. It is our belief that no one system or theory is correct or advisable. Intelligent actors draw from all theories or any theory that assists them in role creation or performance. What works, works! However, personalization is always basic to the training discussed in this book.

Acting: In Person and in Style begins at the logical point of departure in the training of the actor: with the actor's person. The initial step involves the actor's becoming comfortable with himself, or in learning how to use himself as the first acting tool.

Centering

1

. . . naturally and unconsciously put nature to work. And it is only nature itself that can fully control our muscles, tense them properly and relax them.

. . . you must still go on developing, correcting, tuning your bodies until every part of them will respond to the complete task . . . of presenting in external form your invisible feelings.

In ordinary life you walk and sit and talk and look but on stage you lose these faculties. You feel the closeness of the public and you say to yourself, ''Why are they looking at me?''

Constantin Stanislavski

On Centering

The first step in an actor's training program in personalization or self-exploration involves the process of centering. *Centering* is a psychophysical condition whereby an actor finds emotional, mental, and physical freedom. When centered, the actor is in what is called ''a state of heightened awareness.'' This state of heightened awareness is invaluable to the actor because it enhances thinking, physical activity, sensory perception, and emotional availability.

Acting necessitates speaking and behaving in front of other people, activities that usually create excessive nervous tension. The popular label for this tension is ''stage fright.'' Although the term *stage fright* refers to the fear that takes place when an individual is on stage, it is a similar fear one has when soloing a plane, appearing for an interview, attending an important meeting, competing in sports, or embarking on a dangerous trip. Fear becomes harmful only when we become afraid of being afraid. We fall into the trap of thinking normal behavior is abnormal; such thinking produces further psychophysical entanglements that distort honest expression. Consequently, excess energy manifests itself in the form of inordinate tensions through trembling legs, twitching knees, fidgety fingers, facial grimacing, shifting weight from leg to leg, aimless walking, and breathiness. All these events are signals that the actor is not operating from a strong sense of center. He becomes insecure, assuming that someone is judging him, thinking his appearance, manner, intelligence, emotions, and movement are inferior. The reflex response is to become guarded physically and emotionally. The result is unusually artificial behavior that deteriorates an actor's effectiveness and believability. Unnatural behavior is in direct opposition to personalization, which is based on comfort, naturalness, and believability.

A surprising and hopeful thing to note is that emotional tension or anxiety in study, rehearsal, or performance is not necessarily an unfavorable condition provided that it does not become excessive and create the unfavorable conditions just described. Centering prepares the body for better physical, mental, and emotional expression. The body recognizes the necessity for greater energy and prepares itself accordingly. The adrenal gland pumps adrenaline into the system; when adrenaline reaches the muscles, vitality is restored and reaction time is enhanced. The body releases larger quantities of sugar into the bloodstream, giving it greater energy with which to respond to stimuli. Breathing quickens as more oxygen is absorbed, and carbon dioxide is expelled more rapidly. As the pulse rate quickens, more blood arrives at the muscles, the heart, the brain,

and the central nervous system. The blood and the increased oxygen combine to make the brain capable of thinking with greater clarity, perceptiveness, and quickness. The muscles are capable of performing with greater physical effort; and finally, the central nervous system is capable of reacting more quickly. These distinct physiological changes produce a state of heightened awareness that enables the body to respond with greater clarity and vigor.

Centering is the process of focusing and channeling this heightened state into productive resources for the actor. People center in different ways. Actors use a variety of centering processes as preparations for both rehearsal and performance. Some of these methods are group activities, while others are individual exercises. Eventually an actor must discover his own personalized process of centering. Early in the centering process, actors find that they release with greater physical, vocal, emotional, and mental clarity and ease.

It is recommended that you begin the personalization process by keeping a journal to record your evolving exploration, experiences, reactions to the exercises presented, and perceived growth or progress.

The Centering Process

Exercise 1   The Semisupine Position

Lie on the floor. Allow your knees to bend so that your heels and the balls of your feet make solid contact with the floor. Your feet should be as close to your buttocks as possible without causing discomfort or strain. Your feet should be far enough apart to balance the weight of your legs with minimal effort, about shoulder-width apart is a good starting place. Give yourself permission to adjust the arrangement of your legs and feet as you explore a greater sensation of release in the pelvis. Position the knees away from the pelvis so that they are not falling in or out, but pointing towards the ceiling. Place several paperback books underneath your head. The books should be supporting the bony bump at the back of the head near the occiput—the point where the head and neck meet. Experiment with the number of books. If you have too few books, your head will drop down and back, away from the spine. If you have too many books, your chin will press uncomfortably on your throat. Your arms should be bent comfortably at the elbow with palms resting easily on the belly. Allow your body to distribute its weight evenly on the balls of the feet, the back of the pelvis, the shoulder blades, and the back of the head. Inhibit any unnecessary muscular effort as you allow the bones to release into the floor.

You are now ready to begin the activity of "directing." *Directing* is a mental activity where the mind guides the body in a neuromuscular process to a more efficient pattern of self-use. This efficient use of self reflects a position of *mechanical advantage* whereby maximum result is produced with minimal effort. A person functioning from a position of mechanical advantage is working from a strong sense of center. Your job is to mentally suggest that your body move in the given direction by releasing any inhibitory tension that prohibits the lengthening and widening of the body. Allow the neck muscles to release so the head moves away from the spine in a forward and up direction. The directing of the head should facilitate a release in the whole spine. As the spine lengthens, the back will respond by making greater contact with the floor. The knees should be directed toward the ceiling, which will provide a corresponding release in the hip and ankle joints. Allow the heels to release into the floor. Mentally repeat to yourself, "I allow my neck to release so that my head may move forward and up away from my torso as my back lengthens and widens. My knees are moving away from my pelvis as my heels release into the floor." Directing in this manner should be done for at least 5–10 minutes a day. It is important to remember that we are not relaxing the body, but consciously "directing" it on a neuromuscular level to a position of efficiency.

It is essential to inhibit the impulse to daydream as well as to avoid the habitual association of reclining with the activity of sleeping. After lying on the floor, experiment by repeating the process while sitting and standing.

Exercise 2   Centering and Breath

While lying in the semisupine position, direct your attention to your natural breathing rhythm. Observe whether you are breathing from your mouth or your nose. If you are breathing from your nose, allow your jaw to relax so that the breath may enter through your mouth. Notice how a greater sense of release in the jaw encourages a greater sense of release in the belly—the breathing center. Come into contact with your natural breathing rhythm. See if you can observe the natural cycle of your breath without manipulating it. You will notice that there is a need for breath, and the breath drops down to the belly and releases out. There is a slight pause and a need for a new breath, and the process repeats itself. Allow the breath to come and let it go. Wait until it comes back again of its own accord. Notice how the breath moves the body. Inhibit any impulse to force the body to move the breath. Continue

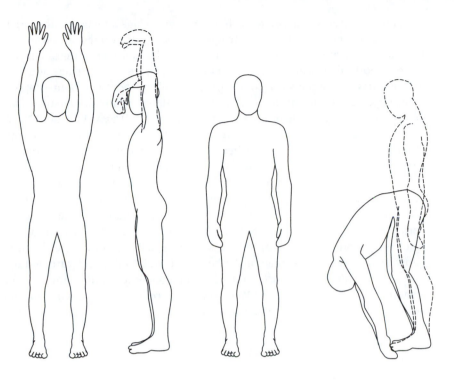

this process for several minutes. Now visualize the place deep within your belly where you feel the breath centering. We will call this place deep within your belly your breathing center. Travel with your breath down to your center and back up and out the mouth. Direct the breath to arrive in the front of the mouth somewhere between the teeth and lips (a very loose "f" sound). Map the distance your breath must travel from its point of entry, all the way down to the center, and back up to its point of exit. Allow any tension restricting the breath's journey to fall away as you continue to allow the breath to come, to let it go, and wait for it to come again. After lying on the floor, experiment with centering the breath while sitting in a chair and, finally, standing.

Exercise 3   Centering and the Spine

While standing, allow your neck to be free so that the head floats forward and up, away from the torso as the back lengthens and widens. Allow your heels to release into the floor as your knees release away from your pelvis. Allow the hand of your choice to take a journey upward so that your arm is fully extended above your head. Allow your other arm to take a similar journey. Allow your fingers on each hand to lengthen and extend up. Inhibit any unnecessary tension in the neck as the head floats forward and up.

Imagine five strings attached to each finger, two strings attached to the wrist, and two at the elbow. Allow the strings to support the weight of your body. Release the strings attached to your fingers while the other strings continue their support. Your hands fall toward the floor. Release the strings attached to your wrist while the strings attached at the elbow continue their support. Your upper arms will fall toward the floor. Allow the remaining strings attached at your elbows to release. Your arms will fall at your sides. Now, allow the weight of your head to release so that your chin drops to your chest. Allow the weight of your head to lead the whole spine, vertebra by vertebra, toward the floor. You will find yourself hanging upside down. Allow your whole torso to release while your knees move away from the pelvis as the heels release into the floor. Hang out. Allow the breath to be free. Inhibit the impulse to fidget. Slowly begin to build back up as each vertebra stacks on top the other like a series of building blocks. Allow the spine to support the body as all excessive muscle tension is released. Finally, allow the last seven vertebrae of the head and neck to float forward and up, away from the torso. Resist the impulse to fidget. Explore this new way of standing. What feels the same? What feels different? Walk around the room noticing what feels the same and what feels different.

Moving with a Sense of Center

Exercise 1   The Journey

Begin in the semisupine position. Once again notice the relationship of your spine to the floor. Yawn, stretch, release. You will begin a journey that will take you from the semisupine position to a standing position. Throughout the course of the journey, give attention to moving in an integrated manner. Allow thought and feeling to initiate the impulse for the spine and breath to move the body from the floor to standing. Begin by discovering how your body feels in relationship to the floor. Curl up, reach overhead, or roll onto your stomach. Continue by exploring all levels and planes of space that surround you. Continue all movement in a forward and up direction. Your journey is a progressive one where attention should be focused on the physical, spatial, emotional, and mental stimuli of the ''now'' as you move continually toward standing. Record your physical and emotional sensations.

Exercise 2   The Flower

Curl up into a fetal position on the floor. Imagine that you are a type of flower seed. Pick any type of flower that reflects in some way your thoughts and feelings in the present moment—a sunflower, a rose, a pansy, an iris, a hibiscus, a tulip, and so on. As you sense the inner impulse to grow, allow your body to expand as the seed takes its journey from germination to full bloom. Record your physical and emotional sensations.

Selective Readings

Aaron, Stephen. *Stage Fright: Its Role On Acting.* Chicago: University of Chicago, 1985.

Alexander, F. Matthias. *The Resurrection of the Body.* Edited by Edward Maisel. New York: University Books, 1969.

Conable, Barbara. *How to Learn the Alexander Technique.* London: STAT Books, 1991.

Feldenkrais, Moshe. *Awareness Through Movement.* New York: Harper & Row, 1972.

Gelb, Michael. *Body Learning.* New York: STAT Books, 1981.

Herrigel, Eugene. *Zen in the Art of Archery.* New York: Random House, 1971.

Leibowithz, Judith, and Connington, Bill. *The Alexander Technique.* New York: Harper Perennial, 1990.

Lessac, Arthur. *Body Wisdom: The Use and Training of the Human Body.* New York: Drama Book Specialists, 1981.

Sensing 2

How can we teach unobservant people to notice what nature and life are trying to show them? First of all, they must be taught to look at, listen to, and to hear what is beautiful.

We can use our inner eye to see all sorts of visual images, living creatures, human faces, their features, landscapes, the material world of objects, settings and so forth. With our inner ear we can hear all sorts of melodies, voices, intonations and so forth. We can feel things in imagination at the prompting of our sensations and emotion memory.

Constantin Stanislavski

On Sensing

The sensory system is composed of five basic senses: seeing, hearing, smelling, tasting, and touching. The sensory system is remarkably powerful in forming the basis of our perceptual understanding of the world. Consequently, an actor's work with his senses extends the personalization process. Every individual consciously or unconsciously selects or rejects specific sensory stimuli in his environment. Beginning sensing work involves developing a heightened awareness of what the individual is seeing, hearing, smelling, tasting, and touching and how that selective process influences reflexive response. After an actor's sensory perception has been awakened, specific application of sense memory can be applied to the acting process. Stanislavski stated that during every moment an actor is on stage, he must be aware of either the external circumstances that surround him (the physical setting), or an inner chain of circumstances that are housed in his memory.

Sensory awareness serves three essential functions in the process of creating a role. It assists the actor's truthful response with the physical environmental stimuli. It provides the actor with a greater sense of public solitude. *Public solitude* is an experiential condition allowing an actor to behave publicly (in front of an audience) with the same freedom, spontaneity, and naturalness he experiences while alone. It elicits a specific need for action and its corresponding emotional expression.

In addition, actors often call upon *sensory recall* to assist them indirectly in the creation of a role. Stanislavski identified this process as ''substitution.'' An actor makes a substitution when he recalls specific sensory experiences from his memory. Through this recollection, a visceral connection with a past emotion is experienced in the present. For example, remembering at this moment the sounds of a holiday, the sight and sounds of fireworks, or the taste of blood may produce an emotional response in the individual. In this respect, ''selective sensory recall'' serves as a trigger to activate feelings in the individual similar to those experienced by the character.

All sensory perception exercises extend an actor's creative development in the disciplines of centering and focusing. It is a mistake to leave this foundational work in the classroom, rehearsal studio, or theater. The art of acting cannot be professionally developed or maintained in a vacuum. It follows that the actor should extend the perceptions and awareness developed into every waking moment. Naturally, the details of occupation, family, and private life may not allow an actor time to practice these exercises frequently. However, if an actor insists upon some planned exercise work during his everyday life, eventually his subconscious perceptions may automatically continue without his being overtly aware of them. This is another way of saying that consciously and subconsciously an actor should be constantly intermingling his life experiences with the practice of his art.

Isolating the Senses

Sight Perception

The initial step in developing heightened sensory awareness involves awareness of the classroom, studio, or theater. Begin with visual perception. A heightened sense of sight involves more than looking at something intently, but requires specific awareness with directed attention to detail and subtle differences. Actors should become aware of what they see in their environment and how they respond to it.

Exercise 1 Seeing Far and Near
Stand in a central location and visually examine every aspect of the room from the ceiling to the walls and all objects and people in it. Take all the time you need. Register in your mind all that you see. Later, move about the room and visually examine everything at close proximity. Again register in your mind all that you see. Discuss your visual examination. Note what others saw that you did not see.

Touch Perception

When an actor becomes visually familiar with the room and its objects, the next step is to begin the process of perception through the sense of touch. Touch perception involves physical contact of any part of the body against or upon any other matter. Touch implies tactile sensory awareness through physical contact. The mind helps interpret the sensory experience of touch.

Exercise 2 Room and Object Contact
Begin by touching walls, furniture, and objects with the fingers and hands. Initially, touch only the room proper and its inanimate objects. Do not touch other actors. Interpersonal touch comes at a later stage of development. Proceed slowly and methodically, attempting to elicit internal as well as external sensitivity as you touch things. After the initial response with your hands, close your eyes and repeat the process. Now feel the objects with the side of the face, nose, chin, and so on. For example, your entire body should be pressed against a wall to gain total perception of it. Do not overlook any

The Glass Menagerie by
Tennessee Williams;
Suzanne Collins as Laura
at the Seattle Repertory
Theatre. Directed by Dan
Sullivan.

object in the room, using both open-eye and closed-eye touch perception.
Your tactile response should clarify the difference in surfaces and textures
of objects.

Exercise 3   Touch Recall

As another exercise in sensory recall, sit in a relaxed position, close your
eyes, and vividly recall both visual and touch perception of the entire room
and all its objects.

Smell Perception

Smelling is perceiving through olfactory nerves to obtain the scent or odor
of something. Smelling is strictly a sensory experience. It cannot reveal
the shape or quality of things. To receive the fullest sensory experience,
the nose, sinus, throat, and chest cavities need to be clear from congestion.

Crimes of the Heart, by Beth Henley, at the Golden Theatre, New York. (L to R) Mary Beth Hurt, Lizbeth MacKay, and Mia Dillon. Directed by Melvin Bernhardt. Photo by Martha Swope.

Exercise 4   Detecting Odor

At a designated time and day, each actor should bring a single object into the room with a particularly distinctive aroma or odor. The object must be concealed in a sack or bag (a plastic bag is best because it is relatively odorless). Blindfolds are used by everyone because sight remains the predominant sensory experience available, and in this instance, you should restrict it. The sacks should be opened and placed in a line; thus, you will not have to touch objects in order to smell them. Move from sack to sack, smelling deeply and registering the smell in memory. When everyone has completed the exercise in silence, blindfolds should be removed, and the smell of each object clarified and explored through discussion.

Taste Perception

Tasting is perceiving the flavor of something by touching with the tongue, utilizing the taste buds. Effective tasting is only possible when we are healthy, particularly without sinus problems, head congestion, or colds.

Exercise 5   Tasting

On a designated time and day, each actor must bring a minimum of three different kinds of fruit. The fruit should be arbitrarily exchanged. Taste the three pieces of fruit in sequence and register those tastes in your memory. When everyone has completed the exercise in silence, the taste of each object should be clarified and explored through discussion.

Hearing Perception

Hearing is perceiving sound through the ear mechanism. Effective hearing is possible only when the mechanism is in a healthy condition, unaffected by congestion or injury.

Exercise 6   Hearing

Everyone sit in a relaxed position. Either close your eyes or use a blindfold, whichever is most comfortable for you. Begin by trying to "listen" to silence (note that hearing is an automatic response, whereas listening requires mental concentration upon what you are hearing). Can you hear it? Your first perception will probably be that you cannot. Do not resist listening to the sounds. Try to perceive precisely what is making the sounds and register them in memory. Occasionally you will note with delight that there are moments without sound, and you will actually "hear" silence. After a comfortable duration of time, open your eyes and clarify and explore through discussion what you have heard.

Combining the Senses

Exercise 1   Sensing with an Object

Select a favorite and easily transportable object that you consider a kind of "extension" of yourself in your environment. Take a relaxed position in front of your peers, and show the object to them. As you do so, describe the object in detail, carefully noting how it feels, smells, sounds, looks, tastes, where you got it, when you got it, and generally what it means to you in terms of both utility and sentiment. Your honest comfort with this object should be demonstrated without any conscious effort.

Exercise 2   Specific Touching

Sit with your colleagues in a line of chairs and relax. The person at the left end of the line rises and faces the next person. Select some specific physical area of the person's *face, head, or hands* to touch and examine, basing your selection on the most natural instinct you have for touching that person in those areas. For example, you may have always wanted to touch a person's hair, chin, lips, or hands. This exercise will permit you to do so with comfort and trust. Proceed down the line of actors until you have made specific physical contact as just instructed with every person. As the first person performing the exercise moves past two or three people, the next person may rise and begin specific touching. Eventually, all of you will be engaged in the activity. Comfortable and directed physical contact heightens sensory awareness and increases trust between actors.

Exercise 3   "Blind" Sensory Experience

Place a blindfold over your eyes. Move carefully around the room touching inanimate objects and the structure of the room, trying to avoid contact with other actors. Remain silent except for breathing and movement sounds. Be extra careful not to injure yourself. Record the things that you touch and the feelings you experience. After the exercise is stopped and blindfolds are removed, sit with your fellow actors and discuss the room and objects touched and the feelings you experienced. Note the variety of emotional activity you underwent, such as giddiness, terror, isolation, loss, excitement, fear. Describe what happened to your breath during moments of trust, relaxation, or tension during the "blind" experience.

Exercise 4   The Mine Field

Imagine that the stage is a field hiding one active land mine buried beneath the surface of the ground. Crawl on your hands and knees over the field searching for the hidden mine. "Probe the ground" with an imaginary bayonet in the manner of a soldier; use the tips of your fingers to search for the "trip wire" that protrudes out of the ground from the mine. Search until your concentration is broken with the futility of the search or until you are certain you have located the mine.

Exercise 5   Barefoot Walk

As you move, imagine that you are walking barefoot on the following kinds of surfaces: wet grass, mud, hot sand, gravel, broken eggshells, a waxed floor, and a thick carpet.

Exercise 6   Weather

As you move, imagine that you are walking in the following kinds of weather conditions: rain, snow, heat, hail, and wind.

Selective Readings

Schafer, R. Murray. *A Sound Education: 100 Exercises in Listening and Sound-Making*. Indian River, Ontario: Arcana Editions, 1992.

Focusing 3

Haven't you felt in real life or on stage, in the course of mutual communication with your partner, that something streamed out of you, some current from your eyes, from the end of your fingers? . . . What name can we give these invisible currents which we use to communicate with one another?

Creativeness on the stage demands complete concentration of all the actor's physical and inner nature, the participation of all his physical and inner faculties.

Intensive observation of an object naturally arouses a desire to do something with it. To do something with it in turn intensifies your observation of it.

Constantin Stanislavski

On Focusing

Focusing is a fundamental skill in the art of acting. Focusing involves selective attention to what actors are seeing, hearing, tasting, smelling, and touching. When an actor's attention is focused on specific environmental stimuli, a creative state, which Stanislavski referred to as "public solitude," is invoked. As discussed in the chapter on sensing, public solitude is an experiential condition allowing an actor to behave publicly (in front of an audience) with the same freedom, spontaneity, and naturalness he experiences while alone. This specific directing of attention eliminates many problems that commonly entangle the actor's instrument.

The process of focusing is begun by selecting *a circle of attention.* Stanislavski placed great stress on circles of attention as a means of focusing the actor. By this he meant that actors must limit attention to specific areas in the environment with assistance from specific physical objects. There are small, medium, and large circles of attention. An actor directs his attention from one circle to another with corresponding shifts in psychological motivation. For example, a person tying his shoe has a relatively small circle of attention. A lawyer pleading his case to a jury would have yet a larger circle of attention. Finally, King Lear on the moor has a circle of attention of cosmic dimensions. By clearly establishing circles of attention, a creative environment is established where a condition emerges that reflects motivation and emotion.

After an actor has selected a circle of attention, Stanislavski suggests that his focus be further directed to a specific place of communion within the circle of attention. These places of communion may be roughly divided as follows: communion with the self; communion with physical objects in the space, including people; communion with the imaginary. Reflecting back to the previous examples, the person tying his shoe is in communion with a physical object in the space, the lawyer with the members of the jury, and perhaps Lear, on the moor, is in shifting points of communion with his internal struggle and the storm raging above him. Communion reflects an interactive condition with specific environmental stimuli that motivate the actor to physical action.

An actor whose focus is misdirected on activities and thoughts that do not further the action of the character in the scene encounters numerous difficulties. When an actor's focus is misdirected on matters of his personal life, his plans after the performance or rehearsal, there is a tendency to forget lines and to mistake blocking or movement patterns. Misdirected focus also leads to imprecise execution of stage business (*stage business* is defined as small, detailed actions of the body, often of the hands, such as handling a cane or smoking a cigarette). Misdirected focus offstage may cause an actor to miss an entrance. Similarly, misdirected focus offstage can result in distracting conversations that may disturb other actors who are on stage or about to enter. Above all, misdirected focus results in an unmotivated and emotionally empty performance.

Good habits become good stage habits. Throughout the day, become aware of your shifting circles of attention as well as the specific places of communion within your circle of attention. How do you move from one circle of attention to the other? What objects, people, memories, or fantasies hold your attention? This type of self-observation is essential in learning about the ongoing, unconscious process of sensory selection and consciousness.

Finally, and perhaps most importantly, work with focus involves interaction with objects, the self, and other people. In order to work with other people and ourselves, we must trust. Trust means possessing an honest confidence in ourselves and inspiring the same in others. The personalization theory necessitates that the actor confront and accept his personality and life experiences, using his strengths confidently and coping with his weaknesses in similar fashion. Hopefully, this awareness will increase with continued, conscientious application.

The Importance of Observation

Preliminary work in the basic skills of observation are necessary before specific and conscientious work on focusing can be explored. Observation exercises are designed to enhance an actor's use of sensory perception and will draw specifically on skills presented in the previous chapter on sensing.

Developing Skills in Observation

Exercise 1 Sharing and Observing a Simple Task

You and a partner are to select any one of the following activities:

peel an orange	tie your shoe
cut out valentines	glue a broken plate
shine a shoe	make a phone call
beat an egg	take a photograph
shuffle cards	set an alarm clock
seal and stamp a letter	polish silverware

As the first person executes the selected physical activity, the partner describes in specific detail a moment to moment verbal commentary on the specific method and manner with which the physical task is executed. Select additional activities taking turns observing and executing the task.

Exercise 2   Alteration

Stand facing another actor. Without speaking, take a few minutes to observe one another. Focus on what the other person is wearing, how he is standing, color of his eyes, and so on. Both partners turn away to make an adjustment/ alteration in appearance (such as switching a ring or watch from one hand to another, pulling one sock higher than the other, leaning to one side). The partners face each other again. Observe and describe any changes discovered. Repeat the exercise with a variety of partners.

Exercise 3   The Visit

Working in groups, select one of the following places for ''the visit'':

go to an airport	go to a bakery
go to a prison	go to a nursery school
go to a church	go to a cathedral
go to an art museum	go to a secondhand store
go to an auction	go to a courthouse

Do not share your selected place with members of other groups. While on the visit, select one specific individual performing a specific task. Notice particular details of the person, place, and activity. Upon returning to class, members of the group will recall the specific details of the visit. All recall statements must be stated in one of the following manners:

I saw . . .
I smelled . . .
I tasted . . .
I heard . . .
I touched . . .

Fellow class members are to determine the specific location, the nature/ manner of the person, and the specific activity being described.

Communion with the Self

Exercise 1   Soloing with the Self

Move into the semisupine position. Begin the centering process. Establish a circle of attention that includes only yourself. Tell yourself a story about the following memories or fantasies:

Remember learning to ride a bike . . .
Remember thoughts and feelings about your first-grade teacher . . .

Remember your first kiss . . .
Remember playing in the rain . . .
Remember being bossy . . .
Remember failing . . .
Fantasize about receiving a million dollars from a relative you dislike . . .
Fantasize about having one specific superhuman power (e.g., ability to
    fly) . . .
Fantasize about being reincarnated . . .
Fantasize about your life if you were an ashtray . . .
Fantasize about meeting the person of your dreams . . .
Fantasize about a new kind of world where . . .
Fantasize about your old age . . .

Exercise 2   Revealing the Self

Choose any one of the above memories or fantasies. Tell your memories and
fantasies to other members of the class.

Communion with Physical Objects

Exercise 1   Small Object

Place several small objects, such as an apple, a set of keys, a comic book, a
photograph, a coffee cup, or so on, in the middle of a circle. Direct your
attention to an object in the circle. Allow your communion with the object
to stimulate you to physical action. Was your physical action honest and
believable? Note your emotional relationship with the object. Note any imaginary circumstances with respect to who, what, when, where, and why.

Communion with the Other

Exercise 1   The Mirror

Stand facing a partner. Make eye contact and maintain it through the entire
exercise. Designate a leader and a follower. Without touching, the leader
performs slow and precise body movements, gestures, and facial expressions.
The follower imitates every movement of the leader precisely. Allow the
leader to change. Subtly and without discussion, play with shifting the initiating and receiving impulses from one partner to the other. Explore this
exercise with a variety of music.

Communion with the Imaginary

Exercise 1   Object Placement

Two actors face each other. One actor initiates the exercise by reaching
forward to pantomime the action of selecting a small cube (small enough to
fit in the palm of one hand). The actor takes the cube in the air and places it

Exemplary and intense stage concentration: Nancy Donohue and Stephen Joyce in *The Runner Stumbles* by Milan Stitt, at the Hartman Theatre, Stamford, Connecticut. Directed by Austin Pendleton.

somewhere in space, carefully and purposefully releasing it for the other actor to retrieve. The pair continues to place and replace the cube, using all the space around them—the floor, the wall, the doorway, the furniture. As the exercise continues, the instructor may change the weight or shape of the cube (object) by calling out new dimensions:

The object is oblong.
The object is alive.
The object is thin.
The object is heavy.
The object is sticky.
The object is a triangle.
The object is larger than the room.
The object is microscopic.
The object is zigzagging out of control.

The second part of this exercise focuses on the relationship between the actor and the object:

The object is a time bomb.
The object is a newborn baby.
The object is a switchblade.

The object is a football.
The object is a warm winter coat.
The object is an orange.

Continue to place and replace the object, allowing for increasingly personalized relationship interaction.

Circles of Attention

Exercise 1   Identifying Focus

Watch a videotape of a movie or a soap opera. Pause the video in specific places noting the actor's specific circle of attention and place of communion. How does the focus shift with respect to character intention and dramatic action? Select several photographs of people in specific environments from magazines. Note the specific circle of attention and places of communion. What is the person doing? What does the person want? How does the person feel? Note the relationship between focus and organic human activity.

Exercise 2   Shifting Focus

Create any one of the following spaces with the rehearsal props and furniture available:

a living room	a bus stop
a park	a bedroom
a bar	a car
an office	a telephone booth
an attic	a graveyard

An actor and a partner are placed in the space created. With the aid of their peers, they are to create specific given circumstances with respect to time, place, activity, character relationship, past history, and conflict. One actor begins by focusing on a specific physical object in the space. His circle of attention includes only himself and the object. The actor communes with the object. At a specific moment in the improvisation, the partner is to elicit the attention of the actor so as to break his communion with the object. The actors now commune with one another in the larger circle of attention. Finally, a third actor enters the space. The first actor changes his relationship to the object and/or his partner. Note any changes in the circle of attention. The circle of attention is widened to include the whole environment and all three actors in a shared circle of attention. One actor decides to leave the environment. The two remaining actors commune with each other. One actor develops a new relationship with the object, and thereby narrows his circle of attention.

Freeing 4

In order to express a most delicate and largely subconscious life, it is necessary to have control of an unusually responsive, excellently prepared vocal and physical apparatus.

. . . naturally and unconsciously put nature to work. And it is only nature itself that can fully control our muscles, tense them properly or relax them.

Always and forever, when you are on the stage, you must play yourself. But it will be in an infinite variety of combinations of objectives, and given circumstances which you have prepared for your part, and which have been smelted in the furnace of your emotional memory.

Constantin Stanislavski

On Freeing

The exercises in this chapter are designed to limber, align, and strengthen the actor's body in an integrated approach that serves the clear and theatrical expression of inner impulse. A natural extension of the centering, focusing, and sensing activities is integrated work with both the internal and external physical and vocal energies. This release work forms the framework for the freeing process, which is designed to liberate the actor's conscious and subconscious physical and vocal response to stimuli while simultaneously strengthening and developing the voice, body, and imagination.

The primary impulse for releasing the body and voice is breath. In this respect, any separation of the body and voice in theory is implausible in practice. The process of voicing is, in fact, movement. Communication between people begins with an impulse—a need to express the self—that results in a complex series of movements that ultimately result in phonation and the formation of thoughts and feelings into words and sentences.

The process of breathing and speaking in organic communication is an unconscious one. F. M. Alexander maintained that correct methods of breathing could not be taught, asserting that any attempt to manipulate the breathing process results in faulty functioning of the entire organism. Because breathing cannot be taught directly, the process of improving the functioning of the voice must be tackled indirectly. This indirect approach involves the removal of habitual and unnecessary tensions that inhibit the effective functioning of the voice-speech mechanism. When the voice and body respond in a reflexive manner to serve inner intention, the impulse moves the body and the voice. Only in a breathing exercise does the reciprocal happen. Consider the inefficient and contrived manner in which the voice would function if the process of phonation began by consciously moving the body to manipulate the voice, thereby producing the impulse. Below you will find a relatively simple account of the very complex physiological process of phonation.

The first step in the process of vocalization occurs when the brain registers an impulse for sound. In this moment the process of inhalation and exhalation assumes a secondary function aside from assisting in the providing of necessary oxygen for the bloodstream. The jaw drops slightly with respect to the amount of breath needed to communicate the desired message of the speaker. As breath is taken in, the vocal cords spread apart to allow the breath to travel through the *trachea,* or windpipe, into the bronchial tubes and reach the lungs. When air reaches the base of the windpipe, the diaphragm is activated. The *diaphragm* is a dome-shaped

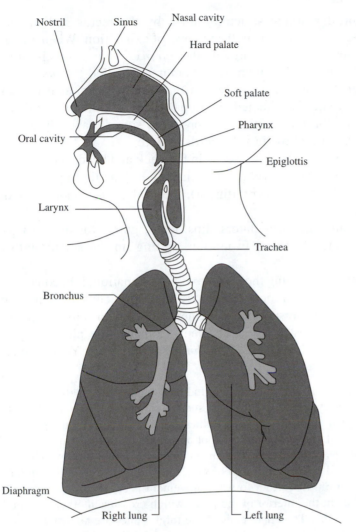

The vocal process.

structure that separates the chest and abdominal cavities. The size of the chest cavity enlarges, creating a partial vacuum. The inhaled air fills this vacuum and expands the lung sacs. The inhalation moves the diaphragm downward, flattening the abdominal muscles and the sides and back of the lower torso. There is an expansion outward, creating the appearance of an inflated abdomen. As the breath is released, the diaphragm moves upward and its dome shape is transformed into a cone shape, reversing the process of inhalation.

The diaphragm structure, aided by the rectus abdominis and other muscle groups, assists in the process of exhalation. When air departs from the lungs, it passes through the *larynx,* where sounds are produced. Housed in the larynx are two membranes called the *vocal cords.* These membranes serve as a bridge for the breath stream as it flows in and out of the mouth. As exhaled breath passes through the vocal cords, they are set in a vibratory motion that produces sound waves. The basic pitch is determined by how fast the cords vibrate.

Resonators, hollow spaces in the neck and head, serve as soundboards that reinforce, modify, and enrich sounds. The three primary human resonators are the pharynx (throat), the oral cavity (mouth), and the nasal cavity (nose).

Finally, the articulators (lips, teeth, gums, tongue, soft palate, hard palate, throat) are set in motion, cutting up the sounds into intelligent speech.

After examining the complexity of phonation, it becomes obvious that this complicated process is impossible for the conscious mind to regulate. Similarly with respect to movement, the subconscious regulation of this function proves the most efficient. Consider the physiology of walking (Cited in Todd, Mable E. *The Thinking Body.* New York: Princeton Book, 1937)

> The foot is arched both longitudinally and transversely, so as to give elasticity, and thus break the sudden shock when the weight of the body is thrown upon it. The ankle-joint is a loose hinge, and the great muscles of the calf can straighten the foot out so far that practiced dancers walk on the tips of their toes. The knee is another hinge-joint, which allows the leg to bend freely, but not to be carried beyond a straight line in the other direction. Its further forward movement is checked by two very powerful cords in the interior of the joint, which cross each other like the letter ''x.'' . . . The upper ends of the thigh bones are almost globes, which are received into deep cup-like cavities of the haunch-bones. They are tied to these last so loosely that, if their ligaments alone held them, they would be half out of their sockets in many positions of the lower limbs. . . . The smooth rounded head of the thigh-bone, moist with glairy fluid, fits so perfectly into the smooth, rounded cavity which received it, that it holds firmly by suction, or atmospheric pressure. . . . Holding in this way by the close apposition of two polished surfaces, the lower extremity swings freely forward and backward like a pendulum. . . . In ordinary walking a man's lower extremity swings essentially by its own weight, requiring little muscular effort to help it.

The complex process of moving and speaking functions most effectively under the direction of our autonomic nervous system. To this end, we will seek to liberate the actor's body and voice through indirect and improvisatory methods. When an actor's body, voice, or imagination is stiff, held, or underdeveloped, it lacks the dexterity and freedom needed to adequately express the essence of the impulse. Oftentimes, the physical and vocal release required of the actor are more demanding than most people routinely encounter. Consequently, freeing work serves to meet the larger physical and vocal requirements of large emotional expression. The freeing process requires a thorough understanding of the centering process, the importance of focus, and sensory perception.

Sounding

Exercise 1   A Return to Center
Repeat the Semisupine Position Exercise, the Centering the Breath Exercise, and the Centering the Spine Exercise presented in chapter 1.

Exercise 2   The Sigh
While lying in the semisupine position, relax your belly and allow your breath to drop deep into your center. From your center, feed in an impulse for a sigh of pleasurable relief. Allow the impulse to move the breath and the breath to move the body. Repeat this exercise in your own time. Explore sighing on breath and then vibration.

Exercise 3   Exploring Vibration
Feed in the impulse for a sigh. Imagine the vibrations streaming out your center like a river. Feed in the impulse again, allowing a stream of vibrations to release. This time, allow the lips to close lightly so that you can register the sensation of vibration on your lips. Luxuriate in the feeling of vibration. Explore vibration on different pitches. Tap your chest lightly to enhance your perception of its resonating function. Place your fingers in your ears. Sense the vibration in your whole head. Allow your teeth to gently touch and register the sensation of vibration there. Place your hands gently over your face, but not touching, registering the sensation on your palms. Pinch your nose open and closed and experience the contrasting sensation of vibration produced by this action. Gently roll your whole head and neck in a circular motion, feeling the vibration awaken and enliven. Finally, roll the vibration through your whole body as you drop up and down your spine as presented in the Centering and the Spine Exercise.

NOTE: A more detailed and thorough exploration of exercises similar in content and scope to those presented above are presented in Kristin Linklater's seminal text *Freeing the Natural Voice*. New York: DBS, 1976.

Sound and Movement Explorations

Exercise 1   Reflections

Find a partner and stand facing each other. Keeping some distance between you, one member of the team begins to initiate and explore slow, sustained movement while the partner mirrors the movement exactly. Maintaining eye contact, discover the space around you. Investigate different planes of space through leaning, bending, crouching, sitting, crawling, and so on. Notice how the breath moves in relation to your slow, physical exploration. Take turns initiating, following, and blending the impulse to lead. This exercise should begin in silence. After working in silence, add sound to the exploration.

Exercise 2   Throwing the Ball

Actors stand in a large circle at least an arm's length from one another. A large beach ball or basketball is passed from one person to another in the manner of a standard basketball pass. In random order the sender passes the ball to any selected receiver. As the ball is passed, a personalized physical and vocal response is released on any vowel that expresses inner intention. In turn, the receiver responds with a personalized physical and vocal response that expresses inner intention. Attention should be directed to the intercommunication between sender and receiver. Experiment with throwing the ball in a variety of ways: high, low, fast, slow, bouncing, rolling, spinning, and so forth. Allow the voice and body to send and receive all the physical and vocal dynamics reflected in the process of passing the ball. Experiment with many different vowels.

Later, explore working with the following sentences:

You are beneath my contempt.
I worship and adore you.
Don't just stand there, Stupid.
None of this is my fault.
I wanna go home.
It's my birthday.
I saw you.
One glad morning when this life is o're, I'll fly away.

Make up your own sentences as you pass the ball.

Exercise 3   Living Sculptures

Working in groups of two or more, build a human sculpture that reflects through physical action the emotional condition prompted by the following words:

love	misery	sickening
hate	nervous	painful
fear	giddy	heat

grief	tedious	cold
joy	lust	disgust
agony	hilarity	desire
terror	obnoxious	

Allow the living sculptures to breathe. Later, add sounds that reflect the thought and feeling of the sculpture. Finally, search for one word, a group of words, a phrase, or a sentence that expresses the essence of the person depicted in the sculpture.

Exercise 4   Drifting

When you are centered, begin to walk slowly about the room. Concentrate initially on your breathing; as you walk, periodically check for undesirable tension in the arms, neck, and shoulders. Be certain your knees are flexing easily and naturally. Wiggle your third and fourth fingers on each hand, which will relax those areas. Remain silent; make no physical or visual contact with other persons. Permit your eyes to drift aimlessly to avoid running into people but do not focus on anything or anyone. Keep your mind occupied with your breathing. As you move, your body is automatically molding your space by moving into it; that is, it is filling empty air with your mass, as well as making waves and abstract impressions in the air around you. In order to perceive your own energy and mass as they imprint themselves upon space, first try to perceive the ''space molding'' that occurs from the impact of other people as they walk past you. Turn your mind from concentration upon your breathing to a conscious search for the feeling of the waves in space from others walking by you. If you really concentrate, you can actually feel their energy in space as it strikes you.

Now shift your focus to your own body. You should begin to feel or perceive your own space. A sense of lightness will ensue; every movement will take on new sensitivity. Your body will feel increasingly weightless, without mass. Instead of an awareness of walking, you will have a feeling of moving and floating, a distinctly different perception.

The first benefit reaped from self-perception in space is a sense of physical and mental freedom. The body will be instinctively more graceful and the mind unburdened. This exercise can eventuate beyond the classroom, rehearsal room, or stage into a perception of the variety of spaces one occupies in all everyday living experiences.

Exercise 5   The Alphabet

Working as a trio, physically create the entire alphabet in space by using your body and voice to formulate each letter. Later, each actor works alone to write the letters of the alphabet in space, using different parts of the body and voice as writing instruments:

| the head | the hands | the knees |
| the elbows | the hips | the legs |

Exercise 6   Question and Answer Scenes

Select one of the following exchanges as a small scene. The actors may explore different situations and intentions for each scene. The purpose is to connect integrated sound and movement dynamics within the context of a short scene. Special attention on centering, focusing, and sensing will assist in the exploration.

1. "Please?"
2. "No."

1. "What are you thinking about?"
2. "None of your business."

1. "How do you feel about me now?"
2. "I am not sure."

Experiment with changing the environment of your scene. How is the movement affected if the scene takes place

in a crowded elevator?
on a mountain top?
in a church?
at a kitchen table?
in a bedroom?

Experiment with exploring the following external physical demands.
How does the addition of an external physical action dictate a change in inner intention? How is the addition of an external physical action reflected in the behavior of the character?

Your character moves quickly.
Your character moves slowly.
Your character does not want to move.
Your character expresses with only the right side of the body.
Your character sways.
Your character bounces.
Your character marches.
Your character is heavy.
Your character is light.
Your character is out of balance.
Your character moves in a low plane of space.
Your character moves in a diagonal direction of space.
Your character moves in circles.
Your character moves in triangles.
Your character contacts the other character.
Your character contacts furniture.
Your character moves with self-contact.

Selective Readings

Balk, H. Wesley. *The Complete Singer-Actor*. Minneapolis: Minnesota Press, 1977.

Davis, Martha. *Understanding Body Movement: An Annotated Bibliography*. New York: Arno Press, 1972.

King, Nancy. *Theatre Movement: The Actor and His Space*. New York: Drama Book Specialists/Publishers, 1971.

Kline, Peter, and Meadows, Nancy. *The Theatre Student: Physical Movement for the Theatre*. New York: Richard Rosen Press, 1971.

Laban, Rudolf. *The Mastery of Movement*. 3d ed. Rev. and enlarged by Lisa Ullman. Boston: Plays, Inc., 1971.

———, and Lawrence, F. C. *Effort*. London: MacDonald and Evan, 1947.

Lessac, Arthur. *The Use and Training of the Human Voice*. New York: Drama Book Specialists/Publishers, 1967.

Linklater, Kristin. *Freeing the Natural Voice*. New York: DBS Publishers, 1976.

Morris, Desmond. *Manwatching: A Field Guide to Human Behavior*. New York: Harry N. Abrams, Inc., 1977.

Pisk, Litz. *The Actor and His Body*. New York: Theatre Arts Books, 1976.

Rubin, Lucille S., ed. *Movement for the Actor*. New York: Drama Book Specialists, 1979.

Shawn, Ted. *Every Little Movement*. A book about Francois Delsarte. 2d ed. Brooklyn: Dance Horizons, 1963.

Speaking 5

After many years of acting and directing experience I arrived at the full realization. . . . that every actor must be in possession of excellent diction and pronunciation, that he must feel not only the phrases and words but also each syllable and each letter.

Our difficulty lies in the fact that many actors lack a well-rounded training in two important elements of speech; on the one side there is smoothness, resonance, fluency, and on the other, rapidity, lightness, clarity, crispness in the pronunciation of words.

Words and the way they are spoken show up much more on the stage than in ordinary life. . . . An actor should know his own tongue in every particular. Of what use will all the subtleties of emotion be if they are expressed in poor speech?

Constantin Stanislavski

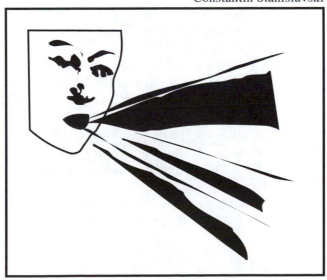

On Speaking

This chapter addresses the task of releasing language in a clear and intelligent manner.

Articulation refers to the manner in which the sound is organized into intelligible speech by the articulators. There are two basic groups of articulators: the movable articulators (lips, lower jaw, tongue, and soft palate) and the immovable articulators (teeth, gum ridge, hard palate, and throat). Clear and effective articulation is achieved by the efficient production of vowel and consonant sounds. A vowel sound is produced with the breath stream open, or uninterrupted or impeded by the articulators. Vowel sounds are produced by varying the shape of the oral passage. Consonants, on the other hand, are produced by stopping the outgoing breath with the assistance of the articulators.

Vowel sounds in spoken English are classified in the following manner: the shape of the tongue, the height of the arch of the tongue and the relative degree of the dropping of the lower jaw, the position of the lips, and potential length and duration of the sound. General guidelines for prescriptive standards of correctness with respect to vowel production are as follows:

1. The tip of the tongue is relaxed and touching the back of the bottom teeth.
2. The belly of the tongue lays flat in the floor of the mouth.
3. The vocal cords vibrate.
4. The breath stream is released from the mouth unimpeded by a lazy soft palate, which diverts vibration into the nasal passages.

Consonants in spoken English are classified in the following manner:

1. vibration
   a. unvoiced: /p/, /t/, /k/
   b. voiced: /b/, /d/, /g/
2. where the sound is made in the mouth
   a. bilabial (both lips): /m/, /b/, /p/, /w/
   b. labio-dental (lower lip/upper teeth): /f/, /v/
   c. dental (tongue tip/upper teeth): /th/
   d. alveolar (gum ridge/tongue tip): /t/, /d/, /s/, /z/
   e. velar (back of tongue/soft palate): /k/, /g/
   f. glottal (articulated in throat): /h/
3. how the sound is made
   a. stop-plosive—the air is stopped and then exploded:
      /b/, /d/, /g/, /p/, /t/, /k/

b. nasals—vibration is sent through the nose: /m/, /n/, /ing/
c. lateral—breath is released over the sides of the tongue: /l/
d. fricative—air is released through a narrow opening formed by the articulators: /f/, /v/, /s/, /z/, /th/

An additional special category of speech sounds are classified as *diphthongs*. Diphthongs are compound vowel sounds produced by combining two simple vowels and occur in the following words: ''hay'', ''I'', ''toy'', ''no'', ''ow.''

The best way to achieve clear and intelligible articulation is to examine the pronunciation, stress, and syllabication of a word in a pronunciation dictionary. Also, the study of phonetics will assist in developing skills necessary for clear articulation. The proper study of phonetics requires extensive time and detailed instruction by a qualified expert. Phonetics, like stage dialects, extends beyond the confines of an introductory chapter on speech. Special symbols, diacritical marks, and the phonetic alphabet must be learned in the examination of words and the process of voice production. (For example, the phonetic symbol [æ] keys to the letter ''a'' in the word ''at'' [æ].) For further, detailed study, refer to books in the Selective Reading list at the conclusion of this chapter.

On Being Heard

When an actor is dealing with spoken words, sentences, and thoughts, the foremost task is to make the audience both hear the words and understand the meaning behind them. The most believable characterization work, the finest emotional creativity, and the most striking interpretation will not suffice if the entire audience cannot hear and understand the actor. Note the distinction between hearing and understanding. First of all, the voice must be heard, that is, the sound of the voice must be fully released to everyone listening. Second, the audience must understand what it hears. For example, a strong, loud voice may carry sound to the back of a 2,000-seat auditorium, but if that sound is slurred or if words are pronounced incorrectly, the sound will be unintelligible.

Invariably, problems with unintelligibility manifest themselves in two common scenarios. Usually, there is some confusion in each of these areas. First and foremost, effective vocal production is directly related to the centering, focusing, and freeing work presented earlier. Second, specific acting choices may be in need of evaluation. Is it possible to redefine intention and thereby produce a physical/vocal action that serves both the

Much Ado About Nothing by William Shakespeare. JoAnn Johnson Patton as Beatrice and John H. Reese as Benedick at the Utah Shakespearean Festival. Directed by Leslie Reidel. Photograph by Boyd D. Redington.

demands of personalization and the physical demands of filling the space? Louder is an external manipulation of the instrument not grounded in inner intention. Consequently, when an actor is given a note to be louder, it is essential that he reexamine his psychological motivation with respect to making the vocal adjustment. A blocked voice is primarily caused by blocked emotions, and poor articulation is a by-product of muddy and unclear thinking. When given voice/speech notes, it is always wise to begin by reviewing the entire acting process. Somewhere along the way, essential steps were missed. In this respect, all voice problems are essentially acting problems. The insightful actor will always attempt to solve all acting problems in an integrated manner.

All of this advice presupposes that conscientious work on centering, focusing, and freeing the body has been a part of the actor's ongoing process and has developed to a mature level that merits application to the process of creating a role. If an actor cannot be heard at the audition, there is little or no reason to believe he will be able to be heard during the performance. The body cannot be fully centered, focused, and freed in a four-week rehearsal.

On Projection

The word "projection" has fallen out of fashion largely due to better training and understanding of the functioning of the voice-speech mechanism. With respect to voice and speech training, there are so many myths, it is often difficult to find healthy and helpful solutions. For example, the diaphragm is a muscle that is not under voluntary control. However, the action of the diaphragm can be inhibited or interrupted by muscles surrounding it in the abdomen. Yet, actors, directors, and even teachers of voice are fond of talking about moving the diaphragm or "projecting from the diaphragm" as if it were something within their conscious control. The only methods to insure effective functioning of the diaphragm are to release the muscles inhibiting its natural and autonomous inclination to serve the impulse of speech. Here again, centering, focusing, and freeing become the foundation of the actor's craft.

The word "project," though still used, regularly sets up patterns of holding in the throat and tightening in the belly as the actor, desperate to be heard, works harder on a conscious level. Good voice/speech reflects a position of mechanical advantage whereby maximum result is produced with minimum effort. In short, by asserting less muscular effort, the body releases to find natural resonance. The "less is more" approach to being heard is a more effective and logical approach than attempting to "throw" the voice to the back of the house. When an actor projects, he has locked himself into a vocal mode that is unable to respond to the subtle complexities and nuances of thought, feeling, and intention. The goal is never to hear the actor's voice, but rather to hear the character living, breathing, and speaking through his open, free, centered, focused instrument.

Developing Skills

Exercise 1 Preparations
Warming up the face:

yawn
lift the upper lip
lift the lower lip
frown
smile
pull the lower lip
pull the upper lip
flutter the lips
knit your eyebrows
wrinkle up your nose

make a figure eight with your tongue
lick your lips
kiss the air
clean teeth with your tongue
swallow
touch the tip of your tongue to your nose
touch the tip of your tongue to your chin
wrinkle your forehead
slap your face
massage your face
tighten all the muscles of your face
yawn and sigh

Exercise 2   Vowel Sounds
Repeat each of the groups of words. Pay particular attention to vowel length.

mee	may	my	mo	moo
tee	tay	tie	toe	too
we	way	why	woe	woo
he	hey	high	ho	who
Dee	day	die	doe	do
Lee	lay	lie	low	Lou
she	shay	shy	show	shoe

Exercise 3   Diphthong Drill
Practice clear use of diphthongs in the following words:

ate	eye	oy	oh	how
jay	sigh	boy	go	cow
dismay	fly	toy	snow	sow
day	die	annoy	throw	vow
stay	sky	enjoy	glow	pow
play	July	employ	woe	drown
gray	defy	coin	doe	town
cliché	guy	broil	row	house

Exercise 4   Gibberish
Working in small groups, engage in the following conversations using only vowel and diphthong sounds to communicate intention:

1. have an argumentative discussion
2. gossip about your teacher
3. tell a secret
4. lie
5. tell a joke
6. give directions

7. apologize
8. defend an important position
9. tell a bedtime story

Exercise 5   Tongue Twisters

Practice the following difficult phrases and sentences individually and as a choral group; increase tempo or speed as you repeat the exercise:

1. Red leather, yellow leather.
2. Big bad bears bleed blue blood.
3. Rubber baby buggy bumpers.
4. Fuzzy Wuzzy wasn't fuzzy, was he?
5. Peter Piper picked a peck of pickled peppers.
6. Sally Sue sells seashells by the seashore.
7. Slippery snake, slithery snake.
8. Thistles whistle as missiles sizzle.
9. Cora Clayworth cooked curly cabbage in copper kettles.
10. Oliver Oodle toodled the stroodle as he strolled with his poodle.

Exercise 6   Consonant Gibberish

Working in small groups, engage in the conversations listed in Exercise 4 using vowels and the following consonant combinations to communicate your intention:

/t/, /d/
/s/, /z/
/k/, /g/
/f/, /v/
/p/, /b/
/sh/, /zh/
/ch/, /j/

Phrasing

Phrasing is speaking two or more words that comprise a pattern of thought or a unit of sense. Clear and intelligible articulation enhance an actor's phrasing. Despite the dictates of iambic pentameter, Hamlet's famous line "To be or not to be, that is the question . . ." has almost infinite possibilities for vocal phrasing. Consider the following possibilities:

To be // or // not to be // that is the question
To be or not to be // that // is the question
To be or not to // be // that is the question
To // be // or // not // to // be // that is the question
To be or not to be // that // is // the // question
To be or not to be that is the question

Exercise 1   Exploring Phrasing

Find at least three different methods of phrasing for each of the following lines:

Note: All punctuation has been omitted except periods.

I left no ring with her what means this lady.

Twelfth Night

Now is the winter of our discontent.

Richard III

I suppose I could start by telling you about my lousy childhood and all that Davey Copperfield kinda crap.

Catcher in the Rye

I saw the storm coming but I didn't think it would burst so soon. Oh what an avalanche of hate you've thrown on my heart. But I'm not old yet. I have five chains for you and this house my father built. So not even the weeds will know of my desolation.

House of Bernada Alba

It's well you know what call I have. It's well you know it's a lonesome thing to be passing small towns with the light shining sideways when the night is down or going in strange places with a dog noising before you and a dog noising behind or drawn to the cities where you'd hear a voice kissing and talking deep love in every shadow of the ditch and passing on with an empty hungry stomach falling from your heart.

Playboy of the Western World

That's right. I owe you an apology. I owe you all an apology. Can't imagine what came over me getting all bitchy like that. Please forgive me. It has to be the vodka no question about it. Goodness my head's just whirling. Let me sit down a moment and then we'll go. I'll buy you all a lovely big meal what'cha say?

The Auction Tomorrow

Context and Vocal Variety

Phrasing is inextricably linked to context. *Context* refers to the possibilities of meaning for each word in each sentence and extends to the possibilities of meaning for each sentence within each paragraph (or speech) in a play. To discover context, an actor must understand the placement of each speech within each scene and, in turn, within an entire play. Proper analysis of character, thought, and structure in a play will permit an actor to determine how best to phrase dialogue. How actors phrase that line determines their interpretation. The importance of contextual under-standing cannot be overemphasized if we are to apply effective phrasing and vocal technique. The clearest and most pleasant speaking voice is rendered worthless if words and speeches are not placed into context.

Context is largely communicated through vocal variety. The ability to modulate, or vary, voice within a pleasant tone range creates a flexible vocal variety, as opposed to a monotone. A flexible voice creates vocal variety by effective use of pitch, range, inflection, intensity, rate or tempo, pause, and rhythm.

Definition of Terms

Pitch and Range

Pitch is how high or how low the voice sounds. Range is the distance measured in notes between the lowest and highest pitch.

Inflection

Inflection is the rise and fall in pitch of the voice.

Intensity

The strength of feeling involved in the quality of speaking combined with manner.

Rate or Tempo

The speed with which one speaks.

Emphasis

Emphasis refers to the amount of stress, force, or vocal weight placed upon a particular word or words within a sentence.

Pause

A brief suspension of the voice, or a hesitation in speech.

Rhythm

The alteration of silence, sound, strength, and weakness in speech.

Vocal Variety in Context

The following exercises combine skills in phrasing, context, and vocal variety to communicate intention. Technical adjustments in vocal delivery such has "louder," "pause," "faster," "with feeling," "raise the energy," often lead to a stilted, mechanical delivery devoid of thought, feeling, and intention. It is best to look to the given circumstances, environmental stimuli, character, scene partner, text, and intention to produce the desired vocal variety.

All the following exercises will use the text listed below as a vehicle for exploring phrasing, context, and vocal variety.

1. Don't go in there.
2. I saw you.
3. I need it.
4. It's coming under the door.
5. I've been wondering about what we were talking about yesterday, and now everything seems perfectly clear to me.
6. When you keep talking and talking, I get so tired of listening I feel like my head will explode, so I've been really busy just pretending you're not here and like I never met you and we have no real relationship at all. Which I know is a pretty lousy thing to do and all. But sometimes, when I am honest I realize that being a nice and polite person . . . is well frankly too much work.
7. When in disgrace and fortune in men's eyes
   I all alone beweep my outcast state
   and trouble deaf heaven with my bootless cries
   and look upon myself and curse my fate . . .
   Shakespeare

Exercise 1   Exploring Character
Communicate all of the phrases listed above as each of the following people:

a bored student
a wild, crazy woman/man
a soldier
a fortune-teller
a priest/nun
a frightened child
a self-absorbed actress/actor
a reference librarian

Exercise 2   Exploring Environment

Communicate all of the phrases listed above, allowing the environment to affect your delivery:

a crowded elevator
a ledge on a high building
in a church service
in a large, wide-open field
at a rock concert
while waiting in a long line
in a fancy restaurant

Exercise 3   Exploring the Senses

Communicate all of the phrases listed above with a heightened sensory awareness of the following conditions:

you are hot and sweaty
your feet are cold
you smell a body odor
you hear a thunderstorm
you taste licorice
you touch a cold windowpane
you feel dizzy
you have a headache
you feel hung over
you smell bread baking
you hear church bells ringing

Exercise 4   Exploring Your Partner

Communicate each of the above phrases to the following partner:

a parent
a lover
a small child
a probation officer
a boss
a teacher
a homeless person
a best friend
a new acquaintance

Selective Readings

Anderson, Virgil. *Training the Speaking Voice.* New York: Oxford University Press, 1961.

Aronson, Arnold. *Clinical Voice Disorders.* 2d ed. New York: Thieme, Inc., 1988.

Bachner, Loris. *Dynamic Singing.* New York: Hill & Wang, 1944.

Bairstow, Edward C., and Greene, Harry Plunket. *Singing Learned From Speech.* New York: St. Martins, n.d.

Balk, H. Wesley. *Performing Power.* Minneapolis: University of Minnesota Press, 1985.

Berry, Cicely. *Voice and the Actor.* New York: MacMillan, 1973.

———. *The Actor and His Text.* London: Harrap, 1987.

Crannell, Kenneth C. *Voice and Articulation.* Belmont, Calif.: Wadsworth, 1985.

Mayer, Lyle V. *Fundamentals of Voice and Diction.* 10th ed. Dubuque, Iowa: Brown and Benchmark Publishers, 1994.

Morrison, Malcolm. *Clear Speech.* London: A. and C. Black, 1989.

Powers, Leland. *Practice Book.* Boston: Thomas Groom & Co., 1913.

Wise, Claude-Merten. *Applied Phonetics.* Englewood Cliffs, N.J.: Arc Books, 1963.

Feeling and Doing 6

On the stage it is necessary to act,
either outwardly or inwardly.

. . . all action in theatre must have
inner justification, be logical,
coherent, and real.

Constantin Stanislavski

On Feeling and Doing

Emotions are manifested in human beings in a physical way. Literally, *emotion* means "outward movement," which implies impulse toward action. Emotion may be either expressed or suppressed. The suppression of emotion reflects a psychophysical denial of self. The expression of emotion manifested in outward physical action is conversely a psychophysical acceptance of the self. We know ourselves to the degree with which we have experienced the release of physical and emotional impulses. Consequently, the personalization process begins with the acknowledgement, acceptance, and release of our feelings without judgment or fear. All physical actions are manifestations of an individual's need to suppress or express emotion. In order for an emotion to find physical expression, habitual patterns of physical holding must be released. These habitual patterns of physical holding serve as defense mechanisms, which circumvent the direct expression of thought and feeling.

The relationship of emotion to physical response is clarified in a theory developed by William James and C. G. Lange early in the twentieth century. The basic point of the theory is that body activity and emotional activity are analogous. In other words, the activity of our muscles is emotional activity. The exercises and discussion in the chapter on freeing are directly related to this theory. The psychological intention for your character—what your character wants at any given moment and how the character feels about that want—assists in the process of creating felt experience. This psychological intention underlies all words spoken and actions taken. With this idea in mind as you explore the following exercises, the question, "What do I want, and how do I feel about it?" will focus your personal emotional response to the specifics of the character and the moment.

Doing and feeling require a commitment of the whole self. This work requires a commitment of the heart, mind, breath, voice, body, past, and present. Personalized acting reflects the supple and inhibited expression of our own humanity.

Exercise 1   Breath and Feeling

While lying in the semisupine position, direct your attention to your natural breathing rhythm. Observe whether you are breathing from your mouth or your nose. If you are breathing from your nose, allow your jaw to relax so that the breath may enter through your mouth. Notice how a greater sense of release in the jaw encourages a greater sense of release in the belly—the breathing center. Come into contact with your natural breathing rhythm. See

Powerful emotions unleashed! Stephen Joyce and Nancy Donohue in *The Runner Stumbles* by Milan Stitt, at the Hartman Theatre, Stamford, Connecticut. Directed by Austin Pendleton.

if you can observe the natural cycle of your breath without manipulating it. You will notice that there is a need for breath, and the breath drops down to the belly and releases out. There is a slight pause and a need for a new breath, and the process repeats itself. Allow the breath to come and let it go. Wait until it comes back again of its own accord. Notice how the breath moves the body. Inhibit any impulse to force the body to move the breath. Continue this process for several minutes. Now visualize the place deep within your belly where you feel the breath releasing. We will call this place deep within your belly your breathing center. Travel with your breath down to your center and back up and out the mouth. Direct the breath to arrive in the front of the mouth somewhere between the teeth and lips (a very loose ''f'' sound). Map the distance your breath must travel from its point of entry all the way down to the center, and back up to its point of exit. Allow any tension restricting the breath's journey to fall away as you continue to allow the breath to come, to let it go, and wait for it to come again. Complete the sentence, "Right now, I am feeling. . . ." Recognition of our own feelings is significant in the personalization process. An awareness of our own emotions is essential to the application of the self to the creative process. In short, "I can only know my character, what my character wants and feels in any given moment, to the degree that I know my own wants and feelings in any given moment."

Exercise 2 Object Exercise

People are inextricably tied to objects. Objects are often endowed with a specific psychological history. As a result, when the sensory system encounters an object with a psychological history, a reflexive emotional response is triggered. This reflexive response is the psychophysical action that forms the foundation of the Stanislavski method.

Select one object of value or importance from your home. This would be the one object you would choose to salvage in the event of a fire. Each person will have an opportunity to relate and respond to his or her object in any manner he or she chooses. Avoid any direct talk about the feelings itself, for example, "I love this watch so much." Ask the following questions: Who do you associate with this object? What do you use it for? When did it come into your life? Where do you keep it? If you have answered who, what, when, and where with truth and integrity, the "why" should be implicit. The answering of the question "Why is this object important to me?" addresses emotion directly. An organic emotional response is best achieved through indirect methods. Consequently, the physical action of responding to the object elicits the emotional response. Discussion of emotion is not necessarily the experience of emotion and should be avoided in the exercise.

Exercise 3 Endowing Objects

An actor's imagination can endow any object with a psychological history. Select an object with no significant psychological history. Answer the who, what, when, where questions. Blend imaginary history with your personal history in order to indirectly elicit an emotional response. Keep playing with the answers to the questions, changing facts and circumstances until you feel satisfied that the question "Why is this object important to me?" is implicit in your response.

Exercise 4 Emotion and Memory

Repeat the centering process. Come to a comfortable, seated position on the floor or on a chair. Select an important experience from your past in which you can sensorially recall the circumstances of the experience. You may select experiences that occurred five to ten years ago. It is best to avoid selecting an experience in which you are uncomfortable with sharing or exploring. Once the experience is vividly recalled, describe it in detail for the class. Do not explain what emotions you felt; rather, focus solely on the circumstances of the experience. In other words, vivid recollection of physical and verbal activity will trigger the internal nervous and muscular systems necessary to activate emotion. Consequently, as you recall and verbally explain what happened to you, it is highly probable that the original emotion will erupt or grow again. Do not be upset if this exercise is not immediately successful. It can be repeated or postponed to a later point of development. Emotion recall is a complex and difficult technique. Since the technique is rooted in the personalization factor, you may require several attempts at affective memory to succeed.

Exercise 5   Objects and Emotion

Establish a personal state of relaxation, concentration, and correct breathing. When you have created this condition by application of selected exercises from chapter 1, accept a personal object from another actor such as a purse, ring, or watch. Examine it in great detail. It is crucial that the object be totally foreign to you and, if it is not, return it and accept another object from someone else. Let your creative imagination work upon the object. Imagine in specific detail where it came from originally, that is, where it was made and by whom. Imaginatively trace the object on its journey to the person you received it from and relate the story verbally to the other actors. Next, using your knowledge and observation of the person who gave it to you, no matter how limited that knowledge and observation may be, imagine a highly emotional experience involving the object and that person and relate it to the group.

Exercise 6   Action and Emotion

Memorize the dialogue to this short scene:

A: What time is it?
B: I don't know.
A: Look at your watch.
B: You look at it.
A: You're kidding.
B: It's 9:30.

Once you have established an identity in your scene and are clear about your relationship to the given circumstances of the script and environment, extend the physicalization of your character by looking at playing any of the verbs listed below. Verbs serve as triggers for action and movement. Select one verb for each moment in the scene.

leaping	nodding	punching
spinning	sweeping	running
crouching	caressing	hitting
leaning	pressing	cradling

reaching	lifting	curving
grasping	bending	waving
dancing	rocking	slouching
kicking	squeezing	dragging
jumping	pouring	squirming
kneeling	tugging	lilting
hugging	gliding	climbing
pointing	covering	massaging
pulling	floating	hiding

Exercise 7   Impromptu Being/Doing Work

Another exercise in rapid, spontaneous work involves reacting immediately with verbal stories to impromptu (i.e., spontaneous or unrehearsed) questions or situations. For example, the following questions and situations may be used by the instructor to stimulate your imaginative response. Respond to the following situations by telling a 3–5 minute imaginative story, doing so as though you had actually experienced the situation described (it is crucial that you accept this exercise with total sincerity and believable involvement when you are responding):

1. Your doctor informs you that you have pernicious anemia and have less than three weeks to live. Describe how you will spend the next three weeks.
2. You are talking to your mother. If you could be anyone in the world, past, present, or future, who would you be? What would you do?
3. You are awakened in the middle of the night by a totally unrecognizable sound in the next room. Describe the sound and what you do.
4. You and your father receive an airmail, special delivery letter postmarked from a foreign city. Describe the message in the letter.
5. On the day of your marriage, your mother tells you that your real father (who lives in another city) will not be able to walk down the aisle with you because he is in a federal penitentiary. How do you respond, and what do you do?
6. You are about to be married when you learn from your brother that your former husband, believed killed in the war, is alive and returning to you. How do you react, and what do you do?
7. You are about to give birth to your first child when you learn from your sister that your husband is having an affair with your best friend. How do you react, and what do you do?
8. You are only one year away from retirement from a twenty-five-year job when your employer is forced to terminate you. How do you react, and what do you do?

9. At the conclusion of a divorce, you learn from your two teenage children that they wish to leave you and live with their father. How do you react, and what do you do?

10. Recently married, you move happily into a new apartment, only to learn from your landlord that your in-laws have rented the apartment below yours. How do you react, and what do you do?

11. You and your brother attend the reading of your father's will. To your amazement, your father leaves you nothing in the will. How do you react, and what do you do?

12. You have been having an affair and cheating on your mate. You decide to confess; you return home to learn from your brother that your mate had discovered your affair and committed suicide. How do you react, and what do you do?

13. You and your child go outside to pick up the morning newspaper and find your pet kitten has been killed by a car in the street. How do you react, and what do you do?

14. You have not seen your sister for twenty years. You open the door and she is standing there. How do you react, and what do you do?

Selective Readings

Berne, Eric. *Games People Play*. New York: Castle, 1964.

———. *What Do You Say After You Say Hello: The Psychology of Human Destiny*. New York: Bantam Books, Inc., 1973.

———. *Transactional Analysis in Psychotherapy*. New York: Castle, 1961.

Darwin, Charles. *The Expression of the Emotions in Man and Animals*. London: John Murray Publishers, 1872.

Davitz, Joel R., and Davitz, Lois Jean. "Nonverbal Vocal Communication of Feeling." *Journal of Communication* 11 (1961): 81–86.

Hagen, Uta. *Challenge For the Actor*. New York: Macmillian, 1992.

James, William. "What Is Emotion?" *Mind* 9 (1884): 188–204.

Kline, Maxine. *Time Space and Designs for Actors*. Boston: Houghton Mifflin, 1975.

Koffa, K. *Principles of Gestalt Psychology*. New York: Harcourt, 1935.

Lange, Carl G., and James, William. *The Emotions*. Facsimile of 1922 ed. New York: Hafner Publishing Co., 1967.

Magarshak, David. *Stanislavski on the Art of the Stage*. New York: Hill and Wang, 1961.

Marowitz, Charles. *The Act of Being*. New York: Taplinger Publishing Co., 1978.

Meisner, Sanford. *Sanford Meisner on Acting*. New York: Random House, 1987.

Perls, Frederick; Hefferline, Ralph F.; and Goodman, Paul. *Gestalt Therapy: Excitement and Growth in the Human Personality.* New York: Dell, 1951.

Wagner, Arthur. *The Drama Review,* Summer 1967, Spring 1969. (Eric Berne theories related to acting.)

Woodbury, Lael J. ''The Externalization of Emotion.'' *Educational Theatre Journal* (October 1960): 177–83.

Synthesizing

7

The objective is the whetter of creativeness, its motive force. The object is the lure of our emotions.

. . . living your part consists of composing a score for your role, of a superobjective, and its active attainment by means of the through line of action.

Constantin Stanislavski

This chapter will provide two efficient, proven approaches to scene study; one approach involves work with four basic acting techniques. The second approach involves following seven simple steps of scene preparation. Both of these approaches are similar and comparable; you may combine elements of both approaches or try each and decide which approach best serves your individual needs.

The material and exercises that follow assume that a considerable amount of exploration in the previously presented material has liberated the physical, mental, psychological, emotional, and vocal resources necessary for scene study.

Selecting a Scene from the Play

Selecting an effective cutting from a play for scene practice is often a difficult task. Many scenes are available in published form in most bookstores (the Selective Readings at the end of this chapter list some of the popularly used scene books). If a scene is extracted or cut from a play, make certain that it is at least five to ten minutes in length and that it is a manageable scene relatively complete within itself. The scene needs to have the kind of abbreviated structure that contains a beginning, a middle, and an end. (A full-length play has the same kind of structure, according to Aristotle; thus, a short, extracted scene from a play needs to be like a small, compressed but complete play.) It is also vital that you read the entire play from which your scene is extracted! Select a scene that seems to have interesting character work and emotional content within your current state of development. Select a character within your present basic age range and physical characteristics. It is also preferable to select a scene from a modern realistic play. Select a play from personal knowledge of dramatic literature; if your experience in this respect is limited, ask your instructor or coach for recommendations. It is usually a good idea to select scenes with two characters for beginning work.

Four Techniques to Prepare a Scene

Four basic techniques suffice to create a character for an extracted scene: personalization, character motivation, pantomimic dramatization, and visualization. These techniques aid in creating a sufficiently believable character.

Personalization and Character in a Scene

Exercise 1   Human Contact from Personal Resources

Two actors create an improvisation in which neither actor is to speak without making physical contact with the other one. Every time a new line of dialogue or new thought is introduced, a corresponding physical contact should be made by each new actor. Only the actor who introduces the vocal line is to make the physical contact. Vocal sounds and noises do not necessitate physical contact.

This exercise is rooted in honesty and intimacy and is designed to develop close communication between actors.

Exercise 2   Autobiography

Sit in a relaxed manner with your scene partner. Take turns relating a short autobiography in which you explain where you were, the various places you have lived, where you received your education, how many people are in your family, the nature of your career goals, and so on. The more you know about one another, the better you can personalize when you begin the scene work.

Motivation and Character in a Scene

The second element for successful acting in scenes is discovering or inventing valid motivations, or reasons, wants, needs, and desires, for everything done on the stage. The character should not seem to be arbitrary; that is, the audience should be able to recognize the purpose behind the behavior of the character. At times, the motivating factor will have occurred at some point in the play prior to the scene being performed. However, because it is generally not necessary to analyze the role in the complete play to perform effectively in the scene, the actor may have to invent appropriate motivation for some of the action. At other times, the motivation may be within the scene itself. To further assist your work involved with motivation and character, we have devised what we call a ''Role Analysis.''

Role Analysis
1. WHO AM I?
   A. Autobiographical facts: parents' upbringing, education, beginnings of major relationships, health, etc. (create specific memories)
   B. Interests, favorite activities, foods, music, idiosyncrasies, etc.
   C. Physical description: age, weight, height, clothing, grooming habits, etc. Name an animal that behaviorally seems analogous to your role.

D. What events constitute victories for you in life? What was a recent victory for you?

E. What events constitute a crisis? What was a recent crisis for you?

F. How does your upbringing affect your present day behavior?

2. WHAT TIME IS IT?

A. Minute, hour, day, season, month, year, century

B. What aspects of time affect me in action?

3. WHERE AM I?

A. What part of the room, house, neighborhood, city, country?

B. Describe your surroundings.

C. What actions are elicited from your relationship to the place?

4. WHAT SURROUNDS ME?

A. What are the objects of significance or interest in the place?

B. What actions are elicited from your relationship to the objects?

5. WHAT ARE THE ACTIONS?

A. What are your activities up to the moment that a scene begins?

B. What is happening in the scene?

  1. What are the struggles? secrets?

  2. What are your expectations and desires?

  3. What ideal future do you fantasize for yourself
     a. in 10 minutes?
     b. tomorrow?
     c. in 1 year?
     d. in 5 years?

6. WHAT ARE MY RELATIONSHIPS?

A. To other characters in the scene

  1. Past contact with others. What has led to present feelings?

  2. How is the relationship important to you?

  3. What do you specifically like and dislike?

  4. In what ways do you need the other person in the scene? In what ways are you vulnerable to the other person?

B. To other characters mentioned in the scene

7. WHAT DO I WISH FOR? NEED? DREAM ABOUT?

A. Super objective—central life needs, driving purpose

B. Scene objective

  1. What do you need at the beginning of the scene? What will you do to try and get what you want?

  2. What will happen if you don't get what you need?

8. WHAT IS IN MY WAY?
   A. Are you encountering obstacles from other characters in the scene?
   B. Are you encountering obstacles within yourself?
9. WHAT DO I DO TO GET WHAT I WANT?
   A. How do my objectives and obstacles change as the scene progresses?
      1. Do my expectations change?
      2. What discoveries do I make?
      3. How am I changed by my discoveries and decisions?
   B. What actions do I pursue in order to reach my goal?
   C. What actions do I consider, but reject?
10. WHAT CAN I DRAW UPON FROM MY OWN LIFE TO HELP CREATE THE CHARACTER'S WANTS, ACTIONS, AND EMOTIONAL LIFE?
    Describe these parallel experiences.

Exercise 1   Motivation

The entire group takes a position onstage, standing or seated as desired. The dramatic situation is that the group is locked in a room for an indefinite period of time and must pass the time waiting for release. No one may wait in total silence; as often as possible, speaking must be included in the improvisational exercise. Your task is to find ways to pass the time without saying or doing things arbitrarily. In other words, all activity (both physical and vocal) must be truthfully and honestly motivated.

Exercise 2   Motivation through Understanding of the "Other" Character

Sit with your scene partner in a relaxed manner. Explain to your partner what you know about his or her character; explain what you think your partner's character *wants* in the scene and *why* he or she wants it. Your partner then reciprocates. When each scene is finished, comment on the observations heard. Are they correct and revealing? Why, or why not?

Pantomimic Dramatization and Character in a Scene

Pantomime and *mime* are specialized kinds of theatre performances or exercises and are considered in their proper place in the chapter on Commedia Dell'Arte. *Pantomimic dramatization,* as it is used here as a beginning acting technique in scene work in the class or studio, implies more than pantomime, which is action without words and more even than mime, which is the imitating of scenes from life (usually as travesty or satire and without dialogue). Pantomimic dramatization is used here to refer to the process of discovering, creating, and using personalized physical action, or business, as it relates to objects. Effective pantomimic dramatization enriches, vitalizes, and adds distinction to the visual and physical impact. Pantomimic dramatization requires an actor to use imagination to determine what to do physically and visually while on stage.

Exercise 1   Pantomimic Dramatization and Characters

Select a role in one of the following scenes. Discover and create personalized physical action, or business, related to objects used in the scene. Write a list of all created action; then practice the scene and incorporate your pantomimic dramatization.

Elma and Grace   opening scene, Act I
    Bus Stop by William Inge
Laura and Jim   Scene viii
    The Glass Menagerie by Tennessee Williams
Willy and Linda   opening scene, Act II
    Death of a Salesman by Arthur Miller
Maggie and Brick   opening scene, Act I
    Cat on a Hot Tin Roof by Tennessee Williams
Biff and Happy   bedroom scene, Act I
    Death of a Salesman by Arthur Miller
Millie and Madge   opening scene, Act II
    Picnic by William Inge
Mel and Edna   beginning of Act II, scene i
    Prisoner of Second Avenue by Neil Simon
George and Martha   opening scene, Act I
    Who's Afraid of Virginia Woolf? by Edward Albee

Visualization and Character in a Scene

Visualization refers to a character's appearance. While the actor's body provides a significant portion of the character appearance, other visual elements are often added to enhance basic characterization. An interesting use of visualization is for an actor to imagine his character as if it were represented in the characteristics of an inanimate object. For example, he could observe the tall, clean lines of a Greek vase and incorporate such characteristics into his posture, movement, and activity. It is similarly helpful to use selected characteristics of animal behavior in visualizing a character.

Exercise 1   The Animal

Recline on a firm surface and establish relaxation and effective breathing. Concentrate only on a specific animal image such as an elephant and its physical attributes and movement. When the animal image is vivid in your mind, rise to your feet and begin moving about in the manner of the animal you selected. Place emphasis on bone structure, rhythm of movement, and facial expressiveness. After a period of time, stop your animal movement and take a relaxed standing position. Walk comfortably in your own manner; then subtly add key characteristics of your animal to your activity. Emphasize bone structure, rhythm, and facial expressiveness again but try to wed them to your own attributes, dropping out of the more excessive imitative factors. You may also use noises or sounds made by the animal.

Exercise 2   You, a Photo, and Your Character

Locate a photograph of a person who seems to resemble your concept of the character you are going to create; sit in front of a mirror and study your face and the photo. Adjust your hair and expressions to match the photo. Use this study to assist your early scene practice.

Seven Steps to Heaven: A Simplified Approach to Preparing a Scene

Another or second approach to preparing a scene for performance in a class, laboratory, or studio involves seven simplified steps that can lead to a happy or "heavenly" conclusion. Before trying these steps, the actor should first observe a few fundamental guidelines: (*a*) Read the entire play from which your scene is selected. (*b*) Keep a personal log or diary of all rehearsals and performances. This will aid you in your "homework" and in your postperformance evaluation. (*c*) Complete "Role Analysis" after completion of Step 4. (*d*) Do not *force* line memorization and do not try to learn lines at the very beginning of the rehearsal period. Let the lines become assimilated into memory over the initial half of the rehearsal period. (*e*) Do not overstructure and "set" blocking or movement patterns too early in the rehearsal period. Let the movement evolve naturally out of your behavior and activity as you work with simplified representations of furniture and hand properties. (*f*) Use costume and hand prop items from the beginning of rehearsals; at least, use facsimiles of actual props. Avoid pantomimic work that becomes an art in itself and usually mitigates against naturalness and believability.

The Seven Steps

1. Accomplish information read-throughs of the scene, using as many as are needed, but at least two or three. Do not exert "effort" or try to "act" the scene at all; do not *work* for characterization or emotion. Simply gather information and facts from the text and discuss these with your partner (What time of day

and season is it? What is the weather like in the scene? What is your character wearing? What has happened just prior to this scene? And so on.)

2. Accomplish several "communion" read-throughs of the scene (e.g., "communion in the sense of intimate interpersonal communication). Use maximum eye contact even if it necessitates reading slowly and paraphrasing. Touch your partner whenever it seems comfortable and natural to do so.

3. Improvise the scene in your own words with free movement and activity. This is a "talk-and-walk-through" rehearsal. You should reveal all the information you learned in Step 1. Focus on covering all the subjects and issues used in the scene by the playwright. Do not consciously try to use the actual lines from the script, although occasionally you may be amazed at how many lines are already becoming part of your memory.

4. Freely explore the scene with script in hand. This process is called "organic combing" or searching for fresh ways to perform each moment of the scene. For example, perform the scene many times with a *single goal* each time; that is, perform it once concentrating solely on the weather and climate. Another time try eating and drinking something throughout the scene; perform it in a value *opposite* to that which seems to be called for in the script (if it is a love scene, perform it as a hate scene, and so on); practice all entrances and exits in several different ways; reverse roles with your partner and see what revelations occur; play music as you do the scene and compare the scene with a painting, a sculpture, dances, and so on. Perform drills bearing on all special problem activity in the scene (such as vocal dialects; limps and handicaps; kisses and love activity; slaps and fighting; nudity; violence; special object and hand prop work; and so on).

5. Set the movement patterns and set all "business" (some directors call this "setting the blocking" and "scoring" or orchestrating/ finalizing all hand prop activity). Make final character and emotional decisions (choices and discarding). Establish a motivating force, that is, know the single most important thing your character *wants* in the *scene* (which may or may not be the single most important thing the character wants in the *play*). The most important thing a character wants in a scene or in the entire play is

often called the character's *intention*. The *MF* (motivating force) is usually *the* most important intention for the character in the entire play, or the *spine* of the character. (A character will usually have a series of secondary wants or intentions that connect to the main one, the MF.)

6. Perform the scene several times without interruption to accomplish a sense of fluidity, a flow, or a rhythm (e.g., a smooth combination of tempo or speed and timing with the proper mood and emotional work). All simplified ''technical'' items are now realized, such as minimal use of performance costumes, props, furniture, and makeup (if used, which is rare in scene practice). Stage lighting is also rarely used in scene work. Step 6 involves full use of characterization and emotion.

7. Perform a couple final ''polish'' run-throughs of the scene (ideally with someone observing, taking and giving notes). ''Preview'' the scene in front of a class, audience, instructor, or coach. Ideally, the performance (or performances) is (are) followed by a written self-evaluation in your journal. Finally, the class, audience, instructor, or coach may discuss and evaluate the performance and offer suggestions for further work.

Personalization will rarely take an actor completely through the creation of a role. At some point, you will be unable to produce or perform an emotion or action. Some kind of traditional acting technique is needed. Such techniques as centering, focusing, sensing, doing and being have all been discussed; any one or all of these techniques can be put to use as part of or an extension of personalization.

A major misunderstanding frequently exists among directors and performers concerning ''personalization'' and ''organic activity.'' The misunderstanding occurs when directors or performers believe that personalization should carry actors completely into performance without benefit of commanded direction of any sort. Personalization and organic activity do *not* imply *total* freedom and nondirection. Rather, the terms imply a restricted period of time early in rehearsals during which the actor may become comfortable and freely express movement and actions. *The actor is not forced to create character and emotion or learn lines and blocking too soon.* By all means, a director should and must guide and eventually refine or even command certain aspects of performance as rehearsals progress to the halfway point or beyond.

Standard Acting Terms

As rehearsals progress toward performance, knowledge of standard terms related to acting and the physical theatre become necessary. The following terminology and definitions are given here for the actor's convenience and assistance during rehearsal of characters in scenes. Note that some of the terms are defined further in the Glossary at the end of this book.

Acting Area

The traditional proscenium stage is generally divided as shown in the accompanying diagram.

The traditional arena stage (central stage) is generally divided according to the accompanying diagram.

Acting Positions

Full-front The actor faces the audience fully. This is a very strong position but can be sustained for long periods of time only in nonrealistic plays and musicals.

Full-back The actor stands with his full back to the audience. Used for special dramatic effect, the position is also very strong but should generally be sustained only for brief periods of time.

One-quarter The actor stands in a quarter turn away from the audience, usually facing another actor. This is a strong position, but less so than full-front. The position increases in strength when the actor makes the one-quarter turn toward the audience rather than away from it. This position can be sustained for the longest period of time in realistic plays.

Profile or One-half Turn The actor stands facing either right or left with his profile in view of the audience. Rarely a strong position, this stance is also used for comic effect.

Three-quarters In this position the actor nearly turns his full back with less than one side of his head and a shoulder toward the audience. This is usually the weakest of the five basic acting positions.

Rehearsal Terms

Stage Business Small, detailed actions of the body (often the hands) such as drinking from a cup, lighting a cigar, mopping the brow, and so on.

Up right	Up center	Up left
Right	Center	Left
Down right	Down center	Down left

The basic acting areas of the traditional proscenium stage.

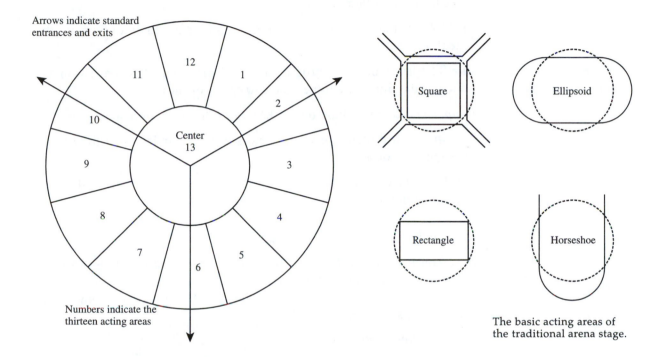

Arrows indicate standard entrances and exits

Numbers indicate the thirteen acting areas

The basic acting areas of the traditional arena stage.

Properties Physical objects used on stage by the actor. The term is usually shortened to props. There are four classifications of props:

1. Hand props: Small objects that actors can carry or handle onstage such as books, drinking glasses, and the like.
2. Personal props: Items on the actor's person such as eyeglasses, jewelry, key chain, and the like.
3. Costume props: Costume accessories such as fans, gloves, handkerchiefs, and the like.
4. Stage props: Major objects related to the physical scene such as stools, pillows, lamps, furniture, and the like.

(The four classifications are interchangeable, depending on how the props are used.)

Ad lib From the Latin *ad libitum* (''at pleasure''), the term applies to lines supplied by the actor when they are lacking in the script but desired in the production (or lines invented when the actor has forgotten the memorized lines).

Aside A line onstage directed at the audience, which is not supposed to be heard by the other characters.

Build An increase in speed or volume in order to reach a climactic theatrical moment.

Cue The last word or words of a speech or the end of an action that indicates the time for another actor to speak or move.

Drop The drop in volume on the last word or words of a speech.

Pickup Cue A direction given to actors to avoid undesirable time lapses between lines or action.

Top Delivery of a line or lines with more volume and intensity than the line preceding it or them.

Terms Related to Movement or Blocking

If personalization works correctly, little or no marking of the script in terms of movement or blocking will be necessary. However, blocking may be marked in the script at an early rehearsal. Following are some of the commonly used notations.

Terms for Proscenium Stage

> D Downstage (forward; toward audience)
> U Upstage (back; away from audience)
> L Stage left (any area left of the performer when facing the audience)
> R Stage right (any area right of the performer when facing the audience)
> C Center stage (the approximate middle of the acting area) (Variations should be self-evident. For example, *UL* indicates upstage left of the acting area.)

Terms for Arena or Central Stage

> C Center stage (the approximate middle of the acting area—the thirteenth area)

Twelve o'clock	Arbitrarily established point of the acting area analogous to the number twelve on a clock (all other eleven acting areas are designated from that point according to the numbers on a clock).

Additional Movement or Blocking Terms

X	Cross (stage)
XC	Cross center (stage)
XDL	Cross down left (stage)
XDR	Cross down right (stage)
XUL, XUR, UDC, etc.	

(A downward arrow ↓ may indicate ''sit'' and an upward arrow ↑ ''rise.'')

Short phrases can also be marked in the script, such as ''close book,'' ''slap him,'' and so on.

Example

''O, woe is me—XDR

Fall—T'have seen what I have seen, seen what

↓to Knees I see''↑Rise—run off DL

OPHELIA in *Hamlet* by William Shakespeare

A Last Comment Concerning Final Rehearsals and Performance of the Scene

As noted earlier, stage properties and furniture in scene study and practice should be kept to a minimum; it is not advisable to spend time and energy creating a believable scenic environment. In scene practice the audience accepts that the focus is upon the actor, with only essential scenic elements provided. These factors also hold true for costuming. What costuming is necessary can probably be provided from personal wardrobes. Also, basic properties and furniture are usually available as part of standard classroom or theatre rehearsal items. Occasionally, actors may have to provide these items as well. In many instances it is acceptable to use substitute facsimiles for properties. Normal room illumination or basic area lighting are sufficient for scenes. Actors in classes often must be content with general room illumination or what is called in the theatre ''work lights'' (meaning non-specialized illumination). Generally, if music and sound effects are necessary or desired, actors must provide them by bringing a cassette player and tape or compact disc player and disc.

Care must also be taken to provide adequate rehearsal time for the person who operates the equipment. As a general rule, stage makeup is not used for scene practice. Audiences for scene performances usually come from the class or acting company. Occasionally, friends, relatives, other students, faculty, or other theatre artists in the company are invited to view a scene performance.

As noted earlier, after a scene is performed before an audience, standard practice is usually to have an informal critique or response from the instructor, director, or coach. Sometimes peers or colleague actors contribute to the response. Additionally, many instructors provide specific written evaluation of scene work, which should complement your self-evaluation. While scene study and practice are invaluable to the beginning actor, it is never abandoned by most successful actors. Many such artists return again and again to a studio or laboratory to explore problems, ''stretch'' their talents, experiment, and ''freshen'' their fundamental skills. (Members of the Actor's Studio do this regularly.) Learn a positive approach to scene study and practice and sustain it through your entire career.

Suggested Characters and Plays for Scene Work

O'Neill, Eugene

Jamie, Edmund, Mary, Tyrone
Long Day's Journey Into Night
Melody, Sarah
A Touch of the Poet
Nina, Dr. Darrell, Sam, Charlie
Strange Interlude
Christine, Lavinia, Ezra, Adam, Orin
Mourning Becomes Electra
Nat, Essie, Richard, Muriel, Lilly, Sid
Ah, Wilderness!
Hickey, Harry, Larry, Don, Pearl, Margie, Lora
The Iceman Cometh
Anna, Chris, Mat
Anna Christie

Miller, Arthur

Chris, Ann, Keller
All My Sons
Willy, Biff, Happy, Linda
Death of a Salesman
Eddie, Catherine, Rudolfo, Beatrice
A View From the Bridge

Proctor, Abigail, Elizabeth, Reverend Hale, Danforth
The Crucible
All characters
The Creation of the World and Other Business
All characters
The American Clock
All characters
Danger: Memory (I Can't Remember Anything and *Clara)*

Williams, Tennesse

Amanda, Laura, Tom, The Gentleman Caller
The Glass Menagerie
Blanche, Stella, Stanley, Mitch
A Streetcar Named Desire
Alma, John
Summer and Smoke
Reverend Shannon, Maxine, Hannah
The Night of the Iguana
Maggie, Brick
Big Daddy, Big Mama
Cat on A Hot Tin Roof
All characters
The Rose Tattoo

All characters
Small Craft Warnings
All characters
Eccentricities of a Nightingale

Kopit, Arthur

Jonathan, Rosalie, Madam
Rosepettle, Commodore
*Oh, Dad, Poor Dad, Mamma's
Hung You in the Closet and
I'm Feelin' So Sad*
Buffalo Bill, Sitting Bull, Wild Bill
Hickok
Indians
Emily Stilson, Amy, Billy, Mr.
Brownstein, Mrs. Timmins
Wings
All characters
Nine
All characters
End of the World

Albee, Edward

Jerry, Peter
The Zoo Story
Martha, George, Nick, Honey
Who's Afraid of Virginia Woolf?
Mommie, Daddy, Grandma, Mrs.
Barker, Young Man
The American Dream
Nancy, Charlie, Leslie, Sarah
Seascape
Tobias, Agnes, Claire, Julia
A Delicate Balance
Miss Alice, Julian, Lawyer,
Cardinal
Tiny Alice
The Wife, The Mistress, The Son,
The Daughter
All Over
All characters
The Lady From Dubuque

Gagliano, Frank

All characters
*Father Uxbridge Wants to
Marry*
Jeremy, Indian, Narrator
Big Sur

Sis, Brother, William Saroyan
O'Neill
*The City Scene: Paradise
Gardens East*
Yam, Jesus
*The City Scene: Conerico Was
Here To Stay*

Inge, William

Elma, Grace, Bo, Cherie
Bus Stop
Doc, Lola
Come Back, Little Sheba
Howard, Rosemary, Hal, Madge
Picnic
All characters
*The Dark At The Top of the
Stairs*

Wilder, Thornton

Sabina, Mr. Antrobus, Mrs.
Antrobus
The Skin of Our Teeth
Emily, George, Stage Manager
Our Town
Dolly, Barnaby, Cornelius,
Minnie, Vandergelder
The Matchmaker

Rabe, David

Harriet, Ozzie, David, Ricky
Sticks and Bones
Ardell, Pavlo
*The Basic Training of Pavlo
Hummel*
Chrissy, Eric, Susan, Al
In the Boom Boom Room
Martin, Richie, Carlyle, Billy,
Roger, Cokes, Rooney
Streamers
All characters
Hurlyburly

Miller, Jason

Tom, George, James, Phil, Coach
That Championship Season

Guare, John

Artie, Bunny, Ronnie, Bananas
The House of Blue Leaves
All characters
Marco Polo Sings A Solo
All characters
Bosoms and Neglect
All characters
Landscape of the Body

Weller, Michael

The Students
Moonchildren
Paul, Susan
Loose Ends

Zindel, Paul

Beatrice, Tillie, Ruth, Nanny
The Effect of Gamma Rays on
Man-In-The-Moon Marigolds
Catherine, Anna, Ceil
And Miss Reardon Drinks a
Little
All characters
The Private Affairs of Mildred
Wild

Gershe, Leonard

Don, Jill, Mrs. Baker, Ralph
Butterflies Are Free

Barry, Julian

Lenny
Lenny

Gilroy, Frank

John, Timmy, Nettie
The Subject Was Roses

Wasserman, Dale

MacMurphy, Nurse, Ratched
One Flew Over the Cuckoo's
Nest
Don Quixote, Sancho, Aldonza
Man of La Mancha

Macleish, Archibald

Zuss, Nickles, J. B., Sarah
J. B.

Wilson, Lanford

The People, The Residents
The Hot L Baltimore
Prof. Howe, Cynthia, Kirsten,
D. K. Eriksen, Dan and Jean
Loggins, Chad
The Mound Builders
All characters
The Fifth of July
Sally, Matt
Talley's Folly
All characters
A Tale Told
All characters
Balm in Gilead
All characters
The Rimers of Eldritch
All characters
The Gingham Dog
All characters
Lemon Sky
All characters
Angels Fall
Talley & Son
Burn This

Anderson, Robert

Gene, Margaret, Alice, Tom
I Never Sang for My Father
Muriel, Herbert
I'm Herbert
Tom, Laura
Tea and Sympathy

Terry, Megan

The Group
Viet Rock
He, She
Comings and Goings

Shepard, Sam

All characters
Operation Side-Winder
Hoss, Crow, Cheyenne, Becky
Lou
The Tooth of Crime
All characters
Suicide in B Flat

All characters
Buried Child
All characters
Curse of the Starving Class
All characters
La Turista
All characters
True West
All characters
Tongues
All characters
Savage Love
All characters
Seduced
All characters
The Unseen Hand
All characters
Fool For Love
All characters
A Lie of the Mind

Shange, Ntozake
All characters
For Colored Girls Who Have Considered Suicide When the Rainbow is Enuf

Hanley, William
Glas, Randell, Rosie
Slow Dance on the Killing Ground

Baldwin, James
Richard, Meridian, Lyle, Parnell, Juanita
Blues for Mister Charlie

Gordone, Charles
Johnny, Gabe, Cora, Shanty, Sweets
No Place to Be Somebody

Mason, Judi, A.
All characters
Livin' Fat

Bullins, Ed
All characters
The Electronic Nigger

All characters
Goin' A Buffalo

Gibson, William
Jerry, Gittle
Two for the Seesaw
Will, Anne, Meg, Kemp
A Cry of Players
All characters
The Miracle Worker
All characters
Monday After The Miracle

Odets, Clifford
Joe, Mr. Bonaparte
Golden Boy
All characters
Awake and Sing!

Gurney, A. R., Jr.
All characters
Children
The Middle Ages
The Golden Fleece
The Dining Room
Sweet Sue
Another Antigone
The Cocktail Hour
The Perfect Party
Love Letters

McCullers, Carson
Bernice, Frankie
Member of the Wedding

Kaufman, George S., and Moss Hart
Penelope, Essie, Grandpa, Mr. DiPina, Ed
You Can't Take It With You

Saroyan, William
Tom, Joe, Kitty, Kit Carson
The Time of Your Life

Cristofer, Michael
The Interviewer, Joe, Steve, Maggie, Brian, Mark, Beverly, Agnes, Felicity
The Shadow Box

Crowley, Mart

    All characters
        The Boys in the Band
    Loraine, Teddy, Michael
        A Breeze From The Gulf

Jones, Preston

    All characters
        A Texas Trilogy (The Last Meeting of the Knights of the White Magnolia; LuAnn Hampton Laverty Oberlander; The Oldest Living Graduate)

Patrick, Robert

    Wanda, Sparger, Carla, Rona, Mark, Bartender
        Kennedy's Children

Innaurato, Albert

    Fran, Francis, Lucille, Bunny, Herschel, Judity, Randy
        Gemini
    Benno, The Old Man, The Girl
        The Transfiguration of Benno Blimpie

Mamet, David

    Robert, John
        A Life in the Theatre
    Charles, Rita, Morton, Lawrence, Mrs. Varec, Mr. Wallace, Bernie, Dave
        The Water Engine
    Mr. Happiness
        Mr. Happiness

Sexual Perversity in Chicago

    Bobby, Teach, Donny
        American Buffalo

Duck Variations

    All characters
        Glengarry Glen Ross
        Edmond
        Speed the Plow

Durang, Christopher

    All characters
        The Vietnamization of New Jersey
        The Actor's Nightmare
    All characters
        A History of the American Film
        Baby With the Bathwater
    Prudence, Bruce
        Beyond Therapy
        Sister Mary Ignatius Explains It All To You

Coburn, D. L.

    All characters
        The Gin Game

Mastrosimone, William

    Rose, Cliff
        The Woolgatherer
    All characters
        Extremities
        Shivaree

Thompson, Ernest

    Norman, Ethel, Charlie, Chelsea, Billy Rae
        On Golden Pond
        The West Side Waltz

Slade, Bernard

    All characters
        Same Time, Next Year
    All characters
        Tribute
    All characters
        Romantic Comedy

Wasserstein, Wendy

    All characters
        Isn't It Romantic?
        The Heidi Chronicles

Fierstein, Harvey

    All characters
        Torch Song Trilogy
        La Cage aux Folles (with Jerry Herman)
        Safe Sex

Mann, Emily
    All characters
        Execution of Justice
        Still Life

Glowacki, Janusz
    All characters
        Cinders
        Hunting Cockroaches

Wolfe, George C.
    All characters
        The Colored Museum

Metcalfe, Stephen
    All characters
        The Incredibly Famous Willy Rivers

Gardner, Herb
    All characters
        A Thousand Clowns
        I'm Not Rappaport

Shawn, Wallace
    All characters
        Aunt Dan & Lemon

Henley, Beth
    All characters
        Crimes of the Heart
        The Miss Firecracker Contest

Foote, Horton
    All characters
        Courtship and Convicts
        Valentine's Day and Lily Dale
        1918 and The Widow Claire
        Roots in a Parched Ground

Howe, Tina
    All characters
        Painting Churches
        The Art of Dining
        Museum
        Costal Disturbances

Bentley, Eric
    All characters
        Are You Now or Have You Ever Been

Bergman, Andrew
    All characters
        Social Security

Brady, Michael
    All characters
        To Gillian On Her 37th Birthday

Fuller, Charles
    All characters
        Zooman and the Sign
        Soldier's Play

Harling, Robert
    All characters
        Steel Magnolias

Heifner, Jack
    All characters
        Vanities

Hoffman, William
    All characters
        As Is

Uhry, Alfred
    Daisy, Hokey
        Driving Miss Daisy

Actor Checklist Eclectic

Voice	Extensive range; effortless articulation and effective vocal production; flexible variation; intermix of many stylistic techniques.
Movement	Total body as communicator; dance, mime, gymnastic, acrobatic, Asian, Tai Chi Chuan, Laban, Suzuki System; spatial activity, improvisational; mix of presentational and representational mode; combination of many stylistic techniques.

Selective Readings

Barlow, Judith E., ed. *Plays by American Women: The Early Years.* New York: Avon, 1981.

Cassady, Marshall. *The Book of Scenes for Acting Practice.* Lincolnwood, Ill.: National Textbook Co., 1992.

Cohen, Lorraine, ed. *Scenes for Young Actors.* New York: Avon, 1973.

Cosgrove, Francis, ed. *Scenes for Student Actors.* Vol. V. New York: Samuel French, Inc., 1942.

Elkind, Samuel, ed. *32 Scenes for Acting Practice.* Glenview, Ill.: Scott, Foresman & Co., 1972.

———. *30 Scenes for Acting Practice.* Glenview, Ill.: Scott, Foresman & Co., 1972.

———. *28 Scenes for Acting Practice.* Glenview, Ill.: Scott, Foresman & Co., 1972.

Emerson, Robert, and Grumback, Jane, eds. *50 Speeches From The Contemporary Theatre.* New York: Drama Book Specialists, 1976.

Grumback, Jane, and Emerson, Robert, eds. *Actors Guide to Scenes.* New York: Drama Book Specialists/Publishers, 1973.

———. *Actors Guide to Monologues.* New York: Drama Book Specialists/Publishers, 1972.

Handman, Wynn, ed. *American Scenes for Student Actors.* New York: Bantam, 1978.

Karton, Joshua, ed. *Film Scenes for Actors.* New York: Bantam Books, 1983.

Lane, Eric. *The Actor's Book of Scenes from New Plays.* New York: Penguin Books, 1988.

Lass, Abraham H., and Levin, Milton, eds. *A Student's Guide to 50 American Plays.* New York: Pocket Books, 1969.

Olfson, Lewy, ed. *50 Great Scenes for Student Actors.* New York: Bantam Books, Inc., 1970.

Rudnicki, Stefan. *The Actor's Book of Classical Scenes.* New York: Penguin Books, 1992.

Schulman, Michael, and Mekler, Eva, eds. *Scenes For Student Actors.*
   New York: Penguin Books, 1980.
———. *The Actor's Scenebook.* New York: Bantam Books, 1984.
Southern, Richard. *Proscenium and Sight Lines.* London: Faber & Faber,
   1939.
Steffensen, James L., Jr., ed. *Great Scenes from World Theatre.* Vols. 1 and
   2. New York: Avon Books, vol. 1, 1965, vol. 2, 1972.
Sullivan, Victoria, and Hatch, James, eds. *Plays By and About Women.*
   New York: Vintage, 1974.

Auditioning

8

The roles for which you haven't the appropriate feelings are those you will never play well. . . . They will be excluded from your repertory.

An Actor must work all his life, cultivate his mind, train his talents systematically, develop his character; he may never despair and never relinquish his main purpose—to love his art with all his strength and love it unselfishly.

Constantin Stanislavski

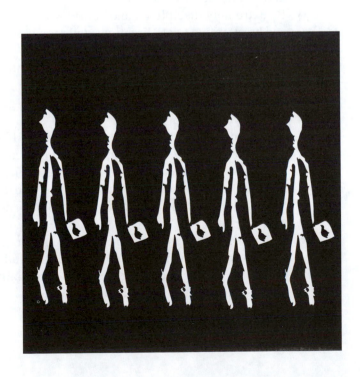

Competition is a necessary aspect of any acting career. Be prepared to accept rejection or defeat and to return with resilience and renewed determination. Playwright Eugene O'Neill said that perseverance and good luck are the key factors to success in the theatre. The sheer volume of actors striving for achievement in the field automatically indicates that even high-quality talent will be overlooked in the scramble and competition for roles and jobs. A classic misconception related to finding work as an actor is the infamous myth of "the casting couch." The connotation in that phrase is obvious, but generally incorrect. The so-called casting couch is neither necessary nor valid in terms of constant work in the theatre any more than in any other walk of life. Actors should never attempt to offer anything less than skill, dedication, and experience as their selling features. While actors should take advantage of honest, ethical contacts to assist in "networking" or gaining work opportunities, they should never sacrifice their personal integrity.

How to Audition

1. If you are auditioning for a written role, read the play in advance.
2. If you are auditioning for a specific part, practice key speeches for that role in advance. It is usually not necessary to memorize speeches unless specified. What is desired is sufficient familiarization in order to demonstrate the proficiency of the actor and his understanding of the character.
3. Be extremely disciplined and courteous at auditions. Be punctual and be attentive to all directions and requests. Be cooperative, but not aggressive.
4. If the audition is open, listen carefully to the competition as it may be beneficial to hear other interpretations. However, if you are particularly impressed by someone, it is generally best not to change your interpretation.
5. Avoid falling into the trap of self-criticism. If you strive for perfection, even one verbal error, for example, can lead to inordinate self-criticism and collapse of an entire audition. Reflection and self-evaluation should occur after the audition is completed. During the audition, remain flexible and good-natured no matter what happens.
6. If the role and scene demand intense emotion, work as honestly and as truthfully within the contexts of the audition. Do not force emotion. Forcing inevitably leads to artificiality. Personal naturalness and comfort should be the guides.

7. When casting is announced, be understanding and cheerful whether you are cast or not. It is juvenile and destructive to allow disappointment to affect progress for any length of time. The only thought an actor should have is what, where, and when is the next audition. It is particularly meaningless to second-guess casting decisions. To do so is debilitating. It is the surest sign of unprofessionalism, and it invariably gains nothing but the possible disfavor of a director and your colleagues. Learn this lesson at the first unsuccessful audition.

Types of Auditions

Auditions will be either open or closed. In an open audition any interested person may participate. Traditionally, also at an open audition actors may watch other actors perform. In a closed audition the general public is usually excluded, and the audition privilege is limited to specific people and groups. Traditionally, at a closed audition actors may not watch other actors perform. In these auditions, actors are usually called at a specific time, and the length of the audition time is rigidly controlled.

Auditions are usually divided into two categories: specific and general. For example, at a specific audition, an actor might audition only for Hamlet and Laertes. At a general audition the actor auditions for any role. Further, a general audition may be for membership in an acting company or group rather than for a specific role or play. For example, when auditioning for a summer stock group or repertory company, the actor may perform one or more short prepared audition pieces to demonstrate general ability.

Selecting an Audition Piece

1. Generally remain within your own basic age range and physical type. While everyone complains about type casting, the practice is used almost exclusively in the professional theatre and much more often than is admitted in educational theatre. How can you best function within the limitations of that concept? Above all, careful, critical understanding of yourself is essential. First, you know how old you are; your age range will generally not vary as a type beyond ten years on either side of your age, provided that you are at least twenty-six or twenty-seven years old (at eighteen years of age, most actors cannot perform the role of an eight-year-old child). You also know your height, weight, and general physical characteristics. Painful though it may be, do not have false illusions about yourself.

2. Select characters with whom you can identify. It will strengthen your audition if you have some understanding and emotional identification with the character you are portraying.
3. Select modern realistic plays for audition unless there are specific directions to the contrary.
4. If your audition permits time for more than one selection, try to provide offerings with distinct contrasts. In other words, if one piece is serious or tragic, the other should probably be light and comic.
5. Do not select a character for an audition that demands a heavy vocal dialect or accent unless there are specific directions to the contrary.
6. An effective audition is usually self-contained, having a beginning, middle, and end. When the requirement is to be extremely brief (e.g., two minutes is the usual time limitation), material should be selected that reflects clarity and unity.
7. Time your selections carefully.

Practical Suggestions

1. You should generally dress for an audition in a comfortable, clean manner. The question arises, Should you dress appropriate to the attire of the character? The answer is in a reasonable way, yes—with qualifications. Dress similarly to the attire of the character. If you are auditioning for the role of a truck driver, jeans, boots, and flannel shirt would be appropriate. If the role is a business woman, a tailored suit would be good. Obviously, if the role is selected from a historical play, you should not attempt to dress in period costume. Generally, it is important not to overdress or underdress and thereby have to compete against your own appearance.
2. Be certain to establish your name clearly. Use the phrase ''My name is. . . .'' These first three nonessential words tune the listener into catching the important phrase, your name.
3. Quickly determine the size of the room in which you are auditioning and adjust accordingly.
4. Never apologize for your appearance, physical condition, or the quality of your work. Self-confidence is desirable.
5. Thank the auditioners.

The Callback

Few actors are cast on the basis of one audition. The format of callbacks vary. The callback may be for another reading or prepared selection. A callback may permit an actor to discuss interpretation and other matters with the director. Answer all questions directly, economically, and honestly.

A recent black-and-white photograph should be attached to the résumé. Eight-by-ten inch prints are preferred. Gloss-finish is preferred to matte-finish photographs because they reproduce better for publicity purposes. A single pose is preferred to a composite, a simple head shot is preferred to a full-length pose, and a natural, unretouched photo is favored over a glamour picture. A final caution concerning photographs: Use an informal, unpretentious pose.

A résumé shouldn't exceed one page regardless of the length of experience. As roles accumulate, an actor becomes more selective as to those he lists. Learn to cite only representative roles and major credits and rarely more than fifteen or twenty. A half-dozen solid roles are more impressive than thirty small ones. The résumé should be neatly typed and easily read. If you have acquired an agent, the agent's and the agency's name or logo usually appear at the top or the side of the résumé. If you have no agent, merely list your own name at the top of the résumé. List your name, full address, and telephone number near the top. Most actors in urban centers utilize an answering service or recording machine to take messages. This is the number you should list on your résumé. Next, list your height, weight, hair color, eye color, and all professional unions to which you belong. Current practice is to eliminate listing your age, age range, and marital status, although some actors still choose to do so. Under *Training,* list schools, degrees, workshops, and well-known acting coaches under whom you have worked. Note any special training (such as voice, mime, improvisation, fencing, dance, and so on). Under the section labeled *Acting Experience,* list just the significant roles you have played, play titles, theaters, theatre locations, and directors if they are well known (list latest roles first). List *Television, Radio,* and *Film* credits (if any) separately. Under *Special Talents* or *Abilities* list only activities, sports, hobbies, or interests that generally reinforce the art of acting, such as musical instruments played, western riding, sports played, and the like. Because putting together an effective résumé is expensive and time-consuming, leave extra room at the top for changes of address and telephone number plus empty space at the bottom to add recent credits and keep the résumé up-to-date.

An actor should usually wear the same clothing to the callback as worn to the original audition, unless specifically asked by the auditioner to wear something else. This minor courtesy of continuity assists the auditioner in remembering the actor and the original audition.

An actor should never let the brief time allotted him for an audition mislead him into thinking that a director will not be able to recognize his ability.

Musical Theatre Auditions

Auditioning for a musical theatre production requires the same procedures of preparation just detailed plus the preparation of a song to sing and dance. A few pertinent guidelines follow.

1. Prepare a song through careful rehearsal with a piano accompanist and, if possible, a singing coach.
2. Select a song within the style and concept of the musical play under audition, but not from the actual play. This procedure will permit you to escape the situation of singing a song from the play under audition contrary to the manner in which the director may prefer to have it sung.
3. However, it would be wise to know one or two songs from the actual play being auditioned in the event the director asks you to try one.
4. Bring your own accompanist to the audition.
5. The factors of dress and appearance apply as described in regular auditioning. However, the clothing *must* permit easy, free movement. Usually, the actor should wear ''dance rehearsal'' clothing.
6. Dance auditions are usually separate from singing auditions and are conducted by the production choreographer. Most dance audition notices carry very specific instructions as to type and requirements (e.g., dress, shoes, music, and so on). However, as a general principle, prepare something within your ability and scope as a dancer.

Gordon Hunt and Michael Shurtleff have provided contemporary actors with particularly helpful written material relative to the special art of auditioning (see Selective Readings at the end of this chapter).

Cold Reading

In the professional theatre, more auditions are based on "cold reading" than on prepared material; that is, the director, producer, or author hands you a script and asks you to read from a designated point. Take a few minutes to look over the material. Make active choices and personalize.

Agents, Contracts, and Unions

Eventually, good actors are located by agents. Selecting an agent is as vital as selecting a career. Ask others in the profession about the quality and reputation of particular agents or seek the counsel of trade unions.

Jay Duffer

Current phone: (702) 555–4123	Height: 5'9"
Permanent phone: (713) 555–7878	Weight: 150 lbs
Voice type: baritone	Eyes: green/Hair: light brown

PERFORMANCE EXPERIENCE:

FOR ME AND MY GAL	George M. Cohan	Acuff Theatre
AIMS MUSICAL THEATRE TOUR	Feature Performer	Graz, Austria
CLOSER THAN EVER	Man 2	Kennedy Center
BROOKSHIRE'S INDUSTRIAL	Feature Performer	Tyler, Texas
CARTOON VOICE-OVER	Rock Rosenberg	Porter Prod.
ROCKIN' AT ROCKVILLE HIGH	Reggie Worthmore	Fiesta, Texas
ROMEO AND JULIET	Romeo	J. Bayley Theatre
THE CRUCIBLE	John Proctor	J. Bayley Theatre
BEST LITTLE WHOREHOUSE...	Governer	J. Bayley Theatre
SUNDAY...PARK W/GEORGE	Soldier/Alex	J. Bayley Theatre
JESUS CHRIST SUPERSTAR	Dancer	J. Bayley Theatre
CABARET	Emcee	Waco Civic
INTO THE WOODS	Wolf/Prince	Jones Theatre
WEST SIDE STORY	Riff	Jones Theatre
SONDHEIM & CO. REVUE	Feature Performer	Jones Theatre
ILLUSIONS DANCE REVUE	Dancer	MCC Community

Theatre Training:
Voice: Paul Kreider, Daniel Scott, Joyce Farwell
Dance: Cheryl Clark, Jerry MacLauchlin, Walter Nicks, Garold
   Gardener, Connie and Cindy Toornburg
Directors: Glenn Cassale, George Malonee, Lewin Goff, Bob Brewer
Stage Voice: Michael Lugering
Musical Theatre: Leta Horan, Cathy Hurst
Stage Movement: Alan Questel, Kenny Raskin
Stage Combat: J.R. Beardsley
Bachelor's of Music Education - Baylor University (Waco, TX)
Currently working towards MFA in Musical Theatre Performance at
   University of Nevada, Las Vegas

Special Skills:
Sight-singing, solo and ensemble jazz singing, composition, music
theory, conducting, dialects, snow-skiing, scuba diving, mountain climbing

Sample Résumé, Actor.

Professional actor Jay Duffer: A sample of a proper professional photograph for casting distribution.
Résumé and photo courtesy of Jay Duffer.

Actors can seek an agent by leaving a photo and résumé with an agent and by asking for an interview. In general practice, actors in the film and television industry must have an agent, especially in the sprawling city of Los Angeles. In New York, the aspiring stage performer need not have an agent in the early years of work.

Contracts are generally complex and beyond the business skills of most actors. An actor who has reached the point in his career in which contracts are involved has usually acquired an agent to handle the contracts. If not, it is advisable to consult an attorney or experienced friend prior to signing any contract.

Many actors now employ personal managers as well as agents or, in some instances, in *place* of agents. The personal manager is usually a person who goes beyond the strictly professional level of involvement used by an agent to matters that might include assisting with personal finances, investments, taxes, developing and marketing a particular image, and advice ranging from contracts to personal issues. A personal manager usually becomes viable after some degree of success in the field is achieved, yet can assist or even replace the agent in launching a career.

STACEY PLASKETT

321 Tamarus #1
New York, New York
212–871–1421

BFA in Acting, UC Santa Barbara
MFA in Music Theatre, UNLV

THEATRE (Selected list)

THE SEAGULL	NINA	*EDWARD ALBEE*
MACBETH	LADY MACBETH	*HAROLD PRINCE*
DANCING AT LUGHNASA	CHRIS	*CATHY HURST*
ROMEO AND JULIET	MERCUTIO	*MICHAEL LUGERING*
THE WORLD GOES 'ROUND	WOMAN 3 (ALTO)	*TOM HUMPHREY*
THE WIZARD OF OZ	DOROTHY	*JON SELOVER*
STAGE DOOR	TERRY RANDALL	*BARBARA BOSCH*
DOLORES	DOLORES	*PETER LACKNER*
THE BOYS FROM SYRACUSE	ADRIANA	*JUDITH OLAUSON*
A MIDSUMMER NIGHT'S DREAM	HELENA	*JUDI DICKERSON*
PIRATES OF PENZANCE	MABEL	*PAUL R. WALDO*
GUYS AND DOLLS	SARAH BROWN	*WALTER SCHOEN*
PETER PAN	PETER PAN	*JON SELOVER*
TANGO	ELEANOR	*JUDITH OLAUSON*
A LITTLE NIGHT MUSIC	CHARLOTTE	*TOM HUMPHREY*

TRAINING

ACTING: Robert Brewer, Cathy Hurst, Frank Condon, Stan Glen, Jane Ridley and James Edmondson
VOICE: Carol Kimball, Catherine Stoltz, and Elizabeth Mannion
SPEECH: Michael Lugering, Judi Dickerson, and Ursula Meyer
MOVEMENT: James Donlon, and Ron and Ludvika Popenhagen
DANCE: MODERN - (Beg/Int) JAZZ - (Beg/Int) TAP - (Beg/Int) BALLET - (Beg)

SPECIAL SKILLS

READ MUSIC, SINGING, WHIP CRACKING, JUGGLING, MASK WORK,
FENCING/STAGE COMBAT, DIALECTS: Standard English, Cockney, Irish,
and Brooklynese, SEWING AND DIVING

Sample Résumé, Actress.

Professional actress Stacey Plaskett: A sample of a proper professional photograph for casting distribution. Résumé and photo courtesy of Stacey Plaskett.

The key to obtaining both an agent and a personal manager is careful, cautious selection based on objective, reliable sources and extensive personal interviewing.

Obtaining membership in theatrical unions usually comes with increased experience, time, and, of course, professional employment. *Actor's Equity Association* (AEA or Equity) and *Screen Actor's Guild* (SAG) are the two most crucial unions for actors. Membership in these unions is the mark of the established professional. Other unions include *Screen Extras Guild* (SEG), *The American Guild of Variety Artists* (AGVA), *The American Federation of Television and Radio Artists* (AFTRA), and *The American Guild of Musical Artists* (AGMA). The AFL-CIO charters all these unions together as *The Associated Actors and Artists of America.*

The Interview

Finally, the most important thing an actor may do outside auditioning is participating in interviews. The actor interviews for casting, to obtain an agent, to negotiate with unions, and so on. The key rule to follow for a successful interview is to conduct yourself with courtesy and honesty. ''Be yourself.''

Auditioning is a perennial affliction of the art of acting—exciting, tormenting, heartbreaking, and rewarding. Always vulnerable, always hopeful, the actor by necessity returns to audition again and again. Following the tenets of this chapter can at least provide an actor with confidence to meet the experience and can enhance the opportunity for success.

Selective Readings

Cohen, Robert. *Acting Professionally.* 4th ed. Palo Alto: Mayfield Publishing Co., 1981.

Hooks, Ed. *The Audition Book.* New York: Watson-Guptill Back Stage Books, 1989.

Markus, Tom. *The Professional Actor: From Audition to Performance.* New York: Drama Book Specialists, 1978.

Matson, Katinka. *The Working Actor: A Guide to the Profession.* New York: Viking, 1976.

Shurtleff, Michael. *Audition.* New York: Walker and Co., 1978.

Silver, Fred. *Auditioning for Musical Theatre.* New York: Penguin Books, 1988.

Rehearsing 9

Our type of creativeness is
conception and birth of new being—
the person in the part. It is a natural
act similar to the birth of a human
being.

Constantin Stanislavski

On Rehearsing

Initial rehearsals are devoted to *play analysis, role analysis, and defining production goals.* Except for role analysis, most of this early process work is initiated and guided by the director and the artistic staff. Although some directors give specific guidelines on role analysis, many directors expect the actor to provide or initiate most of it. The following is an organized, precise, and practical approach to role analysis.

The Steps of Role Analysis

1. Read through the play for basic enjoyment and information.
2. Do some basic reading and research on the playwright.
3. Do some basic study or research on the era in which the play was originally written and produced.
4. Read the play a second time, focusing your attention on your role. Try to locate any and all aspects of the role that you think are similar to your personality. Personalization is the key to truth and believability.
5. Analyze the form, structure, and literal and metaphorical content of the play. Include a basic understanding of the play's type, style, subject, theme and content, exposition, point of attack, conflict, major dramatic question, protagonist or central character, antagonist or opposing force, deciding agent, struggle and complications, major crisis or turn, climax, outcome or denouement, and character drives (most of these terms are defined in the Glossary).
6. Underline all physical action executed by your character. Include "stage directions" as well as action clearly implied by dialogue.
7. Make a D to designate character "discoveries" in the margin of your acting script. A discovery is any new knowledge learned by the character. How does this discovery affect what your character thinks, does, and feels?
8. Visualize your character's physical appearance. Begin with the description provided by the playwright. Use your imagination to fill in a specific and complete visual picture of your character. Some actors complete character visualization by selecting an animal that in appearance, movement, or manner seems analogous to the role they are creating.
9. Select someone you know whose personality is analogous to your character. Do an observation study of this person.

10. Define the motivational force of your character. The motivating force should be stated in one complete sentence, including an active verb; for example, "Willy wants Biff to love him again." Be certain that the statement is specific and involves other characters whenever possible.

11. Write a biographical list of major events in your character's life. This list might include such items as "had no formal education beyond second grade," "mother died when I was age thirteen," "went to work in coal mine at age fourteen," "father was an alcoholic," "fell in love for first time at age fifteen," "joined the army at age seventeen," and so on.

12. Fill in all character activity not specifically provided in the text. Where does your character go when he exits? Why does he come back? What happens to him while he is gone?

13. Create a brief list of major character idiosyncrasies; for example, "loves wine; hates meat; likes fish or fowl; suffers from insomnia; reads classical Spanish literature"; and so on.

14. Maintain a journal concerning your work with your character.

Many directors use the second phase of rehearsals for *blocking*. Often directors plan the blocking for the actor and dictate the movements at rehearsals. However, some directors prefer to take a more flexible, organic approach to blocking. For a week or more, such directors permit actors to move at will according to motivational instincts. Later, the director refines or polishes the movement.

After blocking, *work rehearsals* are devoted to moment-by-moment coaching by the director. When actors are working with a director who rigidly dictates all aspects of character development, an unwritten code of the ethics demands that actors oblige the director. However, in these instances an actor has the right to question and discuss interpretation.

Following work rehearsals, most directors use a number of *runthrough rehearsals*. During "runthroughs" the director no longer stops the action for coaching. He devotes these rehearsals to continuity and rhythm. The actors polish their earlier work. The director takes notes that are communicated to the actors after the runthrough rehearsal.

Finally, *technical rehearsals* are used to implement scenery, lighting, properties, costumes, and makeup.

In the end, it is the job of the actor to sustain a believable performance that meets the demands of the playwright, satisfies the director, and informs the audience of the commonality of our collective struggle to be human. The process work in this book: centering, focusing, sensing, freeing, doing, and feeling work together to sustain and empower the actor in this endeavor. Our sense of artistic truth is inextricably linked to our unique understanding of our personal truth. To this end, we must continually act in person and in style.

Selective Readings

Corson, Richard. *Stage Makeup.* 7th ed. Englewood Cliffs, N.J.: Prentice-Hall, 1986.

Hodge, Francis. *Play Directing: Analysis, Communication, and Style.* 2d. ed. Englewood Cliffs, N.J.: Prentice-Hall, 1982.

Stanislavski, Constantin. *Building a Character.* New York: Theatre Arts Books, 1936.

Stanislavski, Constantin. *Creating A Role.* New York: Theatre Arts Books, 1936.

Yakim, Moni. *Creating A Character: A Physical Approach to Acting.* New York: Back Stage Books, 1990.

Acting: In Style

II

What is "style"? *Style* is a frequently misunderstood and misused word. For example, it is a common mistake to call any nonrealistic play or theatre experience "stylized." It is as though that one highly general term encompasses all possibilities and thereby all nonrealistic theatre activity is swept "by one broom into one basket."

The achievement of style in the theatre, particularly in the art of acting, requires specific analysis. For example, many actors do not know that Realism is as stylized as Romanticism or Expressionism.

No matter the style required, the initial and central problem of an actor is to use personalization to establish comfort and familiarity with the role. Then the actor must communicate the intentions as revealed by the action and characters of the script. Language, environment, emotions, thoughts, and physical activity are all parts of personalizing and communication.

In his important book *Theatre: The Rediscovery of Style,* Michel Saint-Denis discusses how *style* is rooted in the form and content of the play, in its language, and in its historical period.[1] According to Saint-Denis, the style of the play is not determined merely by its language or by the social conventions of the period or by the design of the scenery. The *total* play in historic perspective creates its style, that is, its particular reality.

In its simplest and earliest definition, the word *style* comes from the Latin word *stilus,* a pointed instrument used by the ancients in writing on wax tablets. The stilus made an imprint, a definition, into the wax and left its expression in either design or words. This indentation made a distinct, original, and sometimes artistic impression. We loosely attribute style to a person who is an artist or who is artistic. In this sense, any person can be an artist who is said to have style, from the lady who wears her fox fur elegantly to a sculptor welding a metal collage. Style represents not only a personal stamp, but also a mode of perception by the artist. An artist chooses a recognizable pathway from intention to execution and synthesizes the form and material into a living emotional or intellectual experience that is particular. When a literary or dramatic artist can compel the language to conform to the mode of experience, communication with the audience will be more precise and, therefore, comprehensible.

Finally, some cautionary advice concerning costumes and clothing as they affect movement and performing period style in plays from different time periods: (*a*) Examine all photographic and illustrative evidence available to determine the basic line and flow of garments; then try to assimilate those lines and that flow in garments worn for rehearsal and performance to assist appropriate physical behavior. (*b*) Observe films listed in the Selective Filmography to note how other actors handle period costumes.

Introduction to
Part II
"In Style"

(c) Keep in mind that undergarments were as crucial to people in period times as they are today; undergarments had a direct influence on movement and stature. Tight corsets and girdles were once worn by both men and women; hoop skirts underpinned huge, long dresses; garters for stockings were worn by both men and women; and so on. The actor must do research and, along with director and designers, come to decisions concerning the kind and amount of undergarments to be used on stage as they bear on both physical action and characterization. (d) Remember that the so-called commonfolk, or commonpeople, of any period dressed with fewer and less ornate garments than did royalty or the so-called upper-class people. Thus, costumes and clothing for such characters are freer and easier to wear; also, characterization is affected quite differently relative to speed and quality of action. Most commonfolk characters behave and move similarly to ordinary people today, whereas the aristocracy in period plays tend to behave and move in more restricted, controlled fashion. These specific cautions, or advice, aside, keep firmly in mind that it is a mistake to think we can locate a *definitive* style for *any* period or classification of plays. In other words, a certain amount of "translation" or "adaptation" is always involved in interpreting any "removed" style to the stage for contemporary audiences. The actor, director, and designer must integrate both historical/cultural considerations on "how" theatre was done earlier along with personalized ways of working in contemporary terms. The actor today must confront the task of translating specific stylistic period elements into a modern idiom without undue distortion. It is crucial that you keep this factor about a "definitive style" well in mind as you study and practice the material in each of the ten chapters that follow.

There are two courses open to playwrights when they recreate a particular reality in the theatre. If the playwright chooses a representational technique, the writing brings a truthful image of life into the theatre that establishes and enhances the illusion of the playwright's reality. The actors appear to represent true life by being *oblivious* of the audience and by interacting only with each other. In representational drama, the audience is only permitted to "peek through an illusory fourth wall." The other avenue open to a playwright is to utilize the presentational technique that directs the actor to focus on the audience with *awareness* that it is there watching. This creates a different kind of reality, one that *includes* the audience within it.

Saint-Denis clarified that learning to act in any style means accepting the concept that an acting style is an organic outgrowth of a play. *Style in a theatre production is the truth or essence of the particular play being produced. Primarily, it is the author's particular view of truth or reality.* Even a distorted nightmare depicted on stage is truth and reality to its author. *Obviously, then, style is a direct result of the choices used by the artist in creating the art object.* (It was Aristotle who noted that *identity* is revealed primarily by choice.) *Thus, individual choices are made to create an object or form, controlled by the goals established by the artist, and the result of those choices and goals creates the particular style of the object, form, and artist. It follows that the task of any actor relative to the delineation of style is to understand and find ways to execute or perform the author's/character's choices accurately and with a truthful sense of inevitability.* This entire process is what Professor Roger Gross and others have called ''organic,'' that is, interconnected and fluid.

As Saint-Denis also explained, the style of a play is additionally a process that creatively reflects the mode of some particular era. The author mirrors the hopes, desires, and attitudes of the people living in that age. The playwright is motivated by current psychological, social, religious, and philosophical influences. The playwright is further influenced by the architecture of the theatre, the climate and geography of the country, the technical means of production, the traditions of playwriting, the theories of acting, and the nature of the audiences who see the plays. When an audience is led to identify and accept the reality of the artistic statement, then the mode of presenting the truth of the author and that age becomes the dominant style of the period.

How can we delineate the truths of the past? Style is captured by presenting the author's reality in its own way, not by imposing our own or some other reality on it. Much of the truth of an age resides in the values, personal relationships, and insights into the human condition revealed by its literary and dramatic artists. Also, the prevailing mood, the aesthetic and sensory awareness, the scientific investigation, and the search for knowledge are expressed in an individualized manner by the playwright.

However, all the traditions of a particular age cannot be translated from generation to generation. We can only infuse acting with style by commanding our attention to the plays that in turn will lead us to the spirit of the author and that age. After all, the theatre is not life. The theatre represents life.

How can the actor arrive at an authentic appraisal of the playwright's personal stamp or style? In order for actors to comfortably adopt the original style, they must first examine the dramatic form of a play, either tragedy or comedy, or their derivatives, melodrama, farce, tragicomedy, and other subforms. The reading of plays will help one develop an understanding of the basic classifications of the drama. In addition, study in play analysis can bring awareness of the basic essentials that relate form to the literal and metaphorical content of a play (see Francis Hodge for an in-depth study of play analysis, as well as James H. Clay and Daniel K. Krempel for a metaphorical approach to play analysis).[2] Play analysis (which is specifically a director's responsibility but is invaluable also to an actor) involves study of a play's form, literal and metaphorical content, structure (e.g., plot, character, thought, dialogue, melody, and spectacle), and author's intention. Play analysis precedes style analysis, which is the final clarification of a play's particular reality and its means of expressing that reality (a detailed guide to play analysis is provided in Appendix A). See also the discussion of acting in style in John Harrop's and Sabin Epstein's book, *Acting With Style*.[3]

Your specific study of style begins with the great century of classical antiquity, fifth century B.C., in the country of Greece.

Notes

1. Michel Saint-Denis, *Theatre: The Rediscovery of Style,* (New York: Theatre Arts Books, 1960).
2. Francis Hodge, *Play Directing, Analysis, Communication and Style,* 2d. Ed. (Englewood Cliffs, N.J.: Prentice-Hall, 1982); James H. Clay and Daniel K. Krempel, *The Theatrical Image* (New York: McGraw-Hill Book Co., 1967).
3. John Harrop and Sabin Epstein, *Acting With Style* (Englewood Cliffs, N.J.: Prentice-Hall, 1982).

Classical Antiquity: Restraint 10

Man's life is a day. What is he?
What is he not? A shadow in a
dream
Is man: but when God sheds a
brightness,
Shining light on earth
And life is sweet as honey.

Pindar
The Pythian Odes

Never man again may swear things
shall be as they once were.

Archilochus
from *Ancient Gems in*
Modern Settings

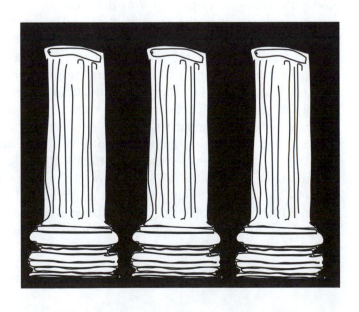

Overview of Greek Tragedy

The origins of Greek drama are generally familiar but extremely speculative. Few matters of scholarship are certain. Vase paintings, some extant plays, and writing fragments provide most of the available information. Greek drama probably evolved from the rites performed in honor of Dionysus by masked worshipers who danced and sang (e.g., Dithyrambs, or hymns to Dionysus) and worked themselves into a frenzy in order to lose their identity and merge with nature and gods. As drama slowly emerged from these ceremonies, it became more and more formalized. So, too, did the physical place evolve as a recognizable area for the presentation of drama. The very earliest *orchestra,* or dancing place, was probably a threshing floor worn smooth by oxen who trod grain upon it. Around the orchestra the *theatron,* or seeing place, developed where the spectators sat on the ground to watch the religious ceremonies. These earliest theatres were always built into a hillside to accommodate large numbers of people. Historical references are also made concerning the custom of having the actors change costumes in a tent, or *skene,* in a sacred wood nearby. As plays grew more complex, the actors were required to enter and leave the orchestra more quickly. Eventually a wooden skene, or scene house, containing dressing rooms and storage space was built directly behind the theatre for the actors. In time, painted set pieces were placed in front of this building to represent scenery. These became more and more intricate with the evolution of the *proskenion,* or central playing area, and the scene building itself became merely a background structure. Wooden and later stone seats were added to the hillside.

The first actor of record was Thespis, who was also a playwright and production manager or precursor of the director. We have evidence that Thespis performed in the first dramatic-religious festivals in Athens around 534 B.C. He probably wore different masks to represent different characters and was the sole actor in a tragedy. These early plays used a chorus or group of singer-dancers who sang odes between the actor's speeches or dialogue. The chorus served ultimately as character, narrator, participant, and ideal spectator. Only men were allowed to act in plays.

In tragedy, three great writers are noteworthy because of their exemplary work and their significant contributions to the development of dramatic art and theatre: Aeschylus (525–456 B.C.), Sophocles (496–406 B.C.), and Euripides (480–406 B.C.). In comedy, Aristophanes (ca. 448–ca. 380 B.C.) was probably the greatest Greek author of Old Comedy (meaning "early"). Later, another writer, Menander (ca. 342–292 B.C.), contributed significantly to the transition from Greek to Roman comedy.

Greek tragedy can be characterized as follows:

1. Use of a limited number of characters acted usually by one to three actors who changed masks to portray different roles. Most scholars agree that Aeschylus used a single actor in his plays; Sophocles, two actors; and Euripides, three or more.
2. Use of a singing-dancing chorus. It should be noted that Aeschylus emphasized the chorus in his plays and Euripides emphasized the actor, giving little attention to the chorus. Sophocles struck a balance of emphasis.
3. Use of iambic trimeter verse for dialogue and for choral odes.
4. Use of a superhuman hero in the plays of Aeschylus, usually a powerful mythological character whose will was continually subjugated to the higher impersonal power of the gods.
5. Use of refined, idealized characters with human problems (rather than religious themes) in the plays of Sophocles, centered on strong, forceful, vehement emotion with which the audience could easily identify.
6. Use of ordinary characters with everyday problems in which thought and emotion were unified in the plays of Euripides, providing the transition from old to new ideas and from religion-myth to human passion.
7. Use of sexual themes in the plays of Euripides to portray man's beginning struggle not with fate and the gods, but with society and his mind and emotions.

Beauty, truth, and grandeur were the objectives of the tragic writers. Greek verse is noble and poetic and stresses a measured cadence. Action is brief and straightforward and concentrates on a single point. Characters are present at any given time on the stage. The Greek authors carefully avoided indiscriminate realism or excessive violence in front of an audience; this action was performed offstage or told in the narrative (note the death of Ajax in Sophocles's *Ajax* and of Evadine in Euripides's *Suppliants*). Greek tragedy penetrates our feelings by its even flow of dialogue interspersed with passages of choral odes and subtle changes of metrical form enhanced by accurate vocal intonation.

Greek acting was characterized by the wearing of masks—large, serious masks for tragedy and somewhat more life-size but grotesque ones for comedy. Early in the development of Greek drama, simple slippers were used on the feet, and the actors may have also performed in bare feet. Later, thick wooden or cork shoes were worn. High shoes or boots called *cothurni* increased an actor's height to larger-than-life size. Long, flowing garments or short simple ones usually in brilliant colors were used. Probably the masks were also very colorful. Later, a high headdress was frequently worn. (Highly simplified scenic equipment may have been available for performances, such as altars, statues, tombs, cranes, scenic prisms, and platforms.)

The exact style of acting in Greek tragedy remains uncertain. Scholars offer a number of theories from which we may determine the attributes of a typical classical Greek actor. We do know that acting was considered a craft by the classical Greek philosopher Socrates. To Plato, his protégé, acting was something that could not, and should not, be learned. The extant play texts reveal that acting in tragedy called for simple, direct action—clear, controlled, and orderly. Some realistic actions are suggested in the plays, such as running, weeping, and falling on the ground. Conventional action was often necessary, as in the choral passages where lyricism and dance are prevalent. While we know that actors had to play many characters within each play and that men took female roles, it may be that females acted minor comedy parts. Although we know that a realistic or lifelike technique of acting was not employed totally by Greek tragic actors, performance of Greek plays today should not be devoid of identifiable human action. It is possible that actors created a sense of realism by discovering expressive and sympathetic characteristics and portrayed them in a somewhat idealized form. The total concept of characterization, then, was truthfulness in a somewhat larger-than-life impersonation.

Voice—Greek Tragedy

Acting techniques for the tragic Greek actor were very specialized due to the tremendous size of the physical theatre. The size can be calculated to be approximately the area of a football stadium and the number of spectators to range from 15,000 to 100,000. Acoustics in this bowl-shaped structure were good. Given a strong, resonant, clear voice, an actor did not exert excessive vocal effort. In effect, the impression created probably tended more toward a recitative or singing mode.

To perform Greek tragedy in present-day theatre requires healthy vocal production. However, you should not de-emphasize the enunciative quality of Greek speech. You may encounter difficulty when working with Greek lyrical passages, especially in key emotional moments. When a long sentence is sustained, it is very difficult to maintain precise diction throughout the line. On the other hand, you also face the possibility of losing the emotional builds at the expense of achieving competence in projection and enuneiation.

Exercise 1   The Voice—Greek Tragedy

1. Each actor sings a musical scale individually. Repeat the exercise as a choral group.
2. Practice speaking the following line individually as though chanting it in an echo chamber. Repeat the exercise singing the line. Finally, repeat the exercise and modify the recitative and sung experience into spoken delivery, but retain the larger-than-life quality of the first two deliveries. Repeat the exercise as a choral group.

   ''Let every man in mankind's frailty
   consider his last day, and let none
   Presume on his good fortune until he finds
   Life, at his death, a memory without pain.''

   Chorus, Sophocles
   Oedipus the King

3. Go outdoors to a large, enclosed patio or to a stadium; practice calling and greeting other actors at long distances. Try the previous speech from *Oedipus the King* in number 2.

Movement—Greek Tragedy

The Greek actor had to carry himself with authority and confidence. Most of his movement was probably slow, majestic, and rhythmic. Movement must have been simplified and broadened to accompany the idealized characterization. Physical contact between actors was probably rare; more than likely the quality of restraint was accentuated by allowing great physical distance between characters. The long monologues in the plays would seem to indicate that body positions were mostly full-front, one-quarter, or profile. The manner of speaking was probably directed more toward the audience than toward other actors (i.e., presentational). Gestures must have been simple, large, or even grand, flowing, and complete, emanating from the upper part of the body. They were probably conventionalized and immediately understood by audiences. It is unlikely that actors ever sat on the stage. It is likely that simple hand props such as a staff, scepter, or sword were carried. At times, certain characters such as a chorus of furies might have carried lighted torches. We can assume that the gods carried their emblems (e.g., a lion skin and club for Heracles).

A Greek tragedy given in today's theatre would probably utilize many of the original Greek conventions. Once again, depending on the size of the theatre, begin from the Greek concept of simple restraint. Generally perform slow, suggestive, rhythmic movements and gestures. The presentational mode of acting should probably dominate, but not to excess. However, a sensible balance between presentational and representational interpretation should be achieved; for example, when one actor turns to respond directly to the audience, the other actor should usually focus on the speaker. Individualized physical movements should be kept to a minimum. While you may move more onstage than your classical Greek counterpart, you must be extremely careful to sustain controlled physical presence. Modern adaptations of the Greek acting style rarely execute a purist concept of the original style. More often than not, you may be required to sit, carry more hand properties than the original Greek style, and relate with other actors more (e.g., touch, stand close, and so on).

It is not known in what exact style the chorus performed its dance functions. Here, too, a modern adaptation might be more flexible than suggested by the traditional Greek chorus. Since we have no record of choral dancing except descriptions that date back to the early religious ceremonies honoring the god Dionysus (e.g., dancing with animallike frenzy), the key to dance adaptation is probably to use controlled, dignified, stately movement with shifting rhythmic patterns.

It is difficult to speak about movements and gestures without again referring to the subject of masks and costumes since they directly affect an actor's physical projection. In the early development of Greek drama, masks may have been made of lightweight linen, wood, or cork. The mask was placed over the head of the actor and undoubtedly gave depth and clarity to facial expression and head movement. (The mask had an open mouth, which a few historians say could have amplified the human voice; however, most recent scholarship does not support this view.) The mask indicated the essence of the character—tragic by an expression of physical or mental suffering and happy by a smile or contented look. In general, the mask showed the specific emotional state of the character. Sometimes, the actor changed masks as the character changed moods or as he changed roles. However, it would seem that the mask could be manipulated by the actor to create shadows that in turn gave an illusion of changing expression. Later in the development of Greek drama, most tragic characters wore a headdress or a wiglike structure called an *onkus*. Together, the mask and the headdress probably restrained flexibility of head movement.

The body garment of the later Greek periods must have presented a problem of mobility. A long-sleeved, ankle-length, heavily embroidered tunic, or *chiton,* was worn by the major characters. According to scenes depicted on vase paintings, other characters wore native dress such as a short tunic, mourning clothes, or ragged garments, all designed to represent the daily clothes of ordinary Greek citizens. Indications are that the chorus wore clothing prescribed by age, sex, and national and social status. Although the clothing in later periods must have been somewhat restrictive due to length and heaviness, this in no way indicates that the actors were unable to move. In fact, costumes remained remarkably similar to the everyday dress of the citizens and did allow freedom of movement and speech and rapid change of roles, particularly during early development of Greek drama.

The modern actor need be concerned only with wearing a costume that does not inhibit freedom of movement. It would be a mistake to use a garment and its accompanying decor (e.g., headdress, boots) that would constrict you in any great way. The main concern is whether masks should be worn in a modern adaptation. Masks should be worn when close fidelity to the original Greek is desired. Heightened, formalized makeup, applied to resemble remotely the look of a mask or half-mask may enhance audience involvement. (See Irene Corey's designs in this chapter.)

Exercise 2   Movement—Greek Tragedy

1. All actors come to an aligned, centered position on their feet. Move through space in the manner of a slow-motion film or in the manner of moving through water or as a spaceman on another planet. Concentrate upon grace, rhythm, fluidity, and a sense of controlled restraint.
2. Repeat number 1 using a modified tempo and permitting the slow motion to evolve into an acceptably believable or realistic tempo.
3. Practice various forms of stereotyped movement gestures that reflect emotional states, such as drawing one arm up slowly with the back of your hand in front of your eyes, your other hand protruding behind you, and your body slowly bending backward to indicate grief. As a welcoming gesture, slowly extend both arms forward and upward with the palms up; the head should elevate somewhat, and the entire body should come to its full height. Freely invent other kinds of movement gestures.
4. Costume yourself in any kind of long robe and/or cape with bare feet, slippers, or sandals, and practice moving with grace and fluidity. Incorporate the garments into your gesturing. This exercise also works well by imagining you are on a space walk in the universe.

Music—Greek Tragedy

It is important to understand the major emphasis placed on musical accompaniment in the original Greek plays. In the beginning, use of music was light, to underscore choral passages. Later, music became more prominent, and actors used a variety of instruments including the flute, whose tone was similar to that of a modern oboe or clarinet, and the lyre, a stringed instrument used for special effects. A flute player probably preceded the chorus into the orchestra and played music as an accompaniment to underscore the emotions described in the choral passages. Occasionally, music might have been used during the episodes or acted segments. Music was extremely important in choral interludes because it made the singing and dancing more harmonious. Additionally, it aided in building choral passages to a climax.

Repeat Exercise 2 to the accompaniment of the extant musical fragments titled "Delphic Hymn" and "Epitaph of Seikilos and Mandi-kiaw."[1] If this recording is not available in your school library, any recording utilizing flutes, drums, and string instruments played in relatively slow tempo will do. Also, many contemporary ethnic composers have created music that can serve to complement the exercises in this chapter. For example, ala Hal im El-Dabh has composed exciting works for the Greek theatre. An actor slowly pounding a rhythm on a drum or tabletop can also serve this exercise well.

Again repeat Exercise 2, but this time *create* "music" through hand-clapping, humming, and fingersnapping.

Character and Emotion—Greek Tragedy

Greek tragedy reveals the author's awareness of each character's underlying motives and justification for action and emotion, but not at the sacrifice of the lyric poetry of the verse.

The problems of a modern actor attempting to physicalize emotions in an ideal way, to maintain believability, and to achieve truthfulness in a Greek role are not insurmountable. Difficulty will arise if you overemphasize the physical aspects of style instead of maintaining a good balance of believable characterization grounded in the reality of the style. Examine the play for primary motivations and justifications, particularly those analogous or similar to yours in order to use personalization at the beginning of rehearsals; find the emotional builds within each scene; discover the intentions of the character as described by the playwright. At times you may encounter conflicting or paradoxical stylistic demands such as restrained versus heightened vocalization and movement. The solution is not to play one quality and eliminate the other. Modify both or adapt them, using both qualities in an appropriate mix of the restrained and the heightened. Role and play analyses will indicate when restraint should dominate the acting and when the acting should be heightened. For example, in the play *Oedipus the King* by Sophocles, the actor portraying Oedipus may effectively use restraint through modern, naturalistic emotion when Oedipus talks to his subjects about the plague early in the play. Oedipus is emotionally under control; he is a proud, majestic king whose voice and movement are characterized by precision and grace. Later in the play,

Studies in makeup design, formalized to resemble the look of the classical Greek mask. Design by Irene Corey for Sophocles's *Electra*; Everyman Players, directed by Orlin Corey.

when Oedipus discovers that calamity is the result of his own actions, greatly heightened emotion, vocalization, and movement should be used, including rapid tempo, strong volume, expansive physicalization, and bold movement. Most Greek playwrights of tragedy wrote to idealize and to transcend the emotions of the ordinary Athenian citizens and to challenge them by exciting their pity for and fear of the character. To use both restrained and heightened emotion in a Greek tragedy requires careful analysis and focus. You will need to adapt your emotion from so-called real-life emotion to the larger-than-life conception of the tragic writer.

Exercise 3   Character and Emotion—Greek Tragedy

1. Examine each of the following phrases that depicts a single idea and an emotional disposition. Establish an immobile physical position that typifies the essence of the emotion or idea. The face and entire body should express the idea or feeling. Once this is successfully accomplished, place the physicalization and attitude into motion through simple walking, sitting, and gesturing. After this is accomplished, invent a complete sentence of dialogue expressing the idea or emotion you are depicting. Memorize the sentence, and as you physicalize and move, vocalize the sentence with different tempos and a variety of expressions ranging from classical restraint to naturalistic intensity.
   a. Excessive pride
   b. Incestuous passion

Oedipus the King by Sophocles. James Barton Hill as Oedipus and Martin Molson as The Priest (up left) at the Hilberry Theatre, Wayne State University. Directed and scenic design by Richard Spear, costumes by Robert Pusilo, and lighting by Gary M. Witt.

    c. Obsessive revenge
    d. Martyred sacrifice
    e. Burial grief
    f. Insane frenzy
    g. Blind drunkenness

2. Select a partner and face one another in a standing position, one of you designated as ''leader.'' Using the concept of the ''mirror'' exercise, mimic one another in the facial depiction of various emotions; repeat the exercise, but this time the ''follower'' should facially express a *contrasting* emotion to that depicted by the ''leader.''

Overview of Satyr Comedy and Old Greek Comedy (Aristophanes)

As the Greek tragic playwrights acquired a following in the fifth century B.C., festival officials required them to present a satyr play when they competed in the festivals. A satyr play was a short comedy that usually burlesqued a Greek myth. This afterpiece utilized a chorus of satyrs who satirized the seriousness of tragic stories by parodying gods, heroes, tragic dances, actions, conventions of acting, costumes, and scenery. The satyrs wore a goatskin loincloth with a phallus (comic imitation of the male sexual organ) in the front and a horse tail in the rear. They wore tight flesh-colored garments that ridiculed tragic costumes. Some characters wore masks with fixed size and expression. In the earlier satyr plays, the masks were not large. Later masks covered the entire head and were decorated with hair, beards, and ornaments. The chorus usually wore identical masks representing animals; the actors wore masks with set human expressions. Characters who did not wear masks, primarily the satyrs, had a snub nose, dark unkempt hair, a beard, and pointed ears, or they were bald and wore horns on top of their head. All action concentrated on lewd pantomime and general buffoonery.

Today we have only one complete satyr play, *Cyclops* by Euripides. It is a parody of the story found in the *Odyssey*.

Greek comedy was officially supported by the State beginning in 486 B.C. (it may have been part of the festival City Dionysia in 501 B.C.). The first professional comedians probably made their debut onstage around 455 B.C., displaying their buffoonery and comic jests. The chorus consisted of twenty-four members whose function was to perform music and dance.

Old Comedy, as exemplified by the works of Aristophanes, differed from tragedy principally in subject matter and in approach. The stories were concerned with contemporary matters of politics or art or with revealing corrupt public and private practices such as sustaining foreign war and the practice of pedantic sophistry. Well-known politicians, philosophers, and playwrights also received a fair share of notoriety in the plays. Usually institutions and public figures were satirized or held up to ridicule for their beliefs or practices. Plot was entirely the invention of the playwright, and unlimited license was the rule. Greek comic plays provided a balance between exaggeration and believability. Caricature was the prominent feature in character portrayal; however, roles of minor stature required closer fidelity to real life. These so-called low characters projected everyday emotional response. Hence, verisimilitude, or fidelity to real life, was vital in Greek comedy, although fantasy was occasionally intermingled (see *The Birds, The Frogs, The Wasps, The Clouds*, etc.).

Voice—Old Greek Comedy

Vocalization in Old Greek Comedy was undoubtedly much more lifelike than was vocalization in tragedy. Since the characters were often members of lower social status, everyday speech was necessary (the exceptions to this were characters such as gods and statesmen). Vocal variety, clarity of diction, and effective projection are standard techniques for successful vocalization of Old Comedy. Occasionally, singing is required as well. Lyricism and rhythm are important in line delivery.

Exercise 4 Voice—Old Greek Comedy

1. Practice the following speech individually and then collectively emphasizing vocal variety, clear diction, and effective vocal production.

> Frogs   Brekekekex Koax Koax
> Brekekekex Koax Koax!
> We are the swamp-children
> Greeny and tiny,
> Fluting our voices
> As all in time we
> Sing our Koax Koax
> Koax Koax Koax

2. Repeat the exercise by *singing* it lyrically and rhythmically, both individually and collectively.
3. Practice various kinds of animal, insect, and bird sounds, calls, and noises (for example, goats, wasps, geese, and so on). Eventually turn these sounds into comic, ''human'' variations of the sounds, including the actual use of words that are easily formed by the sounds (for example, ''bad'' from ''baaa,'' ''fuzz'' from ''bzzz,'' and ''whack'' from ''quaa'').

Movement—Old Greek Comedy

The movement in Old Greek Comedy was mimetic, large or bold, and expressive of a character type; expression undoubtedly developed from highly exaggerated wild-animal movements adapted from religious dances and victory celebrations. Emphasis was probably on kicking the buttocks, slapping the chest or thighs, leaping, high kicking, running, spinning like a top, and beating other actors. Some scholars think that three to five major characters in the play joined the chorus to perform pantomimic tricks and stage business with gusto and fast-paced rhythm. The movement must have depended on the performer executing a variety of skills. Athletic and disciplined, the actors probably reverted to extensive physical action and body contact, relying heavily on farcical and satiric invention and the interpolation of song, dance, and comic acrobatics.

Although comic costumes provided the actor with freer movement, they were not necessarily standard or prescribed. As seen on vase paintings, actors usually wore short, tight-fitting tunics (chitons) over flesh-colored tights to give the illusion of partial nakedness. Nudity and ridiculousness were further emphasized by attaching a phallus to the costumes of most male characters. As in the satyr plays, a mask was a common accoutrement of the comic costume. However, masks were probably more specialized in function, depicting actual persons or representing animals, birds, insects, or exaggerated characteristics such as baldness, skinniness, and obesity.

When Greek comic acting is adapted for modern audiences, very little adjustment is needed. Personalization can again be used effectively in early rehearsals, particularly if you have an instinctive flair for comedy, timing, and laughter and a sense of humor. Major focus should be on the extensive use of physical action and body contact, with corresponding pantomimic business. This simply means to use much burlesque or vaudeville activity. Use music, dance, singing, and acrobatics to provide interpolation between dialogue as well as to punctuate comic lines. Play to the audience slightly more than to one another (e.g., presentational technique slightly dominates representational). Let movements and gestures be energetic, large, and rapid. Coordinate your movements with the satiric speeches to add stress and clarity to the thought. Respond to an emotion when it is appropriate but do not indulge in the feeling, or tempo and pace will be sacrificed. Use costume to simulate nudity, and to provide an illusion of sexuality use a phallus. Most important, you must be physically able to handle the demands of Greek comedy. A high energy level helps provide the correct rhythm to the play; vocal variety, clear diction, and effective vocal production aid in crystallizing satirical points, and a relaxed, well-toned physical posture allows for body control and agility.

Exercise 5   Movement—Old Greek Comedy

1. Repeat vocal Exercise 4, but this time concentrate on executing the following physical activities as you deliver the lines.
   a. Somersaults
   b. Cartwheels
   c. High kicks
   d. Handstands
   e. Leapfrog
   f. Pratfalls
   g. Comic hitting, running, and animallike dancing
   h. Juggling

2. Costume yourself in any kind of short, sacklike garment with or without a waist belt and bare feet, slippers, or sandals. Construct simplified comic "tails," "phalluslike clubs," and "grotesque masks." Practice slapstick clowning, buffoonery, dances, and acrobatics.

Character and Emotion—Old Greek Comedy

Authors of comedy such as Aristophanes focused upon a single obsessive dimension of human character, utilizing it for stereotype or caricature (only occasionally did he create full-dimensional, believable human characters). Aristophanes also used animals, birds, and inanimate objects as character types to represent human beings. He mixed reality and fantasy and treated both in a satiric manner. Examples of his character types include the pompous statesman or philosopher (see Socrates in *The Clouds*), the frustrated lover (see Kinesias in *Lysistrata*), the vulnerable and effeminate god (see Dionysus in *The Frogs*), the comic bird (see Epops in *The Birds*), and the amusing slave or parasite (see Xanthius in *The Frogs*). The emotion depicted by these characters was frequently singular and obsessive; for example, Kinesias's sole interest was in sexual activity with his wife. Accordingly, character and emotion in Old Greek Comedy are much less complex to perform than in Greek tragedy. Emphasis must be on mechanical techniques, physicalization, voice, and movement. However, personalization should support all work with mechanics.

Also note that characters in Greek comedy often make abrupt changes from lyricism to broad farce (see *Lysistrata* as an example). Consequently, acting transitions simply are not provided in the script. This puts extra burden on the actor who often must create transitions or simply change activity without use of them.

Exercise 6   Character and Emotion—Old Greek Comedy

1. Invent one comic emotional characteristic for each of the character types in the list that follows. Establish an immobile physical position that typifies the essence or idea. Your face and entire body should express the essence of the idea or feeling. Once this is successfully accomplished, place the physicalization and attitude into rapid motion through fast walking, sitting, gesturing, tumbling, hitting, and falling. After these movements are accomplished, invent a complete sentence of dialogue expressing the idea or emotion you are depicting. (For example, for pompous statesman, the sentence could be, "I am a great king.") Memorize the sentence and as you move, vocalize the sentence with different tempos and a variety of expressions, ranging from larger-than-life size to modern, naturalistic detail.

a. Pompous statesman
b. Braggart warrior
c. Passionate lover
d. Effeminate god
e. Comic bird
f. Comic frog
g. Comic wasp
h. Comic cloud
i. Comic slave
j. Comic poet

2. Select a character from the list in number 1. Perform an improvisational monologue in which you tell a comic story; depict a variety of emotions with comic expressiveness—all in the mode of the character you have created.

A final word on masks. The director, designer, and actor must decide on the key question "To mask or not to mask?" when transferring any ancient Greek play to the stage. The choices range from the traditional classical Greek full mask to stylized makeup masks to controlled, restrained "facial expression masks" created strictly by the grimaces of the actor. Generally, the choice of mask via makeup or the face of the actor is effective in smaller spaces, unless a "pure" approach is deliberately sought for an outdoor arena or theatre of great size.

Transition—Roman and Medieval Drama

Greece attained its greatest influence during the fifth and fourth centuries B.C. Thereafter, military and economic difficulties eroded the power of Greece, while Rome became the dominant influence in the known world.

Roman Drama

Early Roman theatre utilized a crude form of improvised dialogue. Abusive and obscene, drama was given mostly at harvest and wedding celebrations. Favorite entertainment included chariot races, boxing contests, athletic games, and gladiatorial contests in stadiumlike arenas. The dominant theatre form was the farce play. The farces were heavily influenced by Old Greek Comedy and the so-called Middle or New Comedy of Menander, written during the Hellenistic period of the fourth century. Menander reemphasized the ordinary characters and farce typical of Old Greek Comedy. By the middle of the second century B.C., Rome produced its first major playwrights, Plautus and Terence. Plautus wrote comic farces whose plot devices and low-life characters were of minimal dimension. The plays of Terence were more genteel, and their content was more educational in purpose. Available evidence indicates that the Romans produced comedies and few, if any, tragedies in their theatre. However, Seneca did write several tragedies based on Greek models. These tragedies, while probably never produced, had major influence on Renaissance playwrights hundreds of years later (this influence is discussed in chapter 12).

In serious Roman drama, Seneca's characters, modeled after their classical Greek counterparts, were deeply emotional.

In Roman comedy, the characters were one-dimensional stereotypes, particularly in the plays of Plautus. Plautine farces usually depicted characters of a single emotional bent. The plays of Terence contained a more lifelike human dimension, and the characters were of a slightly more complex emotional level.

Since Roman dramas are rarely produced in the modern theatre and because the style of acting in these dramas is so closely allied to the Greek style, this style of acting is merely summarized here.

Acting Roman Drama

Acting in serious Roman plays was probably closely allied to oratory. Actors probably declaimed to the audience, using little vocal variety. Evidence from Quintilian and Plutarch indicates that meaning and thought were stressed in oratory rather than emotion and feeling.

In Roman comedy, effective vocal production and close attention to comic patterns of speech are necessary. Increased emphasis on words and phrases will intensify the comic meaning.

Movement in serious Roman drama is best handled today by using the techniques explained in the Greek discussion of classical style, with some modification (i.e., less exaggeration in movement and gesture and less vocal size).

Roman comedy should probably be produced as originally presented—broad and lusty and with a large amount of physical contact between performers. Most of the material should be played directly to the audience (presentational). Again, dancing, tumbling, acrobatics, hitting, falling, running, and general slapstick behavior can be used effectively. Great emphasis should be placed on comic precision in the timing of business and dialogue. Many of the Old Greek comic properties such as clapboards, staffs, fans, money pouches, and so on should be used.

Most of the acting style characteristic of Greek drama may be used (with modification) to perform Roman drama. The Roman theatre was important for vitality and entertainment, for perpetuating and adapting Greek drama, and for a heritage that Renaissance playwrights were to use effectively.

Medieval Drama

The power of the Roman empire diminished by the sixth century A.D. Invasions by nomadic barbarians and the influence of the Christian Church splintered Roman power and dispersed popular entertainment and theatre activity. Popular theatre was forbidden during the so-called Dark Ages or Medieval Ages, which ranged generally from the sixth century well into the tenth century A.D. Ironically, the Church helped revive theatre activity by introducing exchanges of dialogue in the form of *tropes,* or hymns, into the mass between the priest and the choir. Later, actual scenery and costumes were used to help teach moral and religious lessons.

As the activity became increasingly secular and involved more participants, drama moved out of the church itself onto the church steps and into streets and courtyards. The mystery plays (biblical stories), miracle plays (stories of saints and martyrs), and morality plays (stories with moral precepts) were produced on a simple platform. In England these kinds of plays were performed on pageant wagons that were drawn by horses through the streets, stopping to perform as a crowd formed. Trade merchants formed guilds that sponsored and produced these religious plays in England and on the Continent.

Eventually, secular, or nonreligious, material became more important than religious material in the plays. Native farce comedy began to dominate theatre activity and was a major development in the transition from the religious plays to the great theatre of the Renaissance. Interludes, another transitional dramatic form, were also performed and were particularly enjoyed by nobles and rich merchants. Interludes were often performed by minstrels or jongleurs (strolling players) who were skilled in singing, dancing, and storytelling. Medieval theatre produced few known playwrights. Authorship was generally anonymous.

Acting Medieval Drama

Several Medieval plays are still produced. *Everyman* (anonymous), *The Second Shepherd's Play* (anonymous), *Pierre Patelin* (anonymous), *The Iron Pot* by Hans Sachs, and the short biblical pieces of Hrosvitha the Nun are among the most popular with audiences. If the limitations caused by negligible information on styles of Medieval acting are recognized, Medieval plays can be a valid acting vehicle if you begin by carefully defining your physical acting area. Since these plays were usually performed on a platform stage, adaptation of a Medieval play requires a similarly limited acting space. Generally, be careful not to perform on a large stage requiring a complicated set. Use smaller areas that limit movement and gesture. Rely essentially on strong, clear vocal work and vivid physicalization to project characterization. (Although characters are clearly and boldly drawn in Medieval plays, some subtle psychological traits, revealed primarily in monologues and isolated scenes, do exist.) Acting in Medieval plays should project a predominately lifelike quality. A study of occupational skills prevalent during the Middle Ages will provide insight into details of everyday life. Since most of these plays emphasize religious allegories and everyday activities (e.g., a monk at study, a carpenter at work, a mason laying bricks, a cobbler making shoes, or a tailor sewing clothes), the modern actor needs to give his character sufficient stage business to develop believable characterization. The rare emotional scenes in these plays make a relatively brief but important contribution to the play's action. Perform these emotions with a direct and simple honesty, whether comic or tragic. Be sincere without belaboring the emotion.

The vocal and physical rhythm of the plays should be expressed in a steadily fluid manner. If the play is written in verse, speak with extra clarity and directness. When comedy appears in the play (e.g., a henpecked husband or a cowardly shepherd), convey the appropriate wide range of comic responses with exaggerated vocal detail and physical action. You must accept archaic conventions when they arise; for example, falling asleep instantly and awakening the next moment. React believably to the entrance of unusual characters such as angels or God in a scene. Be prepared to sing and move with ease. Maintain a realistic base when acting real-life characters by projecting details of human behavior.

Translators and Translations and Adaptations

The key to successful dramatic presentation of Greek, Roman, and most Medieval drama is to use a quality translation by an effective translator. Most plays, particularly verse plays, are performed best in their original language. Greek and Latin plays are particularly difficult to translate into effective English. As a general rule, a wise director, producer, and actor compare several translations of a particular play before deciding which translation should be performed. In this manner you can better judge what reads well, sounds believable, and would seem to interest modern audiences. Some authorities believe the more modern or recent the translation, the better will be the version. In some instances this may be true. However, some nineteenth-century translators remain the most widely used in the theatre today. Another reliable method of determining a good translation is to check which translations are most frequently published in dramatic anthologies.

An adaptation differs from a translation in that it goes beyond language translation into major textual changes. Greek drama, particularly comedy, is frequently adapted as well as translated. For example, there is a version of *Lysistrata* by Aristophanes that has been adapted to an American hillbilly environment. *The Frogs* by the same author has been presented as a 1920 vaudeville production, has been staged in the Yale University swimming pool, and has been played in a boxing ring at the University of Iowa. *The Bacchae* by Euripides has been staged in the manner of the American "hippy" movement of the 1960s. Selecting a translation or an adaptation is primarily the director's decision but is, of course, of major importance to the actor. Your familiarity with different translations and adaptations will greatly assist your development in the art of acting.

Suggested Characters and Plays for Scene Work

Aeschylus

Agamemnon, Clytemnestra, Cassandra
Agamemnon
Orestes, Electra, Clytemnestra
The Eumenides

Sophocles

Oedipus, Jocasta, Tiresias, Messenger
Oedipus Rex
Antigone, Creon, Ismene, Nurse, Messenger
Antigone

Euripides

Medea, Jason
Medea
Hecuba, Andromache, Cassandra, Helen, Menelaus, Talthybius
The Trojan Women

Electra, Orestes
Electra
Phaedre, Nurse, Hippolytus, Aphrodite, Artemis, Theseus
Hippolytus
Dionysus, Cadmus, Tiresias, Pentheus, Agave
The Bacchae
Cyclops, Odysseus
Cyclops

Aristophanes

Dionysius, Xanthias, Aeschylus, Euripides
The Frogs
Lysistrata, Myrinna, Kinesias
Lysistrata
Epops, Peithetairos, Euelpides
The Birds

Additional Suggested Characters and Plays for Scene Work

Plautus

Menaechmus I, Menaechmus II,
Cylindrus, Erotium, Sponge
The Twin Menaechmi
Euclio
The Pot of Gold
Pyrogopolynices, Philocomasium
The Braggart Warrior

Terence

Phormio, Phaedria, Pamphila
Phormio
Micio, Aeschinus, Demea,
Ctesipho, Pamphila
The Brothers

Seneca

Atreus, Thyestes, the Ghost
Thyestes

Anonymous

Abraham, Isaac
Abraham and Isaac
Mak, Gyll
The Second Shepherd's Play

Everyman, Good Deeds
Everyman

Stevenson

Gammer Gurton, Diccon, Dame
Chat
Gammer Gurton's Needle

Anonymous

Pierre Patelin
Pierre Patelin

Hrosvitha

Paphnutius, Thais
Paphnutius

Sackville and Norton

Any role
Gorboduc

Udall, Nicholas

Ralph Roister Doister, Dame
Custance,
Mathewe Merygreeke
Ralph Roister Doister

Actor Checklist   Greek Tragedy

Voice	Heightened word emphasis; precise diction; varied tone qualities; close to declamatory, rhetorical, oratorical, lyrical, or sung mode during the key emotional or lyrical movements.
Movement	Generally slow, suggestive, and rhythmic; rare use of sitting positions; rare use of physical contact with other characters; predominately presentational mode.
Gestures	Restrained, large, fluid, and complete; highly selective and mostly in the upper portion of the body.
Pantomimic Dramatization	Clear, appropriate, limited, and highly selective; rare use of hand props such as staffs and emblems; use of full masks, half-masks, or makeup simulating a mask.

Character	Truthful, though somewhat larger than life; almost exclusively of high rank including gods.
Emotion	Complex and penetrating, particularly Sophocles and Euripides; clearly established and projected; somewhat larger than life; rooted in human psychology, particularly Euripides.
Ideas	Lofty, complex, clear; effectively theatricalized.
Language	Complex, clear, lyric, and rhythmic.
Mood and Atmosphere	Serious, restrained, lofty, passionate, and intense.
Pace and Tempo	Controlled, disciplined, rhythmic, and generally moderate to deliberate.
Special Techniques	Training in singing and dancing highly recommended, particularly for chorus members.

Actor Checklist   Old Greek Comedy

Voice	Clear diction with effective vocal production.
Movement	Energetic, large, extensive physical contact with others; considerable use of sitting; balance of presentation and representational mode.
Gestures	Lifelike but expansive; detailed rather than selective; full use of the entire body.
Pantomimic Dramatization	Extensive interpolation of song, dance, and comedic acrobatics; wild-animal movements; adaptation of religious dances and victory antics, kicking, slapping, and so on; highly inventive use of half-mask or makeup.
Character	Exaggerated to level of caricature, particularly with chorus and minor characters; major characters somewhat closer fidelity to real life. Abrupt transitions.
Emotion	Singular obsession; somewhat more complex in some major characters.
Ideas	Satiric; emphasized; clear.
Language	Mix of prose and verse; generally lifelike.
Mood and Atmosphere	Humorous; unrestrained; common; grotesque; fun.
Pace and Tempo	Rapid to moderate; exuberant.
Special Techniques	Singing, dancing, and acrobatic training highly recommended.

Selective Readings

Aristotle. *Poetics*. Edited by A. Gudemen. Translated by Lane Cooper. Ithaca, N.Y.: Cornell University Press, 1928.

Bieber, Margarette. *The History of the Greek and Roman Theatre*. 2d ed. Princeton, N.J.: Princeton University Press, 1961.

Chambers, E. K. *The Medieval Stage*. 2 vols. London: Oxford University Press, 1963.

Corrigan, Robert W. *Roman Drama*. New York: Dell Publishing Co., 1966.

Flickinger, R. C. *The Greek Theatre and Its Drama*. 6th ed. Chicago: University of Chicago Press, 1960.

Goldberg, Sander M. *The Making of Menander's Comedy*. Berkeley: University of California Press, 1980.

Haigh, A. E. *The Tragic Drama of the Greeks*. New York, 1968.

Hamilton, Edith. *The Greek Way*. New York: W. W. Norton & Company, 1952.

————. *The Roman Way*. New York: W. W. Norton, 1932.

Helterman, Jeffrey. *Symbolic Action in the Plays of the Wakefield Master*. Athens: University of Georgia Press, 1981.

Kitto, H. D. F. *Greek Tragedy*. 2d ed. London: Methuen & Co., Ltd., 1950.

————. *The Greeks*. Baltimore: Penguin, 1964.

Pickard-Cambridge, A. W. *Dithyramb, Tragedy, and Comedy*. 2d ed., rev. by T. B. L. Webster. London: Oxford University Press, 1962.

Price, Jonathan, ed. and trans. *Classic Scenes*. New York: Mentor, 1979.

Salter, F. M. *Medieval Drama in Chester*. Canada: University of Toronto Press, 1955.

Segal, Erich W. *Roman Laughter: The Comedy of Plautus*. Boston: Harvard University Press, 1968.

Wickham, Glynne. *The Medieval Theatre*. London, 1974.

Suggested Filmography

1. *Antigone*. 1961. Playwright—Sophocles. With Irene Papas.
2. *Mourning Becomes Electra*. 1947. Playwright—Eugene O'Neill. Adaptation of *The Oresteia* by Aeschylus. Director—Dudley Nichols. With Rosalind Russell, Kirk Douglas.
3. *Oedipus Rex*. 1956. Playwright—Sophocles. Director—Tyrone Guthrie. With Douglas Campbell.
4. *Oedipus Rex*. 1967. Playwright—Sophocles. Director—Pier Paolo Pasolini. With Silvana Mangano.

5. *The Trojan Women*. 1971. Playwright—Euripides. With Katharine Hepburn.
6. *Year of the Cannibals*. 1970. Based upon *Antigone*. American International Film.

Note

1. RCA Victor Album *History of Music in Sound,* vol. 1, ''Ancient and Oriental Music,'' LM 6057.

Commedia Dell'Arte: Regeneration

11

The snow dissolv'd no more is seen,
The fields, and woods, behold, are green,
the changing year renews the plain,
the rivers know their banks again. . . .

Horace
in *A History of Latin Literature*

A major form of theatre and style of acting, *commedia dell'arte,* regenerated dramatic activity in the sixteenth century. More than a transitional activity, the *commedia dell'arte* became a unique actor-oriented form of theatre. The term *arte* was used to signify professional artists. Commedia performances were improvisational and performed by traveling companies of actors. These companies frequently consisted of members of a single family, such as the famous Gelosi company. The origin of the commedia may be traced to the Atellan farce of Rome or possibly to the plays of Plautus and Terence. Emerging into prominence around the sixteenth century, the influence of the commedia would be important for over two hundred years.

Overview of Commedia Dell'Arte

Commedia was a comedy of intrigue using stock characters, often masked, and largely improvised dialogue based on a brief scenario. (Serious dramatic activity was limited during these years, favored only in erudite court or noble theatres. Commedia was the theatre of the masses.)

Plays were topical, drawn from the immediate time and place. Commedia used considerable pantomime. Speeches were added as an accompaniment to gesture, movement, and stage business. The accent in commedia was on visual performance. Actors were given a standard plot. Memorized lines were used only when they coincided with specifically outlined action. Comic stage business called *lazzi* and comic verbal jokes called *burla* were interspersed throughout the story to provide bits of stage fun or tricky comic turns (e.g., an actor might pretend his hat was filled with cherries, daintily eat them, flick the pits into another actor's face, and remark "a pit in the eye is worth two in the hand").

Commedia scenarios were refined and performed again and again until the last half of the eighteenth century. The most successful plots concerned love and intrigues, disguises and deception.

During its peak years, from approximately 1550 to 1650, about ten or twelve famous commedia dell'arte troupes traveled the Continent. Seven or eight men and three or four women comprised each group. Together they generally formed two sets of lovers, a servant girl, a captain, two zanni (comics), and two old men. Young men and women portrayed "straight" roles, usually romantic in nature; these characters were fashionably dressed and not masked. Other characters such as Pantalone wore tight-fitting red vests, breeches, stockings, and a black, ankle-length matching coat. Pantolone was always depicted wearing a brown mask with a hook nose and having unkempt hair and beard. Dottore's costume always consisted of a long academic gown and a cap. Over the years these costumes were adapted slightly to current trends. Harlequin often shaved his head and wore a comic hat with a black mask. He carried a slapstick or clapboard; originally he wore a suit of colorful diamond-shaped patches. Capitano wore a comic version of a military uniform with lots of green braid; he wore colorful plumes on his hat. Comic female characters such as courtesans wore long, full-length dresses or skirts of current fashion; some were masked. Character roles required special physical traits to help define the older men such as Capitano, Pantalone, and Dottore. The servants or zanni (e.g., Arlecchino or Harlequin) needed to be physically agile and supple in order to project the ridiculous burlesque qualities of these clever comic characters.

Almost eight hundred commedia dell'arte scenarios exist in outline form today. It is virtually impossible to obtain the actual quality of the commedia performance since we have little information concerning its execution. We know, however, that it took great physical skill and clown talent to act in commedia. Although this theatre developed without playwrights, its influence was felt throughout Europe and subsequently had tremendous impact on later actors and playwrights such as Molière (see chapter 13).

Voice

The key aspect of vocal training for commedia is mental acuity for line invention. In other words, it helps to be glib. However, verbal invention must be relevant to the scenario or the contemporary situation. The essentials of good stage speech are vital to delivery. Clear articulation, effective vocal production, rapid tempo, and considerable vocal variety are most important. The presentational mode dominates, necessitating adroit comic timing and direct audience delivery. Establishing reliable verbal burle will greatly assist your ability to emphasize so-called punch lines of comedy.

Exercise 1   Vocal Dexterity and Mental Acuity
1. Recite individually the following comic tongue twisters aloud as rapidly and clearly as possible:
>   Red leather and mellow yellow make wet weather and jolly fellows.
>   Peter Piper picked a peck of pickled peppers; a peck of pickled peppers Peter Piper picked.

   Following this format, invent and practice comic tongue twisters and punch lines.

2. Invent or recall and practice telling comic jokes aloud in under thirty seconds. Every actor must tell at least one joke.

3. Using a current local newspaper, glance over headlines and major captions. Quickly invent and tell comic one-line jokes about each headline and caption.

4. Print several unusual words on slips of paper and place them in a hat or bowl. Each person draws a word and immediately improvises a two-to-three minute comic story based on the word, regardless of whether the definition of the word is known. Suggested words: arbalest; besom; carillon; dado; escudo; flambeau; gewgaw; hamadryad; ichor; jute; kumquat; lintel; mesquite; nanny; Ouija; pariah; quoit; ribald; seism; toucan; uxorious; wildebeest; xebec; yucca; Zouave.

5. Select a series of famous morals or epithets and improvise four-to-five minute comic stories that illustrate and clarify imaginative origins of the morals or epithets. Suggested morals or epithets: ''A bird in the hand is worth two in the bush.'' ''Nothing succeeds like success.'' ''Nothing ventured, nothing gained.'' ''Pound wise and penny foolish.'' ''He who hesitates is lost.'' ''Never put off until tomorrow what you can do today.'' ''He who laughs last, laughs best.''

Movement

Without question, movement is the essence of successful acting in commedia. The style requires acrobatic ability; forceful, flexible, and rapid activity; and, occasionally, gracefully executed dance movements. All of the farce activities of Old Greek and Roman Comedy again apply, with special emphasis on characteristic movements and gestures of stock characters. For example, Pantalone, the old, grumpy father, walks with a hunch using a cane. Capitano, the braggart soldier, struts about with his head held high using grand hand gestures, waving his plumed hat. Harlequin turns cartwheels and somersaults and dances about with great abandon.

Exercise 2 Movement

1. Invent and practice comic movement suitable to each of the following stock commedia characters:
   a. Pantalone, the old merchant, miser, or father
   b. Dottore, pedantic bore
   c. Capitano, braggart soldier
   d. Zanni (comic servant), Harlequin, Pulchinello, Brighella, Scaramouche, Scapin
   e. Fontesca, comic maid
   f. Young lovers (Innamorato—male lover; Innamorata—female lover)

2. Execute a combination or series of acrobatic techniques ranging from tumbling to juggling.
3. To the accompaniment of rapid, high-spirited music (guitars, drums, and flutes are preferable), invent spontaneous and collective group dancing. In the event that music is not available, this exercise can be great fun by improvising the music with the aid of crude instruments such as washboards and metal pipes, bells, wooden sticks or shoes, humming through a piece of paper placed over a comb, and so on.
4. Practice the following ''comic accidents'' or lazzi (use real props or pantomime):
    a. Sit on a basket of eggs.
    b. Slip on a banana skin.
    c. Trip on a rug.
    d. Squirt water in your eye at a fountain.
    e. Brush your teeth with Ben-Gay.
    f. Carry a pie and fall into it.
    g. Drop ice cream on your lap.
    h. Spill hot coffee on your lap.
    i. Sit on a cactus.
    j. Look into a water hose and get squirted.
    k. Laugh and bite your tongue.
    l. Rinse your mouth with shaving lotion.
    m. Trip on your shoelaces.
    n. Get your tie caught in an electric beater.
    o. Hold sour milk in your cheeks while you look for a place to spit.
    p. Miss the nail while hammering and hit your thumb.
    q. Kick yourself in the shin while dancing.
    r. Pick a rose and get a thorn.
    s. Step on a tack.
    t. Slide down a pole and get splinters.
    u. Bite into a pearl in an oyster stew.
    v. Spray under your armpits with extra-strength hair spray.
    w. Get soap in your eyes as you search for a towel.
    x. Spill the bubble bath as you bathe in a tub.
    y. Walk barefoot on hot pavement.
    z. Kick a soccer ball, which turns out to be a bowling ball.
5. Practice ''comic retrievals'' (lazzi) by attaching rubber bands, elastic, or string to a variety of personal objects, such as your cap or hat, a pencil, your purse, your billfold, keys, and so on; drop the object as if by accident and develop ''comic retrievals.''
6. Practice playing ''invisible instruments'' as lazzi; for example, play an invisible violin, tuba, flute, drum, piano, and so on. Your colleagues should dance to your ''invisible instruments'' and ''silent music.''

7. Study the comic pantomime and physical activities of famous clowns and comics; imitate their activities both individually and in groups. For example, study the specialty movement and business of Charlie Chaplin, Buster Keaton, Stan Laurel, Oliver Hardy, Bud Abbott, Lou Costello, The Three Stooges, The Marx Brothers, Red Skelton, and others.

8. Practice a variety of ''safe comic fights'' as lazzi; for example, pillow fights, feather fights, bubble fights, confetti fights, and so on.

9. Practice ''duplicate comic activity'' by performing a variety of routine activities with two (duplicate) items rather than one; for example, drink from two glasses at one time, eat with two forks at one time, smoke two pipes simultaneously, brush with two toothbrushes at the same time, comb your hair with two combs simultaneously, write with two pens in one hand at the same time, and so on.

Character and Emotion

Commedia characters were one-dimensional stereotypes, usually possessive and obsessive, in the tradition of Old Greek and Roman Comedy. Commedia characters differed from their ancient counterparts in that commedia activity was more presentational. Except when performance was repetitive, dialogue and action for commedia characters were almost totally improvisational, and character types were refined and inflexible.

Exercise 3   Character and Emotion

1. Utilizing the work in Exercises 1 and 2, create brief scenarios from the following situational ideas, identifying one actor for each stock character.

   When you have completed discussing the scenario, each actor performs the stock character he or she selected within the context of the scenario. Act the scenario as an improvised play, keeping the performance under five minutes.

   a. A man refuses his daughter's hand in marriage to a young cobbler in favor of an old schoolmaster.

   b. A long-lost twin is reunited with his brother who is identical in appearance.

   c. An old miser is cheated out of his money by a clever servant.

   d. A man masquerades as a doctor of medicine to gain access to the wife of an old merchant.

   e. A soldier returns from the wars to discover his sweetheart has been forced into a marriage with an old attorney-at-law.

2. To create bold, large character types and emotional attitudes, males should practice improvisational characterizations of stock female roles and females should do the same with stock male roles. Create a comic monologue for your ''role reversal,'' depicting a wide range of emotions.

3. Assemble a variety of old clothes, hats, caps, shoes, and boots. Practice fast changes of headdress, outer garments, and footwear individually and as a group. With each change, affect a comic character and emotional trait suitable to that item of clothing.
4. This exercise should be a long-range assignment. Ideally, several weeks or even months should be used to develop this unusual and challenging exercise. Carefully study your features and physique in a mirror. Study your voice by listening to it on tape. Study your walk and habits by observing yourself on videotape. If you were to accentuate portions of your face, body, voice, walk, and habits for comic purposes, what would you choose, and how would you manage the comic accentuation? Would you work with your nose? Ears? Chin? Stomach? Bosom? Legs? Your vocal *quality, pitch,* or *rate?* Your slow walk or your fast walk? The way you eat? Smoke? Drink? Laugh? Make your selections and develop a "comic character and emotion" appropriate to your choices. Over a period of time, carefully create a "comic or clown" character and appropriate scenario to present as part of a final, individual performance in this style. (Later, a group scenario can be invented to incorporate all the "clown characters.")

Transition—Tudor Drama

As the commedia developed and flourished in Italy and elsewhere on the Continent, Europe was prey to barbarism, sacrilege, and selfishness. Despondency was the prevalent mood. The individual became engulfed in the tide of swelling institutional power. Man's life on earth lost meaning except as preparation for an afterlife.

Although Medieval institutions dominated, the spirit that sustained them eventually withered and died. The Holy Roman Empire was crumbling by 1400. Monarchs were subject to foreign invasions and international alliances. Throughout Europe, kingships were suffering paralysis. Economic, social, and political disasters seemed to be without end. Disease, death, suffering, and war took their toll on most of Europe. However, the picture of despair lessened somewhat in England with the presence of Henry VII, founder of the Tudor dynasty, who came to the throne in 1485.

Henry VII was part of the new breed of monarchs on the European continent. He worked to liberate royal government from ecclesiastical interference; he enforced laws, promoted financial solvency, and achieved complete control over the nobility. The violent class turmoil in English life produced by the Wars of the Roses was beginning to settle into a less violent pattern of living in which middle-class gentlemen gained predominance.

In drama, this transitional period produced a combination of Medieval-like Interludes performed by professional actors and classically inspired plays written at universities and Inns of Court performed by students. History was a popular subject, as were Bible stories rewritten in a romantic style. School drama was influenced by the plays of Plautus, Terence, and Seneca, all of which were read or performed in Latin. Original plays were written in both Latin and English, imitating the Roman or classical models. The most popular school plays were *Ralph Roister Doister* by Nicholas Udall and *Gammer Gurton's Needle* by Stevenson. The first known English tragedy was *Gorboduc* by Thomas Sackville and Thomas Norton. Other original native drama combined elements of classical learning (e.g., use of mythological figures) and English low comedy (e.g., use of farcical types). Even prior to Shakespeare's arrival in London, the theatre was under the influence of sophisticated playwriting. In his play *The Spanish Tragedy,* Thomas Kyd revealed the influence of Seneca by use of the revenge motif in combination with supernatural reference and suspenseful plot. (Shakespeare's *Hamlet,* written later, resembled Kyd's play closely.) Christopher Marlowe's contribution was to perfect blank verse as a medium for drama in his plays *Doctor Faustus, Edward II, Tamburlaine the Great,* and *The Jew of Malta.* John Lyly wrote prose comedies with themes from mythology that significantly developed comic playwriting beyond the crude farces of the Tudor period. All playwrights accented the chronological approach to action, emphasizing stage violence, a blend of serious and comic elements, poetic imagery, soliloquy, and short scenes.

Acting Tudor Drama

The Tudor acting style was rooted in specific conventions and verisimilitude (lifelike quality). The major convention was the performing of all female roles by young male actors. Considerable emphasis was placed on realistic contemporary life and manners, especially in the comedies. Actors arrived at an essential truthfulness of what we would term *human psychology;* that is, they created fundamentally convincing characters. However, there are exceptions to realistic character portrayal in these plays. There are roles in Tudor plays that call for a nonrealistic or highly exaggerated acting style, especially the farces in which a bizarre mixture of dramatic and comic elements appears (e.g., mixing serious mythology and low slapstick comedy).

An important outgrowth of Tudor drama in the development of theatrical art was the attention paid to costuming. Following the lead of society, dress for stage use also became quite exaggerated. Men's robes were larger, longer, and more elaborate than during early Medieval times. Young men often dressed in short formfitting tunics, pulled in with a belt. Hose and pointed shoes were worn. Sleeves were ballooned and gathered at the wrist; others were long enough to trail on the ground. Women's bodices also became more formfitting, with pinched waists, and skirts were fuller and heavier. Accordingly, acting style in plays was affected. Walking in a fourteenth-century skirt required extensive knee action. When a curtsy was executed, the front of the skirt was lifted to allow an actress to bend to the ground and rise gracefully. The skirt was held out and the head was inclined slightly to one side or slightly forward.

The men had difficulty executing movements due to their padded breeches. Walking and standing were cumbersome matters. However, men usually walked with a vigorous stride and displayed an athletic physique. Bowing usually occurred in the third ballet position, with toes and knees turned out, the rear knee bent, and the rear heel slightly off the ground; the forward leg was straight with the weight evenly distributed on both feet. Wearing clothes was a pleasure for the Tudor gentlemen. They were dedicated to showing off their legs and general attire.

Women, too, enjoyed elaborate display of clothing by keeping the torso straight and stiff, turning from the waist, and keeping the skirt in line with the shoulders. The head was poised to balance the headdress. The total physical effect of costuming, movement, bowing, and curtsying became a distinctive aspect of Tudor acting.

Late in the sixteenth century as the commedia dell'arte achieved prominence on the Continent, the limited but promising Tudor drama passed gradually into a new and distinct period in theatre activity and style—into the incomparable dramatic Renaissance of Elizabethan England—the age of William Shakespeare.

Suggested Characters and Plays for Scene Work

See any of the many extant commedia dell'arte scenarios. (Refer to Selective Readings at the conclusion of this chapter for titles containing scenarios.)

Actor Checklist   Commedia Dell'Arte

Voice	Comic verbal invention and *burle;* clear articulation; effective vocal production; rapid tempo; considerable vocal variety.
Movement	Acrobatic ability; forceful, flexible, and rapid; occasional dance activity; balance of presentational and representational mode, with slight dominance of presentational.
Gestures	Stock character *lazzi;* considerable physical contact with others; lifelike but expansive; full use of entire body.
Pantomimic Dramatization	Extensive interpolation of song, dance, comedic acrobatics; highly inventive slapstick; use of full mask and half-mask on all characters except young lovers.
Character	Definitive types throughout; young lovers closest to real-life fidelity.
Emotion	Generally limited or one-dimensional; singular obsession.
Ideas	Satiric concerning local and contemporary references; generally light and fun oriented; usually simple, love-triangle basis.
Language	Improvisational prose; generally memorized verse in songs.
Mood and Atmosphere	Humorous; unrestrained; common; grotesque; fun.
Pace and Tempo	Rapid to moderate; exuberant.
Special Techniques	Improvisational skill with dialogue and physical activity; singing, dancing, and acrobatic training highly recommended to relate comic stories.

Selective Readings

Craik, Thomas W. *The Tudor Interlude: Stage, Costume, and Acting.* Leicester: The University Press, 1958.

Disher, Maurice Wilson. *Clowns and Pantomimes.* New York: Benjamin Blom, 1968.

———. *Italian Comedy.* New York: Dover Publications, 1965.

Du Charte, Pierre. *Italian Comedy.* New York: Dover Publications, 1965.

Farley-Hills, David. *The Comic in Renaissance Comedy.* Totowa, N.J.: Barnes & Noble, 1981.

Herrick, Marvin. *Italian Comedy in the Renaissance.* Urbana: University of Illinois Press, 1960.

Lea, Kathleen M. *Italian Popular Comedy: A Study of the Commedia Dell'Arte (1560–1620) with Special Reference to the English Stage.*
2 vols. 1924. Reprint. New York: Russell & Russell Publishers, 1962.

Nicoll, Allardyce. *The World of Harlequin.* New York: Cambridge University Press, 1963.

Oreglia, Giacomo. *The Commedia Dell'Arte.* New York: Hill & Wang, 1968.

Rolfe, Bari. *Commedia Dell'Arte: A Scene Study Book.* Oakland, California: Persona Products, 1976.

———. *Farces, Italian Style.* Oakland, California: Persona Products, 1978.

Salerno, Henry F., ed. and trans. *Scenarios of the Commedia Dell'Arte Flaminio Scala's 11 Theatre Della Favole Rappresentative.* New York: New York University Press, 1967.

Smith, Winifred. *The Commedia Dell'Arte: A Study in Italian Popular Comedy.* New York: Benjamin Blom, 1965.

Suggested Filmography

See any of the films of the great comics/clowns, such as Charlie Chaplin, Buster Keaton, Stan Laurel, Oliver Hardy, Bud Abbott, Lou Costello, Jerry Lewis, The Marx Brothers, The Three Stooges, Red Skelton, and so on.

Elizabethan and Shakespearean Style: Virtuosity

12

The Playgoers

In our assemblies at plays in London you shall see such heaving and shoving, such itching and shouldering, to sit by women—such care for their garments, that they be not trod on—such eyes to their laps that no chips light in them—such pillows to their backs that they take no hurt—such masking in their ears I know not what—such giving them pippins to pass the time—such playing at footsaunt without carts—such ticking, such toying, such smiling, such winking, and such manning them home when the sports are ended.

from *the schoole of abuse*
by Stephen Gosson

A goodly sport

Turner and Dun, two famous fencers, played their prizes this day at the Bankside, but Turner at last ran Dun so far in the brain at the eye that he fell down presently stone dead; a goodly sport in a Christian state, to see one man kill another!

from the diary of John Manningham, a law student in Elizabethan England

Overview of the English Renaissance in Theatre

The English Renaissance in theatre was dominated by a single genius: William Shakespeare, the poet of London from the town of Stratford-on-Avon. Any study of drama in the age of the great Renaissance of learning and progress following the Medieval period must focus upon this great English poet and playwright.

Three fundamental ideas of the period must be kept in mind with this focus. (1) The concept of *ego*. The majesty of man must be exalted! His intellect and ability were believed unmatched among living creatures. (2) The concept of *individuality*. Nothing seemed beyond the vanity and confidence of any Renaissance artist. (3) The concept of *virtuosity*. Man had multiple capability and breadth of vision; art was a business and man practiced the art well.

Shakespeare—The Man, The Theatre, The Art, The Acting

William Shakespeare, the dramatist, was melodic, free, and erratic in his verse. His plays possessed virtuosity. He was aware of space, of people—all kinds of people. With words, Shakespeare was capable of creating a "landscape." He was as brilliant, philosophical, and learned as any master musician of the Renaissance. In Shakespeare, genius and craft were welded in one incredible dramatist. He was the Michelangelo of playwrights.

Shakespeare wrote at least thirty-six plays within a short life span of fifty-two years (1564–1616). These plays and the Bible probably rank as the two richest sets of literary documents in the entire history of Western man. Shakespeare accomplished all this having only what we would term an elementary school education, albeit equivalent to a modern college or graduate education.

During the Renaissance, the Islam Turks (who lacked artistic interest) took Constantinople, and the artists of the city escaped to Venice. There, a true revival of classical art and learning began. Thus, it was Italy, followed by England and Spain, that led the way out of the Middle Ages.

In England, Henry VIII built a strong Protestant nation that continued under Edward VI. Then, in 1558 the stingy but theatre-loving Queen Elizabeth I took the throne. Man became aware again of his "goodness," as well as of his "evil." Sir Francis Drake defeated "the invincible" Spanish Armada in 1588. England became a power and a glory, and her people developed a passion for their own history.

On the Continent in Spain and in Italy, similar impulses brought a flourishing of art, music, and drama led by writers such as Lopé de Vega,

Calderon, and Niccolo Machiavelli. However, only England was able to produce a theatre genius of Shakespeare's magnitude.

As brief background, note that in fifteenth-century England actors were still considered vagabonds. However, by 1482 noblemen employed actors for local entertainment, and by 1572 actors were recognized legally when a statute requiring a license to act in plays was enacted. By 1574 all plays had to be approved for production by the Master of Revels. This form of control or censorship, which survived well into the twentieth century in England, provided both advantages for and limitations to the theatre.

Sponsorship of acting companies by noblemen in England increased, and the profession of acting was reborn, assisted greatly by the royal support of Queen Elizabeth who favored the activity. The strong Puritan element in England opposed the movement, but Elizabeth and the nobility triumphed, at least until well into the seventeenth century. Soon theatre was a prospering public concern. The great period of English Renaissance theatre dates from 1570 to 1620 (in 1642 the Puritans and the Commonwealth closed the theatres until the restoration of the throne to Charles II in 1660).

What were the key influences in the development of dramatic art in the Renaissance?

1. Schools and universities. Formal educational institutions provided translations of Plautus, Terence, and Seneca. The English scholars wrote in imitation of these Roman classics and made a major contribution to dramatic activity.
2. The Inns of Court. Combined residences and training centers for lawyers developed, and there, too, classical drama was studied and imitated.
3. The heritage from English Medieval drama. Old farces, religious plays, and mixed forms of drama were studied. Portions of plays and techniques of writing were borrowed by Renaissance writers.

Certain key dramatists developed, all of whom had a decided influence on Shakespeare. Thomas Kyd and John Lyly were University Wits, or university scholar-artists, who wrote prior to Shakespeare. The youthful Shakespeare undoubtedly studied their work carefully and borrowed techniques, plots, and ideas. Later, literally dozens of fine playwrights developed to compete with Shakespeare, including such writers as Christopher Marlowe, Ben Jonson, Francis Beaumont and John Fletcher, John Webster, Thomas Dekker, and John Ford, among others. Marlowe, unusually adept at blank verse, and Jonson, skilled in comedy of humours (see Glossary), were particularly outstanding dramatists. However, for purposes of clarity and continuity, a study of the acting style of the period should concentrate on Shakespeare, the foremost dramatist of the time and probably unrivaled among playwrights.

The structure of the Elizabethan theater must be noted before we examine Shakespeare, his work, and the acting style necessary to performance of his plays. While evidence concerning these theaters is incomplete and while scholarly disputes have resulted, it is generally accepted that two types of theaters flourished. One was the open-air public theater (such as the famous Globe), and the other was the indoor private theater (such as the Blackfriars). Actually, general audiences could enter both theaters for a fee, but the indoor winter or private theaters tended to be frequented mostly by nobility and royalty. The size of the more popular outdoor or public theaters varied, ranging in seating capacity from 2,000 to 3,000 patrons.

The theaters were enclosed in part by three tiers of roofed *galleries,* which formed the outside of the structure. A large central area, popularly called the *yard* or *pit,* was unroofed. The least-expensive ticket placed the customer in the pit where he stood to watch a play; by paying more, he could sit in one of the galleries. The *stage* itself was about four to six feet in height and thrust forward from one of the sides of the theater (it is likely that the stage was portable or removable in most of the theaters, which permitted the theaters to be used for cruel sporting events such as bullbaiting and bearbaiting). The *roof* of the theater was thatched with straw and wood; to the rear was an area similar to a small balcony called the ''musicians gallery'' where musicians sat and played instruments. It is fairly certain that one or more *trapdoors* were cut in the stage floor and that two large doors at the rear of the stage were used by actors to make entrances and exits. Probably a *pavillion* of some sort stood upon the rear center of the stage. The pavillion was more than likely hung with curtains that could be used to reveal new scenes of action in progress. It would seem that the theater and stage just described permitted a rather continuous flow of dramatic action. There were probably no act or scene divisions in the playing of the scripts (most such divisions were added in later centuries by editors).

It is now believed that some minor scenery and stage machinery were utilized in Shakespearean, or Elizabethan, productions. Documented evidence exists of painted backdrops, rocks, trees, tables, and the like, being kept at the theatre. Scenic effects resembled the freestanding three-dimensional units called mansions, popular during the Medieval period. However, they were probably more detailed than the sets used in Medieval drama. Elizabethans equipped their stage with such articles as trees, thrones, beds, scaffolds, barriers, prison bars, tombs, tents, caves, tables, and chairs. The large central area (the equivalent to the Medieval plateau) could be localized. Set pieces were used when necessary or if they were available. Scenery was probably used when it suited the convenience of the actors, managers, and playwrights rather than to follow any principle of consistent scenic design. As knowledge of the court masques became public and royalty became increasingly interested in acting troupes, theater owners paid more attention to scenic spectacle.

The costuming utilized contemporary Elizabethan street and court dress, with no or very limited attempt at historical accuracy. From 1558 to 1642 costumes were identical to Medieval and Renaissance dress. Attention was paid to correct dress according to rank and to fanciful garments worn by ghosts, fairies, and witches, and traditional kingly attire was copied for such characters as Henry VI, Falstaff, and Richard III. The Elizabethans spared no expense in executing their costumes. Garments were costly and elegant, combining satin, silver, silk, and lace. Color for costumes depended on propriety: foresters wore green, shepherds wore white, royalty wore purple, friars wore brown. In essence, the stage was a glass of fashion—the epitome of the art of wearing clothes.

An Elizabethan acting company was composed of ten to twenty members. The chief actor in Shakespeare's company was Richard Burbage, an accomplished tragedian. Will Kemp was the leading comic actor. Approximately ten members of the company were ''hired'' men. The latter included doorkeepers, musicians, stagehands, and box office personnel, all of whom were paid flat salaries or wages and did not share in profits. There were also three to five boy apprentice actors in the company who played all the female roles (not until the Restoration and the eighteenth century were actresses permitted on the stage). Productions were given at about three o'clock in the afternoon, and natural daylight illuminated the action. A volatile and noisy audience ate and drank during a performance and cheered or jeered their approval or disapproval. As the play ended at twilight, the highly diverse audience dispersed for a drink in a local public house or retired to dinner and conversation. At the end of each performance, the actors sang, danced, and performed comic action, even though the play may have been a tragedy. The theatrical custom was to end the performance on a light, happy note and to send the audience away in a good humor.[1]

Modern adaptation of the original style of Elizabethan acting will probably be minimal, as opposed to the extensive adaptation needed for Greek and Restoration acting styles. The following discussion of language, voice, gestures, movement, pantomimic business, character, emotion, and spectacle provides you with the necessary tools to perform in the acting style of the Elizabethan period, be it in tragedy or comedy.

Voice

In a letter to Mrs. Patrick Campbell, George Bernard Shaw advised the actress, ''When you play Shakespeare, don't worry about the character but go for the music. It was by word-music that he expressed what he wanted to express, and if you get the music right, the whole thing will come right.''[2] Shaw's advice is well taken. An understanding of the verse and poetry in Shakespeare's plays is the key to development of all other acting concepts—character, emotional quality, rhythm, gesture, and movement. In line with the theory of personalization, reducing verse to simple ideas gives you more confidence with your interpretive ability and thus enables you to approach the roots of Shakespeare's reality, which is different from your own only in the manner of utterance and degree of intensity. You need to separate ideas clearly to give the proper shape to the verse, which will give the poetry a pervasive ''music.''

The most common problem an actor encounters with Shakespeare is to maintain personalization while meeting the specific demands of heightened language. The audience must be stirred by the nuances of the poetry. What you must remember is that character and poetry are inseparable. A study of the details and nuances and structure of the lines will enable you to reveal and portray a character in depth.

Verse speaking should be based on an understanding of the structure of the language. To accomplish this task, you must study the organized relationship of words and sounds. During Shakespeare's time, school boys were taught to recognize figures of speech and pronounce them rhetorically with accompanying gestures. Recognition of metaphor is crucial in this task. You cannot circumvent the fact that Shakespearean poetry must be elevated somewhat above a conversational mode to achieve lyricism and beauty. Elevation is aided by permitting the presentational mode to dominate delivery. You need not be confused by all this if you keep in mind the fact that unrhymed iambic pentameter or blank verse is the most malleable and adaptable of forms, open to variety and individuality of expression.

The verse is called *blank* because it allows both the speaker and the listener to anticipate rhymes when the rhythmical pattern is regular and the actor to emphasize sounds to reveal character and emotion.

An *iambus* is a foot of two syllables, a short or unaccented syllable followed by a long or accented syllable—brief, long, brief, long. The human heart, for example, beats in iambs, that is, in two recurring strokes—brief, long, brief, long. Correct stress will result. An example follows:

$$\smile \quad / \quad \smile \quad / \quad \smile \quad / \quad \smile \quad / \quad \smile \quad /$$

Oh,₁what—oh,₂what—oh,₃what—oh,₄what—oh,₅what

Note that the mark ⌣ indicates the short or nonstress syllable; the mark / is the long or accented syllable.

The formalized lines taken together are called iambic pentameter. Sometimes Shakespeare deviated from iambic pentameter in order to surprise or heighten a dramatic situation.

Exercise 1   Iambic Pentameter

Read the following speech aloud with clear articulation and effective vocal production. Note that the iambic pentameter is altered from time to time to keep that pattern from sounding too monotonous and the delivery from sounding too austere.

Sonnet XXXII

When in disgrace with fortune and men's eyes,
I all alone beweep my outcast state,
And trouble deaf Heav'n with my bootless cries,
And look upon myself, and curse my fate,
Wishing me like to one more rich in hope,
Featur'd like him, like him with friends possess'd.
Desiring the man's art, and that man's scope,
With what I most enjoy contented least;
Yet in these thoughts myself almost despising,
Haply I think on thee,—and then my state
(Like to the lark at break of day arising
From sullen earth) sings hymns at heaven's gate;
For thy sweet love remember'd such wealth brings,
That then I scorn to change my state with kings.

Shakespearean language also reveals that clauses are frequently short; for example, Lady Macbeth says:

The raven himself is hoarse
That croaks the fatal entrance of Duncan
Under my battlements
                              Macbeth   Act I, scene v

Pauses are stronger or more imperative; for example, in the prose exchange between Hamlet and Rosencrantz and Guildenstern, Hamlet says:

> You were sent for, and there is a
> kind of confession in your looks, which
> your modesties have not craft enough to
> color. I know the good king and queen
> have sent for you.
>
> *Hamlet*   Act II, scene ii

Transitions are abrupt; for example, the confrontation between Hamlet and Polonius in act 2 reveals such a transition:

> POLONIUS   My lord, I have news to tell you.
> HAMLET   My lord, I have news to tell you.
> When Roscius was an actor in Rome—
> POLONIUS   The actors are come hither, my lord.
> HAMLET   Buzz, Buzz.
> POLONIUS   Upon my honor.
> HAMLET   Then came each actor on his ass—
>
> *Hamlet*   Act II, scene ii

Questions and interjections abound; for example, in the same passage with Hamlet, Rosencrantz, and Guildenstern, Hamlet asks: ''Were you not sent for? Is it your own inclining? Is it a free visitation?''

Imagery is frequently symbolic; for example, the rose is a symbol of youth and the lily is a symbol of purity. Shakespeare often used diverse images to illustrate a single idea. This quality increases the range of concepts and heightens the emotion (e.g., Hamlet's ''To be or not to be'' speech reveals a number of dramatic and diverse images).

Shakespeare often used the half-line in dialogue. A speaker ends his speech in the middle of a metrical line and another speaker takes the line up and completes it.

> HORATIO   Friends to this ground.
> MARCELLUS   And liegemen to the Dane.
>
> *Hamlet*   Act I, scene i

You should note the atmosphere and mood of the scene in order to project the correct feeling of the lines. The illusion, which the poet undertakes, must be understood.

At times you will see repetition of the same sound rather than a play upon different sounds; for example, in *Romeo and Juliet,* Romeo says to the Nurse:

Where is she? and how doth she and what
Says my concealed lady to our cancelled love?
Romeo and Juliet   Act I, scene iii

Puns are words that play upon multiple meanings. They were considered a vital part of Elizabethan word usage. Shakespeare's plays abound in puns (e.g., the dying Mercutio in *Romeo and Juliet* remarks to Romeo, "Ask for me tomorrow, and you shall find me a grave man").

Another peculiarity of Shakespearean language is the *conceit.* The Shakespearean conceit is a piece of extreme, unusual, and often witty poetic imagination.

For example, consider these lines from Romeo and Benvolio in *Romeo and Juliet* in which Romeo discusses the qualities of love:

. . . O brawling love! O loving hate!
O any thing, of nothing first create!
O heavy lightness! serious vanity!
Mis-shapen chaos of well-seeming forms!
Feather of lead, bright smoke, cold fire, sick health!
Still-waking sleep, that is not what it is!
Romeo and Juliet   Act I, scene i

These are conceits in which Shakespeare plays with opposites. Many of his conceits are shocking, melodramatic, and extreme and are usually rooted in the inner conflict of the character speaking the lines.

In his later and better plays, Shakespeare used conceits in an abstract way. In earlier plays, he merely listed apparent contradictions, while in *King Lear,* for example, the Fool's speeches to Lear are used very precisely as commentary on Lear's weaknesses.

Awareness of the conceit device helps to better understand character and to better speak the tricky, ear-challenging, and thought-challenging conceits.

Shakespeare often joined contrasting ideas to make an expressive, compressed statement of equivalence or opposition (e.g., Hamlet's line "A little more than kin and less than kind").

In all the examples just given, meaning and emotion were integral to the structure of the pattern of sound. The most common sound pattern was *rhyme,* often used to end long speeches or scenes. Rhyme is created

Scene from *King Lear* by
William Shakespeare.
Len Cariou as King Lear
and Nicolas Keprose as
the Fool, at The Guthrie
Theatre (Minnesota
Theatre Company),
Minneapolis, Minnesota.

when the end sounds of lines correspond. (Other structures include *as-sonance*—likeness of sound in which the stressed vowel sounds are alike but the consonant sounds are unlike as in *main* and *came;* and *alliteration*—repetition of an initial sound, usually a consonant, in two or more words of a phrase as in "a fair field full of folk.")

When studying the figures of speech in Shakespearean verse, you should discover words designed to simultaneously produce calculated and special emotional reactions. Claudius's soliloquy in *Hamlet* at the end of act 3 is a case in point. The lines depict the sound of anguish:

Oh, wretched state! O bosom black as death!
O liméd soul, that struggling to be free
art more engaged! Help, angels! make assay!
Hamlet   Act III, scene iii

Or note the sensual and romantic lines spoken by Juliet as she waits for Romeo:

Lovers can see to do their amorous rites
By their own beauties; or, if love be blind,
It best agrees with night. Come, civil night,
Thou sober-suited matron, all in black,
And learn me how to lose a winning match,
Played for a pair of stainless maidenhoods.
Hood my unmanned blood bating in my cheeks,
With thy black mantle till strange love grow bold.
Romeo and Juliet   Act III, scene ii

Shakespeare was a master at selecting *the* word and sound to express mood. A classic example is the witches scene in *Macbeth* where supernatural mystery is vividly duplicated:

FIRST WITCH   When shall we three meet again?
                       In thunder, lightning, or in rain?
SECOND WITCH   When the hurlyburly's done,
                       When the battle's lost and won.
THIRD WITCH   That will be ere the set of sun.
FIRST WITCH   Where the place?
SECOND WITCH   Upon the heath.
THIRD WITCH   There to meet with Macbeth.
FIRST WITCH   I come, Graymalkin!
SECOND WITCH   Paddock calls.
THIRD WITCH   Anon!
ALL   Fair is foul, and foul is fair
          Hover through the fog and filthy air.
Macbeth   Act I, scene i

Also note linguistic changes and modern alterations in word meaning as compared with the time of Shakespeare. It is important to study the original meaning of words (i.e., etymology—the additions and losses in vocabulary), semantics (i.e., alterations in meanings and associations of words), accidence and syntax (i.e., changes in inflection and construction of words to form phrases, clauses, and sentences), and phonological changes or equivalents.

A peculiar language situation developed during the Renaissance. Elizabethans loved to borrow phrases from foreign languages. Latin was favored by writers and served to enrich the English language. Latin words were either naturalized or added to the English language. Latin did not replace native words but provided synonyms such as *wonder* and *admiration,* words derived from Latin. It follows that even a slight knowledge of Latin is a great advantage to the correct understanding of Elizabethan writers, especially when we consider that many Latin borrowings of the sixteenth century now have meanings different from the original. For example, the Latin sense of *apparent* no longer means visible or evident, and *intention* does not convey the idea of intentness. Some Latin forms such as the word *objectum* were later changed to conform to English spelling and accent.

French also supplied words and influenced changes in spelling. Commercial, religious, and architectural terms were adopted from the Spanish, Italian, and Dutch languages. Foreign influences on language provided unparalleled freedom of vocabulary and form. However, that freedom also produced confusion, and clarity and precision were often sacrificed. Nevertheless, the English language gained more than it lost by allowing in foreign importations. The number of compound words such as ''homekeeping wits'' was increased, and prefixes such as *dis-, re-,* and *en-* and suffixes such as *-ful, -less, -ness,* and *-hood* were introduced.

Perhaps the greatest problem encountered in the study of Shakespearean verse is not the deciphering of obsolete words, but the difficulty arising from the many times it is possible to get some idea of meaning, however imperfect it might be. It becomes a matter of missing exact shades of meaning and thereby misinterpreting the tone. The following Shakespearean words often differ from their present meaning:

a   he
ability   means, wealth
addition   title
admiration   wonder, care, anxiety
carry   manage
conceit   conception, idea
confusion   overthrow, ruin

fellow   equal
gear   matter, stuff, thing, business
humour   moisture, temperament, whine, caprice
modern   common, ordinary
moe   more
pregnant   resourceful, apt, inclined
prevent   anticipate, hinder

The foregoing analysis of Shakespearean verse and language in which the importance of relationships between words was clarified leads to a consideration of what is technically involved in speaking that verse and language. Once you have learned the details of emphasis, the technique usually becomes second nature. Do not aim solely at reproducing structural patterns because concentration on characterization will suffer. Elizabethan actors may not have had exact patterns or conventions for speaking on the stage, but they did adhere to general attitudes of speech. The actor needed a voice capable of tremendous range of tone and volume. The speaking style was partially influenced by the rhetoric of the Tudor period in that the Elizabethan actor was taught to heighten the simulation of emotion thus to move an audience. (An effective Elizabethan acting voice exhibits spontaneity and beauty of expression.) The speaking style was generally presentational. Verse necessitated a pattern of intonation that ran counter to the metrical pattern of stressed and unstressed syllables. The effect of the actor's delivery was musical, that is, well modulated. The voice was able to convey contrast among words, developing climaxes in tempo and rhythm. Thus, the vocal tone and emotional manner of the character were delineated more clearly. Emotion also played a part in producing the music of the line. Emotion gave color and life to the tones. (Be aware of which emotion is derived from a word or combination of words. An emotion may change just as the sense of a line changes.)

To perform Shakespeare's language you might do well to review Hamlet's advice to the players in act 3, scene 2. Hamlet warns the actors not to chant, whine, or elongate syllables: ". . . but if you mouth it, as many of our players do, I had as lief the town-crier spoke my lines." A fundamentally normal and controlled speaking voice is desired in delivery of Elizabethan prose. A natural vocal quality can best produce a melodic sound. Verse should be heightened somewhat above the conversational mode. However, when the verse is less passionate and emotional, a more natural or conversational mode may be effectively used. It is sometimes difficult for a modern actor to believe in the concept of a natural (as opposed to a declamatory) style of speaking Shakespeare because of the fear that the music of the verse will suffer. If the structural organization of the language is correctly analyzed, the music of the verse can still be maintained with natural speaking. Pitch and length of tone can change quickly and abruptly. Vary your pace according to the needs of the lines. Modern actors often have a tendency to overintellectualize word analysis when speaking Shakespeare by assigning *each word* a definite emotion and objective. A more accurate technique is to let the sense of the whole sentence decide the emphasis on any given word. Elevate or emphasize some words in each sentence and allow the lines to flow. Rarely pause under the pretext of thinking words out, as actors often do in modern naturalistic plays. Modern approaches to performing Shakespeare emphasize character realism within the context of Elizabethan language structure in order to combine the merits of ''modern believability'' with a proper sense of ''classic style.''

Exercise 2   Voice

1. Study the following speech by Prospero from *The Tempest:*

You do look, my son, in a moved sort,
As if you were dismayed. Be cheerful, sir.
Our revels now are ended. These our actors,
As I foretold you, were all spirits and
Are melted into air, into thin air;
And, like the baseless fabric of this vision,
The cloud-capped towers, the gorgeous palaces,
The solemn temples, the great globe itself,
Yea, all which it inherit, shall dissolve,
And, like this insubstantial pageant faded,
Leave not a rack behind. We are such stuff
As dreams are made on, and our little life
Is rounded with a sleep. Sir, I am vexed.
Bear with my weakness. My old brain is troubled.
Be not disturbed with my infirmity.
If you be pleased, retire into my cell
And there repose. A turn or two I'll walk
To still my beating mind.

The Tempest   Act IV, scene i

Practice the speech aloud:
  a. to establish the correct iambic pentameter rhythm.
  b. to focus upon correct pauses and transitions.
  c. to focus upon imagery, figures of speech, repetitions, conceits, and contrasting ideas.
  d. to focus upon emotion and mood (be certain to check an Old English dictionary or a Shakespearean glossary to determine exact meanings of words).

Hal Proske as Prospero in *The Tempest* by William Shakespeare. Directed by Orlin Corey, designed by Irene Corey; Everyman Players.

2. As a lesson through deliberate error, read the Prospero speech aloud once more and consciously adapt the speech to a very modern, naturalistic mode; that is, place pauses and punctuation where there are none, discard some words by murmuring them as though they were unimportant, and so on. This negative lesson may prove comical, but it should reveal the necessity to practice number 1 again.

3. Practice comic vocal timing and a comedic manner by reading aloud the following prose selection:

MACDUFF: What three things does drink especially provoke?
PORTER: Marry, sir, nose-painting,
sleep, and urine. Lechery,
sir, it provokes, and un-
provokes; it provokes the
desire, but it takes away
the performance: therefore,
much drink may be said to be
an equivocator with lechery. . . .
Macbeth Act II, scene iii

Gesture and Movement

Elizabethan actors also used considerable gesture and movement to communicate what was being expressed in words. Gestures were occasionally conventional; they were undoubtedly also natural and precise, revealing the general disposition, humor, and state of mind of the character. The probable view among Elizabethan actors was that if a gesture was seen in daily life, its inclusion onstage was justified. For example, Richard Burbage, leading tragic actor in Shakespeare's company, probably noticed that Elizabethans frequently pointed a great deal with the forefinger; he undoubtedly used the gesture within a play if it was at all appropriate to the text and character. Perhaps this idea contrasts somewhat with the popular notion that in Shakespearean plays a heightened, elevated style of delivery necessitates use of conventional stereotyped gestures. A common misconception among many modern actors is to equate acting of Shakespearean drama with a system of external clichés. On the contrary, Shakespeare's characters exemplified truthful inner emotion, and action was suited to emotion and language. Elizabethans prided themselves on precise, explicit, heightened, and direct action that emanated from within an individual. Elizabethan stage acting surely demonstrated the same concept—expressing externally in a truthful manner what was felt inside.

As gestures acquired an appropriate, natural, though somewhat elevated appearance, so too, did stage movements. Movements were characterized as full, fluid, and controlled. A consideration of the physical aspects of the Elizabethan stage and audience indicates the necessity to maximize all physical action. Since the acting areas were small and audiences were rowdy and loud, Elizabethan actors were trained in strong stage action such as fencing. The actor had to handle a heavy rapier in one hand and a dagger for parrying in the other. All fencing movements were highly calculated. Thrusting was accomplished at close quarters from the wrist and forearm and was usually aimed at the opponent's eye or below the ribs. In fencing, the actor had to achieve brutal reality to please the crowd. His training for theatrical fencing was highly rigorous and his physical coordination was excellent. Action was rapid and intensified.

The modern actor playing in an Elizabethan drama finds stage movement immediately restricted simply because of the incredible weight of the costumes. It is commonly noted that Elizabethan clothes could ''stand up by themselves.'' If we generalize the typical Elizabethan man as assertive, arrogant, and physically well toned, we create a picture of someone moving with confidence and vigor. However, he is attired in clothes that are difficult for us to wear. His doublet fits tightly to the body, the ruff fits stiffly around the neck, stockings reach to above the knee and are fastened up to the waistline by points or laces. Although physical action is startlingly limited within these confines, an actor must try to give the illusion of a rapid flow of movement. Continual practice in Elizabethan costume is the only solution for an actor who must be ''swaggering and virile.'' Physical strength is further inhibited by the excessive padding under the garments, which tends to throw modern actors completely off balance.

Women also have their share of difficulty moving in costume. An immense amount of space is absorbed by the shape of the skirt (e.g., a bell-shaped skirt with a farthingale worn underneath, literally, a series of hoops that start at the waist and become progressively larger toward the ground). Moving through doors is awkward, approaching a chair and sitting in it pose problems, turning excessively is next to impossible, and hanging the arms at the sides is difficult. All stage movement must be taken in stride—no forced action or sudden moving. Women wear a long, tight bodice and tight *stomacher* (stiff front waist piece). They glide fluidly along the stage, holding the torso and head straight. (A wired ruff at the back of the head precludes excessive head movement; it also shields the face from the audience.) Hands can rest lightly on the top of the farthingale or strike a pose on top of each other, palms up, at the waist, or hands can be brought together at the waist with the thumbs on top and knuckles pointing down. Because of the stiff roll at the top of sleeves, underarms are held away from the body. Ladies usually carry a fan, which is moved from the shoulder or from the wrist, depending on the cut of the costume. Fan movement usually involves the entire arm, not just the wrist, due to the tight-fitting sleeves.

Exercise 3   The Bow

Two types of bows and two types of curtsies should be learned to accommodate these important social customs used in most Elizabethan plays.

1. To execute a full or formal bow, stand with the feet astraddle in a normal standing position; withdraw either foot behind the other leg about twelve inches, turning the rear foot to form a 45-degree angle behind the other foot. The rear knee should now be bent. Remove the hat and drop that hand to one side or to the rear as you bend or, depending on circumstances, leave the hat on your head as you bend; turn the other hand palm forward to the person being addressed. Lower the head toward the chest, and bend the back forward slightly.
2. A less formal version of this bow is to simply remove the hat while bending the head and back slightly forward. The feet remain astraddle. This bow was used for respect to peers or for hurried recognition, while the full or formal bow was used to address noblemen or royalty.

Exercise 4   The Curtsy

1. To execute a full or formal curtsy, rest the hands on top of the farthingale or skirt. Withdraw one foot behind the other several inches; bend both knees, the head, and the back. If you are addressing a queen, your body might bend to the point where you are sitting on the rear foot with the head inclined forward to the floor and the arms outstretched. To curtsy to one's peers, usually bend the knees only six to twelve inches with the head slightly inclined.
2. A less formal version of this curtsy can be accomplished by lowering the head slightly and bending both knees a few inches with the feet in a straddled position. This curtsy was used for making quick acknowledgments or for entering or leaving a room.

Exercise 5   Pantomimic Greetings

Practice the following:

1. Greet another man with both arms extended while grasping one another simultaneously with both hands above the elbows or about the wrists.

2. Greet another woman by kissing her on the cheek as you meet.
3. One man extends his hand to a lady while walking by putting an arm forward at the elbow, palm down; the lady places her fingertips on top of his wrist or hand. As you walk by other couples, nod heads in informal greeting.

Using a course of movement in Elizabethan plays that is direct and decisive applies also to handling soliloquies (solo monologues) and asides (short addresses to the audience).

A popular opinion holds that an actor speaking a soliloquy must come downstage center to deliver his innermost thoughts directly to the audience. However, there is nothing sacred concerning the way an actor delivers a soliloquy. There is no special stage area where this intimate, intensive, and personal revelation must take place. Sometimes it may not be appropriate to address your character's thought to the audience at all, although the Elizabethan actor probably oriented much of his action in that manner. There are exceptions to the presentational directness of stage movements in every play, including Elizabethan plays.

Exercise 6   The Soliloquy

Practice the following soliloquies by performing them at various stage locations, alternating direct presentation to the audience with self-reflective representational delivery. Invent your own movement and gestures.

The spirit that I have seen
May be the devil: and the devil hath power
To assume a pleasing shape; yea, and perhaps
Out of my weakness and my melancholy,
As he is very potent with such spirits,
Abuses me to damn me: I'll have grounds
more relative than this: the play's the thing
Wherein I'll catch the conscience of the King
       HAMLET   *Hamlet*   Act II, scene iii

How easy it is for the proper false
In women's waxen hearts to set their forms!
Alas, our frailty is the cause, not we!
For such as we are made of, such we be.
How will this fadge? My master loves her dearly;
And I (poor monster) fond as much on him;
And she (mistaken) seems to dote on me.
       VIOLA   *Twelfth Night*   Act II, scene ii

The *aside* is an expression of thought spoken privately to the audience while other characters are present. Depending upon the circumstances in the play, the character may or may not move away from the other character or characters onstage. The actor delivering the aside may simply turn the body or face or change the voice. Asides can be spoken from all areas of the stage—from the rear to the front. An aside might be performed during action or other actors can *freeze* when the aside is delivered. It is not always believable to move away from other actors in an aside; however, the speaker *usually* remains stationary.

Exercise 7   The Aside

Practice the following asides using the various methods of delivery just discussed. Invent any necessary movement or gesture.

HAMLET   Let her not walk i' the sun: conception is a blessing: but not as your daughter may conceive. Friend, look to 't.

POLONIUS *(aside)*   How say you by that? Still harping on my daughter . . .

HAMLET   . . . for yourself, sir, should be old as I am, if like a crab you could go backward.

POLONIUS *(aside)*   Though this be madness, yet there is method in 't. . . .

Hamlet   Act II, scene ii

TOBY   . . . Therefore draw for the supportance of his vow. He protests he will not hurt you.

VIOLA *(aside)*   Pray God defend me! A little thing would make me tell them how much I lack of a man.

Twelfth Night   Act III, scene iv

Elizabethan actors were highly selective concerning the use of pantomimic business. Tragic plays did not require use of extensive and detailed stage business; conversely, comic plays tended toward use of highly inventive and extensive business. In tragedy, the Elizabethan audience loved to see an actor simulate running a sword through another actor's body or "tearing out his entrails." They cheered at the slight of hand. They wanted to see "real blood" (usually sheep's blood), which was put into a bladder with a hollow handle or slipped inside a white leather jerkin painted to look like human skin and punctured at the appropriate moment.

The play text itself will usually provide you with definite circumstances for stage business (e.g., knocking at a door, sword fighting, striking a bell, reading a book, holding a skull, holding a candle). Banquet scenes are frequently called for, as well as receptions, funerals, and *dumb shows*. Sometimes Shakespeare implied pantomimic business by mentioning the use of a book, dagger, or some other prop; at other times, more expansive physical action such as falling down was implied.

Note should be made concerning pantomimic dumb shows. These shows were performed in true commedia dell'arte style, using masks, appropriate costumes for stock characters, and detailed slapstick burlesque activities. Following the traditional Roman pantomime, no words were spoken. Movements were slow, precise, and exaggerated. For actors a dumb show should be truly improvisational. Later, the action can be set in order to perfect the precision of the pantomime.

Comedy permitted more flexibility in the use of stage properties and accessories; therefore, business was more inventive and detailed. Articles that an actor may utilize in comedy include handkerchiefs, keys, purses or notecases, letters, combs, and fans with mirrors hidden in them. Costume properties can also be considered material for stage business; for example, gloves sometimes concealed ''poison.'' Comedy often called for disguise—for example, adding a hood or a hat or a mask to cover the head and face. It is characteristic in comic plays for actors to consider the circumstances of a situation and create appropriate pantomimic business to add interest and heighten the humor.

Exercise 8 Dumb Show

Read and study the following dumb show performed by the players in *Hamlet,* act 3, scene 2:

Enter a King and a Queen very lovingly; the Queen embracing him. She kneels, and makes show of protestation unto him. He takes her up and declines his head upon her neck. He lays him down upon a bank of flowers. She, seeing him asleep, leaves him. Anon comes in a fellow, takes off his crown, kisses it, pours poison in the King's ears, and exits. The Queen returns, finds the King dead, and makes passionate action. The Poisoner, with some two or three Mutes, comes in again, seeming to lament with her. The dead body is carried away. The Poisoner woos the Queen with gifts; she seems loath and unwilling awhile, but in the end accepts his love.

Exeunt

Form several casts of players and create the action called for in the dumb show. Improvise pantomimic dramatization as needed, including the use of any necessary props.

Character and Emotion

Shakespeare did not provide character description as many modern playwrights do. Nor did he provide many stages directions. It will be your and the director's responsibility to decide the quantity and quality of personality characteristics necessary for the development of character. Observe how the style of the speech affects the formality or informality of the person. You will often find that both qualities are fused. Although the formality does not necessarily mean a less natural performance, you must remain conscious of your character's emotions and actions. Again, the personalization technique permits you to rehearse the role first as if the character were you. The degree of realism will be determined by what the character says and how much he says. Natural acting orientated toward truthfully expressed emotion is essential to acting in an Elizabethan play, just as it has been in most plays throughout history.

Shakespeare's characters are extraordinarily well defined in the text and extremely varied and complex. The characters are usually multidimensional. The verse is an unusually sensitive gauge of the character's disposition and humor. Shakespeare's plays blend standardized fictional character types with well-known historical figures. Because Shakespeare's stories were usually based on existing stories or earlier plays, his characters retain a classical kind of clarity. A character comes from a definite place; he has traceable literary and historical progeny, fixed attitudes, indicative bearing, and pronounced temperament (e.g., think of Iago, Hamlet, Macbeth, Desdemona, and Falstaff). Shakespeare also utilized the Elizabethan society well by presenting the psychological and philosophical foundations prevalent in his milieu. Characters fit into a generic group whose behavior tends to conform to specific social classes. Shakespeare also differentiated characters within each class. For example, gentlewomen and ladies-in-waiting bore the signs of the upper class, yet they were given internal qualities and distinct characterization (e.g., Maria in *Twelfth Night* and Emilia in *Othello* may be portrayed as women of a certain social position in a particular social scheme and as highly individualized characters).

The difficulty encountered in delineating character development in any play need not concern you unnecessarily if the character's state of being is clear at the beginning of the play. Character development will come organically out of the whole play. Shakespeare was particularly careful to base character motivation on the broad desires that all men might experience. As with the Greeks, it was a belief of the Elizabethan society that affections or emotions *should* be controlled by reason. When passions rule, disaster follows. Individuals are motivated by specific ends and universal emotions—greed, love, hate, revenge, and jealousy. Reason remains powerless before the volatile and pervasive nature of emotion that can destroy the moral and political world.

Shakespeare defined his characters more by their emotion than by their reason. *How* the character speaks is often more important than what is said. To accomplish this precept, use a carefully selected psychological intention. Again, *all* acting in *all* styles rests upon that fundamental selection. Often the poetry seems to consume the character. Rhythmic and melodic recitation affect the emotions of the character and may be heightened by close physical proximity to the audience. It is through the verse that impressions of dignity, suffering, grandeur, and human significance are created. However, there is no need to portray Shakespearean emotion melodramatically or unconvincingly. The guide for today's actor is control and precision when handling Shakespearean emotion. Place your focus on the spoken word and the verbal display such as in soliloquies, orations, descriptions, repartee, and puns. Concentrate on emphasizing and elevating key words in sentences. Try not to "think the emotion out;" imagine the emotion of an actual person in a real situation. The outcome should result in contagious response of clear, disciplined, and appropriate emotion.

Exercise 9　Character and Emotion

1. Select a character from the list at the end of this chapter. Read the play and study the character with special focus on character development, character personality, and character emotion. Write a one-to-two-page paper in which you clarify what you learned from your study about the character and emotion. The paper should be read and discussed by your instructor and colleagues. Later you may wish to perform a representative scene or monologue to complete this exercise.
2. Practice creating emotional complexity in each of the following speeches:

IMOGEN:　I would have broke mine eye-strings; crack'd them, but
　　　To look upon him, till the diminution
　　　Of space had painted him sharp as my needle,
　　　　　Nay, follow'd him, till he had melted from
　　　The smallness of a gnat to air, and then
　　　Have turn'd mine eye and wept.
　　　　　　　　　　Cymbeline Act I, scene iii

ULYSSES:　Time, hath, my lord, a wallet at his back,
　　　Wherein he puts alms for oblivion,
　　　A great-sized monster of ingratitudes:
　　　Those scraps are good deeds past, which are devour'd

As fast as they are made, forgot as soon
As done: perseverance, dear my lord,
Keeps honor bright: to have done is to hang
Quite out of fashion, like a rusty nail
In monumental mockery.

Troilus and Cressida
Act III, scene iii

Dance and Music

Elizabethan men were excellent dancers. In addition, some men, especially the nobility, were accomplished musicians. Elizabethan society was exceptionally conscious of the role that music and dance played in helping formulate the temperament of the times. Execution of dances was skillful and intricate. Dancing became a test of quick intelligence and physical agility. There are many extant Elizabethan dances that can be performed either before a play, during intermission, or after a play. Performances traditionally ended with a dance called the *jig.* This was a violent, spectacular dance with many intricate steps. Actors executed exaggerated leaps called *caprioles* and violent lifts of one's partner high into the air called *voltes.* Other known dances were the *Pavane* (after the peacock's pride of bearing), the *galliarde* (a lively, nimble movement), and the *alman* or *allemande* (German or heavy type of movement with the feet).

The richness of the Elizabethan period was fully exemplified by its music. Nearly everyone sang and performed. Class distinctions ceased to exist when it came to music. The most popular kind of music was the *madrigal,* a song written with up to seven parts. There were drinking songs and solo love ballads. Unfortunately, many of Shakespeare's songs have to be adapted to modern music because the original melodies are lost. However, most scholars believe Shakespeare considered music to be supportive, not dominant, in his plays. Music was created for effect, to underscore some point, to add character dimension, or to introduce scenery and characters. Occasionally instruments were played by stage characters to add color. Musicians were used in dumb shows for entrances and exits of special (usually royal) characters, to underscore alliterative verse or repetition of phrases, and to intensify emotional effects. Mad or insane people also were associated with music, for example, Lear and Ophelia. Music was used for moments of fantasy (e.g., *The Tempest* and *A Midsummer Night's Dream*). In general, music was classified into three groups: fanfares, dances, and songs. The instruments varied greatly, but the main ones were the virginal, the lute, the viola da gamba, and the

recorder. We are most familiar with the lute and the recorder. The lute was similar in shape to a bowl and was slung across the shoulders by brightly colored ribbons. The strings were plucked, and it was used primarily to accompany singing of love songs. The recorder, a thin-sounding instrument, has regained popularity in recent times. The virginal was played by the ladies who plucked the strings with quills to actuate the keyboard. The viol (viola da gamba) was a stringed instrument suitable for chamber music. Flageolets, or penny whistles, were also used to produce a sweet, melodic tone. The hautboy, a reed instrument, was rather shrill and harsh. Horns were used for hunting music; trumpets and drums were used as ''alarums'' and ''flourishes'' to announce royalty. Violins, cornets, flutes, hautboys, and drums were traditionally used in dumb shows. Instruments might be grouped by families, or small mixed combinations of three or four instruments with or without voices. The organ was used by itself primarily. It was a small instrument consisting of flute pipes and beating reeds, which produced a harsh sound.

Learning to dance to Elizabethan music is a highly specialized technique that should not be undertaken in a single acting exercise. Extensive study and practice with a trained choreographer or director are required (study references are given in Selective Readings at the end of this chapter).

Music and dance in Shakespeare's plays should always be considered in the light of how clearly and appropriately they support character, action, and mood and should rarely be used as spectacles in their own right. Music and dance are only supportive and must never dominate or destroy the power of what is inherently Shakespearean in terms of brilliant verse and characterization.

Suggested Characters and Plays for Scene Work

Shakespeare, William

Hamlet, Ophelia, Claudius, Gertrude, Polonius, Laertes, Horatio, Ghost, First Gravedigger
Hamlet

Othello, Desdemona, Iago, Emilia
Othello

Romeo, Juliet, Mercutio, Nurse
Romeo and Juliet

Anthony, Brutus, Cassius, Caesar, Calpurnia, Portia
Julius Caesar

Richard III, Clarence, Lady Anne
Richard III

Bottom, Puck
A Midsummer Night's Dream

Shylock, Portia, Jessica
The Merchant of Venice

Falstaff, Hotspur, Henry IV, Mistress Quickly
Henry IV, Part I

Henry V, Katherine
The Life of King Henry V

Rosalind, Jaques
As You Like It

Malvolio, Feste, Sir Toby Belch, Sir Andrew Aguecheek, Viola, Olivia, Maria, Duke Orsino
Twelfth Night

Lear, Edmund, The Fool, Gloucester, Goneril, Regan, Cordelia
King Lear

Macbeth, Banquo, Macduff, Lady Macbeth, The Witches
Macbeth

Antony, Cleopatra
Antony and Cleopatra

Prospero, Caliban, Ariel
The Tempest

Jonson, Ben

Volpone, Mosca
Volpone

Morose, Epicoene
Epicoene

Jeremy, Subtle, Dol Common
Alchemist

Dekker, Thomas

Lacy, Rafe
The Shoemaker's Holiday

Webster, John

Duchess of Malfi, Bosola
The Duchess of Malfi

Marlowe, Christopher

Dr. Faustus, Mephistophilis, Wagner, Helen
Tragical History of Dr. Faustus

Barabas, Abigail, Ithamore
The Jew of Malta

King Edward the Second, Queen Isabella
Reign of Edward the Second

Actor Checklist   Elizabethan and Shakespearean Style

Voice	Clear articulation; effective vocal production; varied; slightly elevated tone.
Movement	Full and fluid; appropriate to character; slightly elevated but natural and comfortable; highly selective for tragedy; free and spontaneous for comedy; presentational delivery generally used in soliloquy and aside; representational mode dominates slightly in both tragedy and comedy.
Gestures	Use of full body; clear, fluid, and appropriate; slightly elevated; highly selective in tragedy; flexible in comedy.
Pantomimic Dramatization	Clear, appropriate; use of hand and costume props, particularly in comedy; highly selective for tragedy; highly inventive for comedy.
Character	Truthful and believable; clear; empathic, if appropriate; appropriate dimension.
Emotion	Complex and multidimensional; clear; disciplined; rooted in human psychology.
Ideas	Complex and clear; rooted in Renaissance and Elizabethan social, philosophical, and theological thought; effectively theatricalized.
Language	Often unusual vocabulary; clear and understandable; iambic pentameter rhythmically intact with interpretative freedom permitted; correct pronunciation; lyrical and musical when intended.
Pace and Tempo	Varied; rhythmic; disciplined.
Special Techniques	Specialized dancing and singing depending on context; specialized musical instruments when required; language requires unusual vocal dexterity; unusual attention to movement in costume.

Selective Readings

Adams, John C. *The Globe Playhouse: Its Design and Equipment.* 2d ed. New York: Barnes & Noble, 1961.

Baxter, John. *Shakespeare's Poetic Styles: Verse Into Drama.* Boston: Routledge and Kegan Paul, 1980.

Beckerman, Bernard. *Shakespeare at the Globe, 1500–1609.* New York: Macmillan Co., 1962.

Bentley, Gerald E. *Shakespeare, A Biographical Handbook.* New Haven: Yale University Press, 1961.

Berry, Ralph. *Shakespearean Structures.* Totowa, N.J.: Barnes & Noble, 1981.

Brown, John Russell. *Shakespeare in Performance.* New York: Harcourt, Brace Jovanovich, 1976.

Chute, Marchette. *Shakespeare of London.* New York: E. P. Dutton & Co., 1949.

Clurman, Harold. "Actors in Style and Style in Actors." New York *Times Magazine,* December 7, 1952.

Gibson, William. *Shakespeare's Game.* New York: Atheneum, 1978.

Granville-Barker, H. *Prefaces to Shakespeare.* 4 vols. Princeton, N.J.: Princeton University Press, 1947.

———, and Harrison, G. B. *A Companion to Shakespeare.* New York: Doubleday & Co., 1960.

Harbage, Alfred. *Shakespeare's Audience.* New York: Columbia University Press, 1961.

Hibbard, G. R. *The Making of Shakespeare's Dramatic Poetry.* Toronto: University of Toronto Press, 1981.

Hodges, C. W. *The Globe Restored.* rev. ed. New York: Coward, McCann & Geoghegan, 1968.

Horst, Louis. *Pre-Classic Dance Forms.* New York: Kamin Dance Publishers, 1953.

Joseph, Bertram. *Elizabethan Acting.* London: Oxford University Press, 1951.

———. *Acting Shakespeare.* New York: Theatre Arts Books, 1969.

———. *A Shakespeare Workbook.* 2 vols. New York: Theatre Arts Books, 1981.

Kokeritz, Helge. *Shakespeare's Names: A Pronouncing Dictionary.* New Haven: Yale University Press, 1959.

———. *Shakespeare's Pronunciation.* New Haven: Yale University Press, 1953.

Nagler, A. M. *Shakespeare's Stage.* New Haven, Conn: Yale University Press, 1958.

Nevo, Ruth. *Comic Transformations in Shakespeare.* New York: Methuen, 1980.

Pilkington, Ace G. *Screening Shakespeare.* Doctoral thesis, University of Oxford, 1988. (Focuses on Shakespeare's plays on film and contains an excellent bibliography related to acting Shakespeare.)

Pitt, Angela. *Shakespeare's Women.* Totowa, N.J.: Barnes & Noble, 1981.

Robinson, Marion Parsons, ed. *Scenes for Women from the Plays of Shakespeare.* Boston, Mass.: Walter H. Baker Co., 1967.

Rudnicki, Stefan, ed. *Classical Monologues: 1 Shakespeare.* New York: Drama Book Specialists, 1979.

Schmidgall, Gary. *Shakespeare and the Courtly Aesthetic.* Berkeley: University of California Press, 1981.

Schoenbaum, S. *Shakespeare The Globe and the World.* Oxford: University Press Folger Shakespeare Library, 1979.

Schofield, Martin. *The Ghosts of Hamlet: The Play and Modern Writers.* New York: Cambridge University Press, 1980.

''Shakespeare: An Annotated Bibliography,'' *Shakespeare Quarterly (1924– 19—). [SQ was originally called The Shakespeare Association Bulletin.]* Annual bibliography of writings about Shakespeare.

Shakespeare Survey: An Annual Survey of Shakespearean Study and Production. Cambridge: Harvard University Press, 1948.

Speaight, Robert. *Shakespeare on the Stage: An Illustrated History of Shakespearean Performance.* New York: William Collins Sons & Co., Ltd., 1972.

Webster, Margaret. *Shakespeare without Tears.* Greenwich, Conn.: Fawcett World Library, 1955.

Wickham, Glynne. *Early English Stages, 1300–1660.* 2 vols. New York: Columbia University Press, 1959–1962.

Suggested Filmography

1. *Antony and Cleopatra.* 1972. British. Directed by and starring Charlton Heston.
2. *Catch My Soul.* 1974. Based upon *Othello.* Written and directed by Patrick McGoohan.
3. *Chimes at Midnight.* British. (*Falstaff* in U.S.). 1966. Adapted from *Richard II, Henry IV, Pts. 1 & 2, Henry V, The Merry Wives of Windsor,* with narration from Holinshed's *Chronicles.* Director— Orson Welles. With Orson Welles.
4. *Dr. Faustus.* 1967. Columbia. Playwright—Christopher Marlowe. Director—Richard Burton. With Burton, Elizabeth Taylor.
5. *Forbidden Planet.* 1956. MGM. Director—Fred M. Wilcox. With Walter Pidgeon, Anne Francis, Leslie Nielsen. A ''fifties'' science-fiction version of *The Tempest,* with Caliban as a monster from the subconscious.
6. *Hamlet.* 1948. Universal-International. Director—Sir Laurence Olivier. With Olivier and Jean Simmons.
7. *Henry V.* 1944. U. A. Director—Sir Laurence Olivier. With Olivier.

8. *Macbeth.* 1987. British. Royal Shakespeare Company. Director—Trevor Nunn. With Ian McKellen.
9. *Macbeth.* 1971. British. Director—Roman Polanski. With John Finch, Francessca Annis.
10. *A Midsummer Night's Dream.* 1935. Warners. Director—Max Reinhardt and Wm. Dieterle. With James Cagney.
11. *Othello.* 1952. Directed by and starring Orson Welles.
12. *Othello.* With Laurence Olivier. 1965.
13. *Richard III.* 1956. London Films. Director—Sir Laurence Olivier. With Olivier.
14. *Ran.* 1987. Based on *King Lear.* Directed by Akira Kurosawa.
15. *Romeo and Juliet.* 1968. British. Paramount. Director—Franco Zeffirelli. With Olivia Hussey, Michael York.
16. *The Taming of the Shrew,* 1967. With Elizabeth Taylor and Richard Burton.
17. *Tempest.* 1982. Columbia. Adapted from Shakespeare's play, *The Tempest.* Director—Paul Mazursky. With John Cassavetes, Gena Rowlands, Raul Julia.
18. *The Tempest.* 1980. British. Writer/director Derek Jarman. A "punk" version of Shakespeare's play.
19. *Throne of Blood.* 1957. (From *Macbeth.*) Director—Akira Kurosawa. With Toshiro Mifune.

Notes

1. For further, more detailed discussion of the Elizabethan theater and audience, see C. Walter Hodges, *The Globe Restored,* 2d ed. (London: Oxford University Press, 1968); Alois Nagler, *Shakespeare's Stage* (New Haven, Conn.: Yale University Press, 1958); Alfred Harbage, *Shakespeare's Audience* (New York: Columbia University Press, 1961).
2. Marowitz, Charles, *The Method as Means* (London: Herbert Jenkins, 1961) p. 77.

Seventeenth-Century French Neoclassicism: Restraint Again

13

. . . Indeed, I think that it is much easier to soar with grand sentiments, to brave fortune in verse, to arraign destiny and reproach the Gods, than to broach ridicule in a fit manner, and to make the faults of all mankind seem pleasant on the stage. When you paint heroes you can do as you like.

Dorante in *School for Wives*
by Molière

. . . Aristotle laid down the rules of dramatic poetry, and Socrates, the wisest of the philosophers, did not disdain to speak of the tragedies of Euripides. We should like our works to be as solid and full of useful instruction as were those of antiquity. This might be a means to reconcile tragedy to a number of celebrated persons . . . who would undoubtedly cast a more favorable eye upon it [tragedy] if the dramatists endeavored to instruct as well as please their auditors, and so came nearer to the true end of all tragedy.

Racine in Preface to *Phaedra*

Molière's delightful female character Dorante expresses the key problem confronting the comic playwright—how to reveal man's ridiculous nature, lower sentiments, and human faults in a humorous and, therefore, pleasant statement on a stage. Perhaps no comic playwright, with the possible exceptions of Aristophanes, Shakespeare, and Shaw, has succeeded in mastering this problem as well as the genius of the seventeenth-century French stage, Molière. Molière wrote a host of brilliant comedies with infinite dramatic variety. In tragedy, his chief counterpart, Jean Racine, in following the so-called new or Neoclassic bent, abandoned the flexible forms of Renaissance tragedy and returned to a restrained imitation of the ancient Greeks (refined through the influence of the Romans). Pierre Corneille in his plays also contributed to the reform of French tragedy, but the finest examples were those of Racine. The plays of Molière and Racine are the best for an actor to study when learning how to act seventeenth-century French Neoclassic drama.

Overview of French Neoclassicism (Seventeenth Century)

The period of French Neoclassicism (i.e., *New* Classicism) began in the third decade of the seventeenth century when Cardinal Richelieu became primate to King Louis XIV. (The French often delete *Neo* from the name and refer only to the French *Classicism.*) During this period France was flush with a fierce nationalism that spilled into the cultural heritage of the nation. In 1630 under the guidance of Richelieu, a revolution in the arts was forged whose pattern of cultural development was modeled on the Italian Renaissance and derived primarily from the work of Castelvetro, a sixteenth-century Italian scholar. Neoclassic drama began with the study of classical Roman plays in the late fifteenth century and continued with the writing of Latin imitations of classical works in the early sixteenth century, and its influence spread to French drama after 1550. The principle of Neoclassicism was dramatization of abstract concepts. Plays were concerned with ideas and their effect on human beings—ideas such as honor and dishonor, sin and innocence, loyalty and treachery, will and necessity, respect and contempt, authority and servility. In Neoclassic plays, the concept of verisimilitude (likelife quality) was paramount in exemplifying generalized ideals. French playwrights wanted the audience to see the ''appearance'' of reality—a world perceived by the senses, a particularized world that the playwright allowed to be seen. The classical unities of time, place, and action were strictly supported. The *unities* were attributed erroneously to Aristotle when actually they were misinterpretations of his writing by Italian Renaissance critics who studied Horace more than Aristotle. Emphasis was on the universal aspects of character and situation. Character was synonymous with status, rank, and code of behavior. This concept of character became known as *decorum* or appropriateness of characterization. To Neoclassicists, verisimilitude and decorum were essential to achieve complete universality in drama.

Neoclassic playwrights produced virile drama. Most plays were based on the models of Alexandre Hardy (ca. 1572–1632). Hardy was the innovator of the Alexandrine line, the basic verse used in Neoclassic drama (i.e., six iambic feet). Romantic character dominated in his plays, whose trademark was a highly narrative elegiac style.

The first exponent of Neoclassic drama in France was Corneille (1604–1684). Corneille's use of simple characters and complex plots made him a highly popular playwright. *The Cid,* written in 1636, typified Corneille's use of a hero with an indomitable will. *The Cid* is perhaps most famous for having been the center of a controversy in the French Academy (formed in 1635 by Cardinal Richelieu to set cultural standards in France). Corneille's highly successful play was rejected by the Academy because it violated the unities. Subsequently, Corneille set out to write other plays that adhered to the Neoclassical rules of playwriting. However, they were singularly unimpressive as viable drama.

Jean Racine (1639–1673) was a much more impressive Neoclassic playwright. Racine's plays possessed a natural sense of order and good taste. He achieved the epitome of the Neoclassic style of tragedy in his plays—in effect, the Neoclassic form was truly an expression of his natural style of writing. His plays contained little external action. The drama resulted from internal psychological conflict centered on a single complex character. Racine de-emphasized the physical appearance of characters, emphasizing instead the psychological and moral states of the hero or heroine. Characters portrayed intense emotional depth that was manifested in great conflicts of passion and willpower (e.g., Phaedra). Human weakness and strength were exposed by simple dramatic passages. Departure from established decorum brought about the downfall of a character.

Comedy was very popular in France during the seventeenth century. True to the Neoclassic demands of the French Academy, Molière (christened Jean-Baptiste Poquelin; 1622–1673) wrote plays that conformed to the classical ideal of having five acts and adhering to the unities. His plays were usually set in a drawing room (rarely out-of-doors). Molière created dramatic action through the impact of events on character, which in turn reacted and created new events for counterimpact (i.e., *Tartuffe*). Molière drew his characters from all levels of society. Psychology was the mainspring of his plays, exposing humanized and vulnerable man in a weakened condition. Molière was essentially a satirist devoted to truth. He used satire to expose the pretentions of the world while attempting to bring about change. It is important to keep in mind that Molière was a great admirer of the commedia dell'arte (he toured with a commedia troupe as an actor). Many characters in Molière's comedies were based on commedia types (for example, Harpagon in *The Miser* is a Pantalone figure). Molière's farces also borrowed from Plautus and Terence and from Spanish and Italian sources. Although he wrote other types of plays such as ballets and tragedies, Molière's appeal has endured strictly because of his comedies.

The major theatres of Paris included the Hotel de Bourgogne, the Theatre du Marais, and the Palais-Royal (first theatre in France to use a proscenium arch). Tennis courts were often converted into temporary theatres, with a simple platform for acting at one end of the court, while galleries and benches were placed on the sides and down the length of the court for spectators. The Hotel de Bourgogne was simply a long, narrow room with galleries on the sides and benches in front of a raised platform at one end. The Marais and Palais-Royal resembled the kind of theatres generally used today. The spectators sat on a sloping floor or in one of the three gallery levels on the sides. Some people sat in the pit below the apron or upon the stage itself (thereby severely limiting the acting area). Scenic demands were simple, ranging from curtains and small three-dimensional units to painted representations of rooms, streets, and gardens. All scenic changes were executed in full view of the audience. Footlights as well as overhead lighting utilized candles and oil lamps. Poor lighting forced actors to play primarily downstage center. Movement was limited also by lighting and the spectators onstage.

Actors and actresses wore contemporary costumes except for well-known historic, fantastic, and allegorical characters. A variety of elaborateness prevailed in costuming, depending upon the character and the financial status of the acting troupe. Most characters wore long, full wigs. In a few plays the commedia influence resulted in the retention of masks by some characters. Costuming and contemporary dress were generally beautiful and elaborate, emphasizing lace, brocade, and other fineries.

Voice—French Neoclassic Tragedy

The acting style in France during the seventeenth century was generally characterized as highly formal and conventionalized, with great emphasis on vocal recitation. The tradition for performing in plays by Corneille was to use grandiose recitation while standing rigidly in one place. On the

Hume Cronyn as Harpagon in *The Miser* by Molière. Directed by Douglas Campbell, designed by Tanya Moiseiwitsch, at The Guthrie Theatre (Minnesota Theatre Company), Minneapolis, Minnesota.

other hand, for Racine's plays a less declamatory vocal delivery was necessary. Because Racine's characters explored the subconscious passions of the mind, the actor had to develop a new and fairly subtle naturalness in the voice. A free voice is the key requirement for successful performance of Neoclassic French tragedy. The voice must vary with respect to passions and with differing parts of the classical oration; it also must vary with figures of rhetoric, unusual sentences and unique words. Racine's art is a formal one contrived of human passion within strict linguistic limitations. In Alexandrine verse, recitation must achieve a balance of the rhymed couplet and the individual line. The line may or may not be broken in the middle by the caesura. The verse is "sculptured" to help compress passion into one major crisis. For example, Phaedra is a tormented woman trying to find a way to control her incestuous passion in act 4 as she speaks to Oenone:

> Hypocrisy and incest breathe at once through all I do. My hands are ripe for murder. To spill the guiltless blood of innocence. Do I still live, a wretch, and dare to face the holy sun, from whom I have my being? My father's father was the king of gods; My race is spread through all the universe.—Where can I hide? In the dark realms of Pluto? But there my father holds the fatal urn.

> *Phaedra* by Racine

Language is probably the most difficult problem in studying the acting style of Racine and Neoclassic French tragedy. The magnificent quality of his style with language can only be conveyed indirectly in English. Any translator of Racine begins by apologizing. Racine's language is considered to be the most nearly perfect example of purity of style of all French literature.

Alexandrine poetry was written in a twelve-syllable line of qualitative rather than quantitative verse, with a thirteenth unpronounced syllable permitted in a feminine line. The line was further divided into two hemistichs (one-half of the verse line), with a caesura after the sixth syllable. Boileau-Despreaux, French dramatic critic, stated it this way for the actor:

> Have an ear for cadence,
> Always let your meaning, cutting off your words,
> Halt at the hemistich, mark it with a stop.

There was also a requirement, extremely difficult to fulfill, that each line should terminate a logical sequence of thought with no carryover to the next line. Such a carryover, an *enjambement,* was considered a defect of style and a flaw in the writing. A kind of carryover was allowed, in rare cases, for a special effect and was then called a *rejet.* A famous example of a successful *rejet* occurs in *Phaedra* in the scene between Phaedra and Hippolytus in the second act in which Phaedra makes five *rejets*. By use of this devise at precisely these points, Racine called attention to the fact that Phaedra is distraught. She can no longer arrest her speech normally as a lady should. The five *rejets* that Racine used indicate to the audience that Phaedra is being carried away by her emotions.

The language of Neoclassic tragedy was aristocratic and removed from daily life. The poet spoke abstractly, with rarified elegance and great formality. Today this language is considered rather affected and is one of the difficulties in performing Neoclassic tragedy adequately for modern taste. A good English translation naturally accomplishes a great deal in making the verse palatable but, just as naturally, also sacrifices much of the great beauty and meaning of the language in the process. However, awareness of the precision, beauty, and special effects as just described is a valuable part of an actor's training as he or she prepares to act Neoclassic tragedy.

Exercise 1   Voice—Neoclassic Tragedy

1. Practice the following selections aloud, emphasizing highly grandiose, declamatory delivery. Work to achieve balance of rhythm and rhyme. Try to achieve termination of thought in each line. Be highly selective in where you place emotion, inflection, and variety. Later repeat the exercise by modifying it to a level of what might be considered palatable or natural for contemporary audiences:

PHAEDRA   Although you hate me, I shall not
complain, My lord: for you have seen me
bent to harm you.
You could not read the tables of my heart.
I've taken care to invite your enmity,
And could not bear your presence where I
dwelt.
In public, and in private, your known foe,
I've wished the seas to part us, and even
forbidden
The mention of your name within my hearing.
But if one measures punishment by the offense,
If only hatred can attract your hate,
Never was woman who deserved more pity,
My lord, and less deserved your enmity.

HIPPOLYTUS   A mother jealous for her children's
rights
Seldom forgives her stepson. I know it,
madam.

Nagging suspicions are the commonest fruits
Of second marriage; and another wife
Would have disliked me just the same; and I
Might well have had to swallow greater wrongs.

Phaedra by Racine

2. Using the selection from *Phaedra* in number 1, *sing* the speeches in an improvised melody. Try to create a serious and fluid melody to assist you in grasping the level of grandeur inherent within the style. Then repeat the speeches in regular speaking patterns but utilize a *stage whisper*. This may assist you in locating the delicate, psychological depths inherent within the style. Finally, attempt to combine vocal grandeur and delicate, psychological shadings into a rich and appropriate style of delivery.

Movement—French Neoclassic Tragedy

All movement in Neoclassic tragedy is confined by linguistic demands. That confinement requires that the actor achieve poetic and precise command of gestures and movements highly elevated to a larger-than-life level. The elevation should coincide with the formality of the words. Movement should be characterized by elegance and gracefulness of manner and bearing, reminiscent of the classic Greek style. Modern actors can benefit greatly from studying the paintings of such seventeenth-century artists as Peter Rubens, Nicolas Poussin, and Charles Lebrun. These artists depicted the dress and costumes of the time well and also captured gestures and facial expressions that might be helpful. Movement was probably very limited on the seventeenth-century French stage because of the poor lighting, small acting area, and emphasis on language. The physical focus was on the upper portion of the body, particularly the face, hands, and arms. Naturally, in today's theatre more movement is employed in the staging. However, emphasis remains on voice and character. Modern directors employ more use of sitting positions and handling of properties than in the original style. Movement, sitting, and use of properties must be handled discreetly; it is a mistake to use a great deal of realistic activity in a Neoclassic French tragedy. Similar to the seventeenth century, selective use of hand and costume properties such as fans, handkerchiefs, staffs, canes, goblets, capes, swords, and so on, is advisable today. Movement was generally slow with rare physical contact with other characters. The presentational mode dominated almost exclusively in the original style but is, of course, modified today.

Exercise 2   Movement—Neoclassic Tragedy

1. Perform the following action as a review of classical Greek movement, which relates closely to Neoclassic movement.

    a. From a centered position on your feet, move through space in a slow-motion manner concentrating upon grace, rhythm, fluidity, and sense of controlled restraint.

    b. Repeat the foregoing exercise in a modified tempo permitting the slow motion to evolve into an acceptably believable or natural tempo.

2. Locate a book on the history of art that contains photographs of paintings by Rubens, Poussin, and Lebrun. Create stage replicas of these paintings that depict posture and expressions similar to those seen in the paintings. Then put these ''portraits'' and ''tableaux'' into graceful, restrained motion.

Character and Emotion—French Neoclassic Tragedy

Except for the psychology of their emotion, characters in Racine's plays were not realistically conceived. They are contained in a condition of artistic purity. We see very little of their daily routine; they seem not to sleep, eat, or drink. They speak with an elevated and artificial (meaning ''contrived by art'') language. Their soliloquies are rational pieces of literature or rhetoric. However, close examination reveals shivering emotion beneath the reason. That emotion was based on valid human psychology having full, rich motivation. An intelligent approach to character and emotion in French Neoclassic tragedy is to establish a believable characterization beginning with the use of personalization. The personalization is best used in this style only for the sake of comfort in early rehearsals. While the language will dominate, the style works best in today's theatre with believable characterization. The language in itself will keep the character and emotion at a necessary larger-than-life level.

Exercise 3   Character and Emotion—Neoclassic Tragedy

1. Invent and perform a series of improvisations in pairs in which you explore the levels of human psychology concerning the following character and emotional states. Be certain that a goal or an objective is established for each improvisation. For example, the goal of a *greed* improvisation might be a wife discovers her husband has hidden a million-dollar inheritance from her.

    a. Greed

    b. Ambition

    c. Incestuous love

    d. Pride

    e. Jealousy

    f. Grief

    g. Hatred

    h. Love

2. Using the eight emotions listed in the foregoing exercise, "overact" a highly contrived physical manifestation of each emotion; improvise a highly artificial verbal expression or phrase to coincide with your physicalization. Finally, use personalization to modify your previous effort in order to make the character and emotion palatable and believable, with some "elevation" lingering from the exaggerated work.

Voice—French Neoclassic Comedy

French Neoclassic comedy as exemplified by Molière was concerned with the manners and customs of the court and those persons who lived on the edge of the social life of the period. It was fashionable to be impious and licentious about serious subjects. Audiences probably enjoyed seeing their manners and customs mirrored. The focus of the acting style is on language, but due to the genius of Molière, equal focus comes to bear on character. Molière's plays conform to Neoclassic rules of structure and the unities; some of his plays were written in verse and others in prose. Rhythm and pace are crucial considerations when delivering Molière's comic lines.

His characters generally interacted rapidly. The vocal tempo is usually rapid and precise. Again it is necessary to check vocabulary carefully. Soliloquies and asides were frequently used. Unusually clear articulation, pronunciation, and effective vocal production are necessary to handle the rapid line delivery and varied language of Molière. Complex inflections and vocal variety are absolutely necessary in performing the language of Molière, who wrote primarily in Alexandrine couplets (some translators adapt his writing to prose at great damage to rhythm and lyricism).

Exercise 4   Voice—Neoclassic Comedy

1. Practice the following speeches for rapid delivery; comic repartee and inflection; clear articulation, pronunciation, effective vocal production; and variety. Perform entirely presentational; then modify and repeat the exercise with balanced use of representational and presentational modes.

CLÉANTÉ   . . . You agreed of late
That young Valere might have your
daughter's hand.

ORGON   I did.

CLÉANTÉ   You've not postponed it; is that true?

ORGON   No doubt.

CLÉANTÉ   The match no longer pleases you?

ORGON   Who knows?

CLÉANTÉ   D'you mean to go back on your word?

ORGON   I won't say that.

CLÉANTÉ   Has anything occurred
Which might entitle you to break your pledge?

ORGON   Perhaps.

Tartuffe Act I, scene v, by Molière

MARIANNE   Oh, you turn my blood to ice!
Stop torturing me, and give me your advice.

DORINE   *(threatening to go)* Your servant,
Madam.

MARIANNE   Dorine, I beg of you . . .

DORINE   No, you deserve it; this
marriage must go through.

MARIANNE   Dorine!

DORINE   No.

MARIANNE   Not Tartuffe! You know I think him . . .

DORINE   Tartuffe's your cup of tea,
and you shall drink him.

MARIANNE   I've always told you everything,
and relied . . .

DORINE   No. You deserve to be tartuffified.

Tartuffe Act III, scene iii, by Molière

2. To enhance vocal rhythm, practice the foregoing speeches by improvising a melody and singing them. Try to create a light, rapid, and fun
melody.

3. Repeat the same speeches from *Tartuffe* and toss a tennis ball to your
partner as you say the last word of each speech; the partner does the
same in return. This exercise can enhance timing and cuing.

Movement—French Neoclassic Comedy

Two points must be kept in mind when movement in Molière comedy is
discussed. One, when heavy commedia dell'arte influence is obvious,
commedia acting style should dominate; for example, *The Physician in
Spite of Himself,* a farcical short play by Molière, is frequently performed
in the commedia style (commedia style is discussed in chapter 11). Two,

a unique, elaborate acting style is necessary in most of Molière's character comedies because they are rich in social satire. His character and social comedies were rooted in precise, inventive activity, and therefore movement should be selective and rapid in tempo. A highly theatrical, presentational mode should be used. For example, movement should focus on firm stride and erect standing position or posture (weight resting on the back foot with the front foot forward and to the side). Men walked with virility and used elaborate finger gestures. Gestures were broad and punctuated by use of fluid movements of the wrist and hand. Maids and servants bounced and pranced a great deal; central female characters generally glided in a highly elevated and charming manner. Clothing generally emphasized the figure.

Unlike Neoclassic tragedy, there was considerable stage movement, particularly in the plays influenced by commedia. Bowing and curtsying were used frequently. Pantomimic dramatization was inventive, emphasizing facial grimacing and extensive use of hand and costume properties. Hands were usually held high to reveal lace cuffs. Personal objects were handled with flourish: handkerchiefs were waved between the fingers; fans were fluttered at crucial moments of anxiety, discovery, or flirtation; half-masks were deployed at gala public affairs and out-of-doors; canes and staffs were swung about for emphasis or humor; and snuff was taken by most characters, male and female. Snuff was usually a mixture of tobacco and dried herbs or powders and occasionally drugs. Snuff was used to attract attention. Its use was a matter of great ceremony and social custom. On a practical level, taking snuff usually caused one to sneeze, thereby cleaning the nasal passages. It also had a slightly intoxicating and pleasant effect. Most people of upper society carried a small box of snuff with them. A snuffbox was taken from the waistcoat pocket, tapped at the top to make the particles fall to the bottom, and a pinch was taken with the thumb and second finger and either applied to the nose and inhaled or placed on the back of the hand and sniffed. The cuffs were then shaken or snapped at with a handkerchief to remove any clinging particles of snuff.

The male bow was slightly modified from that used in the Renaissance. A gentleman stepped back, bent one knee, and placed his right hand over his heart while bending slightly. Some men used a more elaborate bow by bending more deeply and sweeping their hats behind them. The female curtsy used the same variations as the Renaissance, and the use of fans and handkerchiefs made the curtsies more elaborate.

Soliloquies and asides were handled basically as they were in Elizabethan drama (see chapter 12).

Exercise 5   Movement—Neoclassic Comedy

1. Review all steps of Exercise 2 in chapter 11 on commedia movement.
2. Practice the modified bows and curtsies just described.
3. Study and practice the following:
   a. Take snuff according to the directions just given (see *Movement— French Neoclassic Comedy*).
   b. Assume the male standing position with weight resting on the rear foot, the front foot forward and to the side. With arms extending slightly to the side, move rapidly about the stage with precision and elegance. If they are available, use walking staffs, canes, handkerchiefs, and costume properties. (Execute these movements with considerable male virility.)
   c. Assume an elegant and graceful female pose. The weight should be balanced on both feet with the arms and hands extended away from the body. Move gracefully and rapidly about the stage with precision and elegance. If they are available, use fans, handkerchiefs, and costume properties.
   d. Using the speeches from *Tartuffe* in Exercise 4, create fun, lively dances to perform *as you deliver lines.*

Character and Emotion—French Neoclassic Comedy

Stock characters prevail in the plays of Molière influenced by commedia. In these plays, such as *The Physician In Spite of Himself,* your main concern will again be with singular obsession and usually one-dimensional personality characteristics.

However, the genius of Molière is exemplified in his great character creations in the social comedies such as *The Misanthrope, Tartuffe,* and *The Would-Be Gentleman.* The central characters in these plays are multidimensional, complex, and rooted in human psychology. The humanity of Molière's characters permit effective use of personalization in early rehearsals and in some instances beyond. Full-scale role analysis is necessary to create these characters. Molière's brilliant language in both prose and verse provides the key to character delineation. His characters have biographical background, clear attitudes, and temperament. They represent clear facets of seventeenth-century society and current political, philosophic, and theological thought and run the gamut of human feelings. Molière characters are highly motivated by clear emotional hungers and desires. Your approach to these roles must be serious and in no way mocking, detached, or superficial. The wit and comic situations tend to render the characters ludicrous and humorous, although a serious point of view underlies the comic facade. Create a complete human being; take the roles seriously and reveal the various emotional desires that drive them

Tartuffe by Molière. John Rensenhouse as Tartuffe and Edith Elliott as Elmire at the University of Wisconsin–Milwaukee. Directed by Nagle Jackson, scenery by R. H. Graham, costumes by Liz Covey. Photograph by Alan Magayne-Roshak.

such as greed, love, lust, avarice, and so on. If you play a role as though you or the character know you are humorous, you may destroy Molière's satire. The audience and other characters must recognize the ludicrous and comic element, but the actor and the character must not be aware of it. For example, Tartuffe in *Tartuffe* and Alceste in *The Misanthrope* are deadly earnest concerning their desires and problems. The situations Molière put them into, combined with his language and wit, turn the rich human characterizations into comedy. However, without detracting from foregoing points, it should be noted that Molière's characterizations are not totally natural. Behavior is altered; it is different from real life. It is magnified life. In other words, it is a perfect marriage of content and form.

Exercise 6 Character and Emotion—Neoclassic Comedy

1. Select a character from the list of Molière plays provided at the end of this chapter. Read the play and study the character, with special focus on character background, development, personality, and emotional hungers. Carefully identify the obsessive aspects of the hunger that ultimately render the character ludicrous or comic. Write a brief paper in which you clarify your study. After the paper is read and discussed, perform a representative scene or monologue to complete this exercise.

2. Using the character you selected in number 1 of this exercise, identify a stock commedia character type suitable as a stereotypical model for this character. Practice a speech from the play using a one-dimensional, commedia approach. Repeat the speech using the full-dimensional, personalization efforts reflective of the work done in number 1, yet retaining the commedia factor as a foundation for the role.

Music and Translations—French Neoclassicism

Most of Molière's plays called for use of some music and dance; for example, a form of ballet interlude was required in *The School For Husbands*. In seventeenth-century France, orchestral music was usually quite lavish, ranging from chamber groups to complete stringed orchestras. Viols, lutes, and organs were popular, along with wind instruments. Choral singing was also enjoyed.

While Racine and French Neoclassic tragedy are only occasionally performed today, Molière's comedies remain among the most popularly produced plays in the theatre. Effective translations are difficult to find because the elegant French language and meter suffer greatly when transposed into English. In recent years, poet Richard Wilbur has written highly acclaimed translations of Molière plays including *The Misanthrope* and *Tartuffe*.

French Neoclassic acting styles were influential on the Continent. Their influence was also seen in England with the restoration of the crown in 1660. However, as discussed in chapter 14, the glory of the French style was modified and uniquely adapted and altered by the artists of the Restoration.

Suggested Characters and Plays for Scene Work

Molière

Tartuffe, Orgon, Elmire, Dorine, Marianne, Cléanté
Tartuffe
Alceste, Célimène
The Misanthrope

Harpagon, Cléanté, Marianne
The Miser
M. Jourdain, Cléanté, Covielle
The Would-Be Gentleman

Scapin, Octavio, Leander
 Scapin
Sganarelle, Isabella, Valère, Ariste
 The School for Husbands
Argon, Angelique
 The Imaginery Invalid
Arnolphe, Agnes, Horace, Oronte
 The School for Wives

Racine, Jean
 Phaedra, Hippolytus, Oenone,
 Theseus
  Phaedra
 Andromache, Hermoine
  Andromache

Corneille, Pierre
 Chimene, Don Rodrique
  The Cid

Actor Checklist French Neoclassic Tragedy (Racine)

Voice	Clear diction; oratorical, rhetorical, and declamatory; varied; highly elevated; smooth and polished delivery; generally restrained except for *rejet* moments.
Movement	Highly restrained; elevated; appropriate; graceful; coordinated with linguistic demands; highly selective; presentational mode dominates; slow-to-moderate tempo, but accelerated at emotional moments.
Gestures	Selective; elevated; restrained except when emotion overcomes reason as in the vocal *rejet;* focus on the upper part of the body; rare use of sitting position.
Pantomimic Dramatization	Clear; appropriate; elevated; restrained; use of hand and costume properties; selective.
Character	Psychological; believable and truthful; clear; emphatic, if appropriate; full dimension in Racine; somewhat larger than life.
Emotion	Rooted in human psychology; well motivated; at times larger than life; controlled until moments of outburst.
Ideas	Exemplify Neoclassic mandates of verisimilitude and decorum; focus on reason over emotion.
Language	Lyrical; controlled Alexandrine verse; aristocratic, removed from daily life; abstract; elegant; formal; precise; beautiful.
Mood and Atmosphere	Correct and clear in terms of being supportive of character and action; no mix of comedy; pure in its seriousness.

Pace and Tempo	Moderate to slow except for moments of high emotion.
Special Techniques	Verse complexity requires great vocal dexterity.

Actor Checklist   French Neoclassic Comedy (Molière)

Voice	Exaggerated melodic patterns and inflections; rapid but clear; smooth and polished line delivery; precise diction, particularly in verse.
Movement	Elegant; elevated; graceful; controlled; well-executed use of bows, curtsies, asides, and soliloquies; balance of presentational and representational mode; generally rapid tempo.
Gestures	Hand, head, facial dominate; clear; elevated.
Pantomimic Dramatization	Clear and highly inventive; extensive use of period costumes and props such as fans, staffs, handkerchiefs, half-masks, snuff, and so on.
Character	Major characters are well motivated, multidimensional, complex, and rooted in human psychology; clear background, attitude, and temperament; representative social facet clear; serious actor involvement.
Emotion	Complex and multidimensional in major characters; clear; at times obsessive; rooted in human psychology.
Ideas	Clear; satiric; witty; to correct social injustices.
Language	Witty; rhythmic, brilliant vocabulary, and rich imagery; correct pronunciation; lyrical and musical when intended.
Mood and Atmosphere	Clear in terms of comic satire, farce or repartee and wit, as script demands; supportive of situation, action, character; generally comic with serious undertones.
Pace and Tempo	Generally rapid.
Special Techniques	Wit and language demand unusual vocal dexterity; singing and dancing usually required of some characters; unusual attention to movement in costume.
For Commedia Influence	See chapter 11.

Selective Readings

Gossip, C. J. *An Introduction to French Classical Tragedy.* Totowa, N.J.: Barnes & Noble, 1981.

Gossman, Lionel. *Men and Masks: A Study of Molière.* Baltimore: Johns Hopkins University Press, 1963.

Hubert, Judd D. *Molière and the Comedy of Intellect.* Reprint of 1962 ed. New York: Russell & Russell, 1971.

Lancaster, H. C. *A History of French Dramatic Literature in the Seventeenth Century.* 9 vols. Reprint of 1942 ed. Staten Island, N.Y.: Gordian Press, 1966.

Palmer, John. *Molière.* New York: Brewer & Warren, 1930.

Reiss, Timothy J. *Tragedy and Truth: Studies in the Development of a Renaissance and Neo-Classical Discourse.* New Haven: Yale University Press, 1980.

Turnell, Martin. *The Classical Moment: Studies in Corneille, Molière, and Racine.* Reprint of 1948 ed. Westport, Conn.: Greenwood Press, 1971.

Suggested Filmography

1. *Phaedre.* 1961. Adaptation of Racine's *Phaedre.* Directed by Jules Dassin. With Melina Mercouri and Anthony Perkins.

Restoration Comedy: Vitality 14

Our Galleries too, were finely us'd of late,
Where roosting Masques sat cackling for a Mate;
They came not to see Plays but act their own,
And had throng'd Audiences when we had none.
Our Plays it was impossible to hear,
Confound you, give your bawdy prating o're,
Or Zounds, I'le fling you i' the Pit, you bawling Whore,

Crowne Epilogue to *Sir Courtly Nice*

Leaning over other ladies awhile to whisper with the King, she rose out of the box and went into the King's right hand, between the King and the Duke of York; which . . . put the King himself, as well as every body else out of countenence. . . . She did it only to show the world that she is not out of favour yet, as was believed.

Samuel Pepys *Diary*

Crowne's view of the boisterous and unruly theatre audiences of Resto-ration England typifies the excitement and vitality that characterized the revival of dramatic activity and the reopening of the theatres after their closing by the Puritans and Commonwealth government between 1642 and 1660. The accession to the throne of Charles II brought a fun-loving, woman-loving, theatre-loving king to power. Dramatic activity flourished again. As Pepys notes, the king was a frequent visitor to London theatres. He and his entourage played many of the same flirtatious games in the royal box as did the aristocratic populace in the galleries and pit. Elegant dandies and fops sat upon the stage itself to exhibit their clothing and other fineries.

Restoration drama was noteworthy primarily for its comedies, al-though authors such as John Dryden, Thomas Otway, and others produced some interesting serious plays categorized Heroic Tragedy. Dryden's *The Conquest of Granada* was a notable example, although his tragedy about Antony and Cleopatra, *All for Love,* has proved more stageworthy. Ex-cessively bombastic and written in rhymed heroic couplets, the tragedies are rarely if ever produced in the contemporary theatre. Were they to be produced, directors and actors could well utilize the acting style employed in seventeenth-century French Neoclassic tragedy.

Overview of Restoration Comedy

The following discussion is based on the work of Lyn Oxenford in *Playing Period Plays* and Charles A. Gildon in *The Life of Mr. Thomas Betterton* (see Selective Readings at the end of this chapter for specific bibliographic information).

There are many similarities between theatre development in England and in France during the seventeenth and eighteenth centuries. Although the English Commonwealth under Cromwell suppressed plays and players from 1642 to 1660, theatre activity was not completely destroyed. Bandit actors and theatre managers provided a limited public with live ''under-ground'' entertainment. When Charles II was restored to the monarchy in 1660, the granting of theatre monopolies to William D'Avenant (Duke's Men) and Thomas Killigrew (King's Men) ensured competent manage-ment of plays, playwrights, actors, and theatres. Audiences attending the Restoration theaters (approximately 1660 to 1710) were predominately the aristocracy who demanded heroics in their tragedies and imitation of their own manners in their comedies.

Theatre structures in England were similar in style to the French theatres. Theatres were arranged in a semicircle ending in a gallery about midway in the auditorium. Most buildings provided a second gallery and a sloping pit with rows of seats arranged in a semicircle. The deep apron was backed by a raked stage whose depth from the front of the apron to the back wall was slightly less than half the total length of the building. The second Drury Lane theatre had four proscenium doors, two on either side of the apron with a box above each door (musicians usually sat in one of the boxes and spectators sat in the other box). In 1696, the apron was shortened by four feet and the downstage proscenium doors were converted into boxes. Additional benches were installed in the pit.

A feature of the French theatres not duplicated was the characteristic manner of moving scenery and producing scenic effect. On the Continent, scenery was moved by a pole-and-chariot system; in England a wing-and-backdrop system of sliding scenery was used. Grooves were inserted in the stage floor to receive the wing flats and shutters that formed the set. They were spaced to allow room between each set of scenes for placing furniture and assembling actors in a tableau. Sometimes scenes were cut out and set one behind the other to provide vistas and give the illusion of depth. Actors entered and exited through the proscenium doors. There was no act curtain; a front curtain was lowered and raised to begin and end the play. The audience never waited between scenes. The action was continuous due to the streamlined execution of scenery and the inclusion of songs and musical interludes between scenes.

Scenic demands for tragedies and comedies in seventeenth-century England were more elaborate than in France. Scenes were usually painted in perspective on wings, borders, and backdrops. However, the Neoclassic demand for universality was satisfied by the generality of the localized settings. As in France, few realistic set designs were needed for plays. The first move toward scenic realism came late in the eighteenth century (1771) when the scenic artist Phillip James de Loutherbourg was employed by the actor-manager David Garrick. Following the trend toward naturalism, Garrick removed all spectators from the stage (Voltaire accomplished the same thing in France).

The Restoration stage was generally lit poorly. Hooplike chandeliers obstructed the vision of the audience in the gallery seats. Oil lamps and candles were also used, and illumination was hazy. Later in the eighteenth century, Garrick removed the chandeliers from the front of the proscenium and placed them in the upstage area, out of sight of the audience, which thus was given a clear view of the stage. Garrick was also able to illuminate the backstage area to heighten dramatic effects. In addition, he placed light behind the wings on a level with the actors, introduced lanterns and wall brackets as integral parts of the set, provided greater use of oil lamps, and used colored transparent silks to produce lighting effects in color.

Restoration comedy, or comedy of manners, was preeminent on the English stage from 1660 to approximately 1710. The English aristocracy were enthralled with the accurate imitation of their customs and manners mirrored on the stage. Restoration actors and actresses captured their audience with a flamboyant display of witty, bluntly sexual dialogue, boudoir intrigues, sensual innuendos, and rakish behavior. A narrow set of conventions entirely dominated Restoration comedy: constancy in love, especially in marriage, was a bore; sex should be tempting; love thrived on variety; genuine sexual feelings (e.g., sentimentalism) had no place on the stage. In play after play, characters clashed with other characters in situations selected to produce love entanglements and intrigues. Dorimant, a character in Etherege's *The Man of Mode,* summarized the Restoration philosophy: ''Next to coming to a good understanding with a new mistress, I love a quarrel with an old one.''

Country life was considered boring. The clergy and professional men were treated with indifference or condescension. The most popular Restoration playwrights of the comedy of manners were William Wycherley, George Etherege, William Congreve, Thomas Shadwell, and John Vanbrugh. (George Farquhar was also a noted Restoration playwright, but one who might better be considered a ''transition'' author between Restoration and Sentimental Drama [see under Transition—Eighteenth-Century Sentimentalism and Nineteenth-Century Romanticism and Melodrama, later in this chapter].) These and many other comic authors proved once again that man was corruptible. The humor was in the satiric treatment of people who allowed themselves to be deceived or attempted to deceive others. Laughter was directed against the fop, the pretender at wit and sophistication, the old trying to be young, and the old man with a young and beautiful wife. For the most part, any standard of moral behavior was acceptable, but rewards and punishments were clearly meted out in accordance with the ability to achieve self-knowledge.

Prologues and epilogues were especially important in plays throughout the Restoration and well into the eighteenth century. Playwrights and actors-comedians continued the ancient stage tradition of introducing and concluding plays with special pieces, usually poetic, performed in a coarse, boisterous, hilarious manner.

The prevailing costume style in Restoration comedy was the contemporary dress of the late seventeenth and early eighteenth centuries. Every conceivable part of the human body was adorned. The actor wore a large-brimmed, plumed hat; a heavy periwig with curls over his forehead and down to his shoulders; a square-cut coat and a waistcoat hanging to the knees; wide, stiff cuffs and ruffles reaching to the knuckles; and ribbons on every available unmarked surface. The actress wore a gown with bell-shaped skirt and sleeves. A high mantilla and veil covered her head. Women were allowed to show their face, hands, and neck (and, of course, much of their bosom) when indoors. However, when appearing outside, ladies wore large hooded cloaks. As the years passed, men's tights revealed more muscular contour of the legs. Women's dresses became more clinging and revealed more of the female body. Sumptuous costumes were worn by heroes and heroines. Eye patches were seen regularly. Both sexes wore excessive makeup, false noses, beards, mustaches, powder, rouge, pencil, lipstick, and beauty patches. Obviously, little attempt was made at facial expression; to do so meant risking a cracked face.

Voice

In Restoration comedy the focus was unquestionably on brilliant, brittle, witty language, usually in prose. The style of Restoration acting was characterized by harmonious fusion of heightened oratory and rapid repartee. Vocal tone was important to denote emotional quality. For example, a soft and charming voice reflected love to an audience; a sharp, sullen, severe voice denoted hate or anger; a full, flowing, brisk voice denoted joy. English actors deliberately imitated the Parisian aristocratic style of address with its rich heritage from Molière. Phrasing and precise pronunciation were anglicized and became the fashionable language of British upper society and aristocracy. Training in British schools included singing, dancing, posture, gesture, walking, and all the arts of deportment. Because of the spectators on the stage and the inadequate lighting, actors learned to use the downstage center portion of the apron area with proficiency and aplomb. Intricate vocal pauses and timing were developed. Vocal tempo was usually rapid. Articulation, pronunciation, and effective vocal production were clear and precise. Vocal asides and soliloquies (particularly in the prologues and epilogues) took on new dimension with the heightened presentational intimacy between performer and audience. Vocal inflection and variety were uniquely expansive.

Exercise 1   Voice—Restoration Comedy

1. Practice the following verses individually and then collectively, stressing a variety of vocal tones. Repeat the exercise stressing precise

phrasing, clear articulation, pronunciation, and effective vocal production. Repeat the exercise stressing pauses, timing, and rapid tempo. Finally, repeat the exercise stressing expansive vocal inflection and variety.

King Charles, and who'll do him right now?
King Charles, and who's ripe for fight now?
Give a rouse: here's, in hell's despite now,
King Charles!

Who gave me the goods that went since?
Who raised me the house that sank once?
Who helped me to gold I spent since?
Who found me in wine you drank once?

> King Charles, and who'll do him right now?
> King Charles, and who's ripe for fight now?
> Give me a rouse: here's in hell's despite now,
> King Charles!

To whom used by boy George quaff else,
By the old fool's side that begot him?
For whom did he cheer and laugh else,
While Noll's damned troopers shot him.

> King Charles, and who'll do him right now?
> King Charles, and who's ripe for fight now?
> Give me a rouse: here's, in hell's despite now,
> King Charles!
>
> Anonymous English song

2. Improvise fast, lively, fun music for the English song in number 1 and practice singing it as an individual and within a group. Finally, incorporate exaggerated postures, gestures, and facial expressions to accompany the song and perform it as both a presentational solo and as a presentational chorus.

Movement

As originally staged, Restoration comedies were almost entirely presentational. Most movement was concerned with entering through the proscenium doors and exiting through the doors later. Much of the action took place downstage center on the apron. When adapting Restoration comedy to the modern stage, you and your director should not confine your action exclusively to the apron. You should probably utilize the area behind the proscenium arch in addition to the forestage. Movement in

Restoration comedy should be characterized by highly elevated, graceful patterns. All physical activity should be precise and inventive. A wide range of uniquely conventional gestures must be employed. For example, in the Restoration theatre an actor would point to his head to indicate reason and to his heart to indicate love or passion, raise his eyes or hands upward when evoking the gods, or extend his arms forward, palms out, to indicate horror or surprise. An elaborate system of facial grimacing, winking, and smiling was used both for humor and for intimate communication to the audience.

The *fop* was a very fashionable character and the butt of much sarcastic humor. Actors playing fops minced, strutted, and performed myriad flourishing hand and facial gestures. Outlandish posturing and posing were employed in a static presentational position. Actresses flirted continually over and behind fans, half-masks, and handkerchiefs.

Bows and curtsies in the seventeenth-century French manner were used throughout a play and were directed to other characters as well as to the audience. When one character passed another, they frequently performed the *en passant,* which was a slight bow from the waist with one foot sweeping in an arc around the other foot without losing the pace of the walk.

Taking snuff, a very popular social custom enjoyed by both men and women of society, was frequently performed on the stage. (Utilize the instructions for taking snuff provided in chapter 13, page 182.)

A gentlemen always kissed a lady's hand when leaving her. Men always held their hands high and away from their body to emphasize their lace cuffs, handkerchiefs, and ornate walking sticks and canes. This was done in a masculine and virile manner, except by fops. Men also swaggered elegantly in high-heeled shoes and relished their expansive movement. While controlled, these movements were vital and zestful. The women balanced enormous and outlandish hats upon their heads. Most women carried a muff, which was used not only for warming the hands, but also as a place to hide objects such as love letters. The women walked in slightly curved, graceful patterns, their dresses held slightly off the floor in a delicate manner.

In modern adaptation of Restoration comedy, more extensive use of pantomimic dramatization is necessary than in the original plays; for example, more furniture is used. Use of the sitting position is fairly common although women find it difficult to manage because of the size of the long, full skirts. Similarly, hand properties are used more frequently today. Drinking tea is a common example of this kind of activity. Movement in Restoration comedy is perhaps the most decorous and theatricalized of any stage movement in the history of theatre and reflects an affected, artificial manner almost without modern parallel. The possible exception is the exaggerated, satirical presentation of cocktail parties and events of so-called high society (e.g., recall the Ascot racetrack scene from *My Fair Lady*). However, beneath the externals of highly elevated, stylized movement, characters should be portrayed who are realistically rooted in their society; that is, care must be taken not to reduce characters to the level of robots. While many characters were one-dimensional (often reflected in their names), moving and speaking artifically by today's standards, they nevertheless reflected real counterparts within their society. The skill of the playwrights was often reflected in the focus upon and accentuation of single traits of those realistic counterparts.

Exercise 2   Movement—Restoration Comedy

1. Review and practice Exercise 5, chapter 13, page 189.
2. Organize and perform a group improvisation called ''The President's Cocktail Party.'' Pantomine all activity in a highly exaggerated manner. Improvise dialogue and movement and overdo every action in an extremely decorous but theatrical way. An actor and an actress should be designated host and hostess, while everyone else arrives and participates. The improvisation ends when the president of the United States departs.
3. Repeat Exercise 2 in the manner of a Restoration high-society party. Employ all available Restoration properties and costumes or facsimiles. The improvisation ends with the departure of King Charles II.
4. As described earlier in this chapter, practice bows, curtsies, *en passants,* taking snuff, wearing lace cuffs, flicking handkerchiefs, and walking with sticks and canes. Exaggerate the execution of these actions by elevating each one to a theatrical size, which is much larger than behavior used today. Specifically, bows and curtsies should be larger and deeper with great flourishes of hands and arms; fans should be ''popped'' open and shut loudly and crisply and fluttered with great speed while being embellished with flourishes. Handkerchiefs should be dangled at length from the fingers or wrists and swirled in the air; walking sticks and canes should be elaborately placed and used to pose while creating ''living portraits'' in grand positions of body attitude. The elevated or expansive use of costume and prop accessories relates directly to the enlarged, artificial quality of many one-dimensional Restoration comedy characters. Thus, clothing and accessories directly affect characterization as well as movement. (For example, huge wigs and elaborate hats restricted head activity due to unusual weight and the need for special balance and

control. This fact restricts actor work to some degree from the neck upward. Accordingly, the actor must practice with wigs and hats in order to integrate these items into characterization and physical activity.)

Character and Emotion

Many characters in Restoration comedy were notoriously one-dimensional, frequently caricatured by the implication in their name such as Snake, Lady Wishfort, Sir Fopling Flutter, Fainall, Lady Loveit, Sullen, Aimwell, Pinchwife, Manly, Lady Brute, Lady Fanciful, and so on. Characters were usually obsessed by a single emotional drive such as seduction, deception, gossip, greed, lust, and so on. *A major distinction between characterization in Restoration comedy and French Neoclassic comedy is the actor's sense of involvement with a character. Whereas serious involvement is necessary for playing most of the major roles in Molière, in Restoration comedy, performance will probably be more successful if a certain level of detached objectivity is retained.* Even with personalization and subtextual role analysis, it is difficult to become involved with Restoration characters because of their lack of depth and subservience to plot situation and because of the mechanistic language. This is somewhat less true of the more intelligent Restoration characters such as Millamant and Mirabell in Congreve's *The Way of the World.* The question arises, How far does the actor take the sense of detachment or objectivity? Is everything an artificial mockery or put-on? Actually, a highly affected, theatricalized performance that appears to be a kind of comment on itself can be very effective in staging Restoration comedy. However, a more discerning director or actor probably will not carry the detachment to that extent. In other words, *the advice given for playing Molière's major characters may again be the best advice. Take your character and his emotional obsession or foible seriously enough for genuine human portrayal. Retain enough detachment to execute the role using the various stylistic mannerisms necessary to engage comic response.* Characters were not defined realistically but created according to conventional decorum. Despite this, Restoration comic characters do possess an element of believability and natural emotion. However, more often than not, characters built on principles, as they tend to be in Restoration comedy, rarely create a true illusion of reality. Audiences enjoy the dramatic vitality of extremely witty characters and laugh at the foolishness of those who would be witty but are not.

Although the aristocratic manners of the time were "realistically" portrayed on the Restoration stage, it is a mistake to interpret late seventeenth-century *realism* as the word is defined today. In other words, what was represented on the Restoration stage was an exaggeration of what happened in life (albeit in a small section of society). The wit, repartee, precision of language, and elegance of manners were realistic *in terms* of appearance before the Restoration audience. Bawdy, sensual situations were not new to English drama. The only innovative ingredient was the realism of sensuality given by the appearance of women onstage. The inclusion of women allowed the dramatist greater freedom to develop situations that had heretofore been denied him. Sex play was a favorite aristocratic pastime. The female was displayed onstage for provocation (e.g., witness the many examples in Restoration plays of partial exposure of a female bosom or of a girl wearing breeches disguised as a boy). These sexual conventions simply mirrored the practices of society. Frequently, court ladies dressed as boys in order to arrange a rendezvous with a lover. (Sexual flirtation was pursued just as vigorously in the auditorium among the spectators as onstage!)

Exercise 3 Character and Emotion—Restoration Comedy

1. Select a Restoration character from the list that follows and determine a singular emotional obsession appropriate to the implication in the name. Perform an improvised soliloquy in the manner of a Restoration prologue or epilogue in which you explain and pantomimically dramatize your emotional obsession, what you want, and how you are going to get it.

Sullen	Lord Plausible
Snake	Witwood
Lady Wishfort	Petulant
Scandal	Waitwell
Tattle	Foible
Mrs. Frail	Constant
Lady Pliant	Heartfree
Lady Fidget	Lady Fanciful
Mrs. Squeamish	Sir Novelty Fashion
Sparkish	Mr. Smirk
Pinchwife	Loveless
Horner	Sir Clumsey
Manly	Bull

2. Select a character from the list in number 1. Locate the play in which this character is written. Select a long speech or two from your character's dialogue and practice singular emotional obsession for the character. Thereafter, expand that singularity through personalization and subtext.

Transition—Eighteenth-Century Sentimentalism and Nineteenth-Century Romanticism and Melodrama

The turn of the century (specifically by 1710) saw the ushering in of sentimental treatment for both serious and comic material. By the beginning of the eighteenth century, the number of people attending the theatre had increased (the population of Britain increased from six million in 1650 to ten million in 1800) and included many middle-class patrons. During the reign of Queen Anne (1702–1714), standards of decorum were higher. As interest in the court's activities lessened, middle-class self-awareness grew. No longer were theatre audiences predominately aristocratic. The purpose of sentimental drama was to show the middle classes the disparity between the real world and the ideal world. The sentimentalists believed that it was a part of Christian morality to see oneself as a moral paragon whose behavior was in many respects Christlike. Playwrights stressed the rewards of virtue and need for gentility. Great emphasis was placed on arousing sympathetic response to the misfortunes of others, and it was considered healthy to display emotion and to test one's virtues.

Opposition to the Restoration high comedy of manners came first from the playwright Colley Cibber in his play *Love's Last Shift* (1696). Shortly thereafter, other playwrights adopted the sentimental theme. Although George Farquhar is considered a Restoration author, his plays *The Recruiting Officer* and *The Beaux' Stratagem* delineated high moral standards for the middle class. Sir Richard Steele's *The Conscious Lovers* aroused kindly laughter and tears, as did Richard Cumberland's *The West Indian*. Sir Richard Sheridan's *The Rivals* and *The School for Scandal* pointed out the distinction between true virtue and pious remarks and satirized human shortsightedness and frailty. In Oliver Goldsmith's *She Stoops to Conquer*, deviations from morality were punished and traditional Christian values were upheld. George Lillo in *George Barnwell: The London Merchant* exalted the merchant class and presented a central character who was weak and pathetic and thus established the first bourgeois tragedy.[1]

New comic forms provided alternate entertainment during the eighteenth century; for example, the ballad opera, exemplified by John Gay in *The Beggar's Opera* in 1728. John Rich created pantomimes in which dancing and silent mimicry were performed to musical accompaniment. Burlesque was written by Henry Fielding (*Tom Thumb*). These forms of theatre entertainment required detailed scenery and special effects. They were highly popular with the middle classes and much admired for their dance and music.

Wild Oats by John O'Keefe. Bruce Evers as Twitch, Mark Tymchyshyn as Rover, and Barbara Acker as Amelia at the Hilberry Theatre, Wayne State University. Directed by Robert Emmett McGill, scenery by Jeffery R. Thomson, costumes by Jackie Durbin, lighting by Richard S. Latta. Regional American College Theatre Festival winner.

Later, the Licensing Act of 1737 placed all English drama under the regulations of censorship. The ballad opera and burlesques were replaced by the comic opera, a more sentimental play/entertainment utilizing music and comedy. Sheridan's *The Duenna* was in this vein, as was the work of John O'Keeffe (*The Poor Soldier* and *Wild Oats*).

The prologue acting piece reached its height of popularity in David Garrick. The epilogue was more strategically important than the prologue. It literally "saved" the play. The epilogue was usually assigned to an actress; the prologue, to an actor. Both pieces were accompanied by stage business, by noisy encounters of actors at the stage doors, and by a plea to judge the play by emotion and not by reason.

During the middle and late eighteenth century, periodic attempts at acting reform toward a more natural or lifelike style were made. A number of individual actors began to revolt against the traditions and conventions of acting styles. This emphasis on the individual artist coincided with other theatre developments. Newly constructed theatres such as the Haymarket used a smaller apron—a feature that in the earlier years of the Drury Lane, Covent Garden, and other theatres had severely limited the actors' freedom of movement. With Garrick's reforms in lighting, actors were moving away from the apron and behind the proscenium. Realistic details were more vivid in the upstage areas against a more naturalistic painted backdrop. When the spectators were finally removed from the stage, actors could give their characters a more realistic base and thereby could pay more attention to the play than to the audience. Eighteenth-century dramatists began to write about middle-class characters who were undergoing personality change. Granted, the writing was strictly sentimental and stressed the rewards of virtuous behavior. The character traits, however, were grounded in reality. Unfortunately, playwrights detracted from realistic detail by emphasizing disguises, surprises, and generally superficial characters.

Except for the modifications just mentioned, throughout the eighteenth century, emphasis was on rant or cadence in theatrical speech. Rant produces declamatory monotone. In a declamatory style, the actor runs on with little regard for accent or emphasis. Passion is revealed by turgid vocalization or effeminate whine.

Actors studied ancient orations, moral philosophy, and paintings of the period to learn manners and to delineate passion. The study of passion was highly scientific and systematized. Accompanying gestures were copied from prints and paintings; for example, the hands were never raised about the head unless for some extraordinary occasion, and a woman had to veil her face when expressing grief. As late as 1744, acting style was entrenched in exaggerated characterization, cadence, rant, and traditional convention. (Garrick offered some reforms in these areas.)

However, in 1750, a change in theatrical speech somewhat supplanted cadence with natural speaking, and actors began creating specific characters. There was little sense of historical accuracy, but costumes were no longer based strictly on current fashion. Perhaps the most famous actor to discard contemporary dress was Charles Macklin who made history by wearing historically accurate costumes in his portrayal of Macbeth. Thereafter, most actors leaned toward realistic propriety in costuming.

In Italy, a great eighteenth-century writer, Carlo Goldoni, provided the world with several remarkable comedies in the best tradition of commedia dell'arte and scripted material combined. Goldoni humanized the commedia characters, abandoned masks, and improved stage speaking. His plays are witty, fun, and still play well on the modern stage. *The Servant of Two Masters* and *Il Campiello* are representative of his fine work.

The eighteenth-century German playwright and critic Gotthold Lessing provided the foremost dramatic criticism of the period in his document *The Hamburg Dramaturgy* (1767–1769). His influential plays include *Miss Sara Sampson* and *Minna von Barnhelm*. He also wrote a famous treatise on dramatic theory, *Laokoon,* an opposition to the Neoclassic aesthetic.

Il Campiello a Venetian Comedy by Carlo Goldoni, adapted by Richard Nelson. Lori Putnam as Lucietta with The Acting Company on Tour for the John F. Kennedy Center for the Performing Arts. A continental representative of eighteenth-century comedy in transition (with a strong commedia dell'arte influence). Directed by Liviu Ciulei. Photograph by Martha Swope.

In the eighteenth century it was Denis Diderot, French encyclopedist, who above all argued against the limitations of Neoclassic drama. Diderot advocated reform in staging, in plays, and in acting and was instrumental in introducing the concept of the ''fourth wall'' in which the stage picture was filled with realistic detail and the audience peeked through an imaginary fourth wall to observe the action. His famous document *The Paradox of Acting* was revolutionary in articulating a philosophy of acting based on minimizing the actor's emotional involvement. Diderot believed that the actor should feel nothing himself but rather render the external signs of emotion in such a way as to convince the audience of the reality of the illusion (hence, the *paradox*)—an audience that is convinced it is seeing real emotion or feeling when in fact it is only the truthful *appearance* of reality. In an age when the acting style was still highly presentational and declamatory, Diderot's total insistence upon representational style brought adamant opposition from many critics and audiences. Diderot emphasized natural speech and pauses for thought and stressed use of lifelike gestures, pantomime, silence, and emotion. Diderot argued the revolutionary idea of conscious identification by the actor with his character through the use of imagination and impersonation. While little heed was paid at the time, Diderot's theories on acting were preparation for the turn-of-the-century movement toward realistic and naturalistic styles of acting.

In the Western world, the nineteenth century was largely a century of revolution and turmoil. After a century of emphasis on nature and reason, the nineteenth century, often called the Romantic Age, was an emotional, passionate time. The term *romance* implies emotional attractions, affairs of the heart, religious ideals, freedom, and strong emphasis on the needs of both the masses and the individual. This was the time of Napoleon and the French Revolution, a time in which the aristocracy was challenged by the middle and lower classes. It was as well a century of scientific innovation leading to the Industrial Revolution, to the evolutionary theories of Charles Darwin, and to the psychological insights of Sigmund Freud. In England, it was the era of the great Romantic poets such as Wordsworth, Coleridge, Byron, Shelley, and Keats; in Germany, of the poets and dramatists Johann von Goethe and Friedrich Schiller; in France, of the Romantic poet, novelist, and dramatist Victor Hugo; in America, of Henry Wadsworth Longfellow.

Romanticism encouraged the exploration of fantasy in juxtaposition to the world of natural phenomena. Romanticism reflected a belief in religious transcendentalism, or the affinity of man and spirit and of man and nature. The Romantics believed in the autonomy of inspired genius, the necessity of releasing the imagination, the spontaneity of intuitive feeling, the freedom of artistic expression, and a vision of nature as part of a unified cosmos. Romantic idealism culminated in the notion of organic growth and development arising from an interest in the past, particularly in the Middle Ages. In Germany the Romantic movement was called *Sturm und Drang,* or Storm and Stress. Goethe wrote both Romantic and Neoclassic plays such as *Faustus* and *Iphigenia at Tauris.* Schiller wrote *William Tell* in the Romantic vein. Goethe is considered one of the precursors of what is now called the director in the theatre. In his theatre at Weimar, Goethe succeeded in classifying many acting techniques.

Movement toward Realism

During the eighteenth and nineteenth centuries, acting style in German theatre continued to move toward naturalness. Actors became interested in techniques of role creation and in disciplined vocal and emotional work. Acting style was moving closer to Realism (discussed in chapter 15). Part of the transition toward Realism was accomplished by changes in the content and structure of plays. August von Kotzbue wrote the first melo-dramas, which were a combination of music and drama in the form of a three-act play accompanied by a musical score.

Finally, in mid-nineteenth century, theatre in Germany reached a new level of supremacy with the achievements of Richard Wagner and, late in the nineteenth century, with the Duke of Saxe-Meiningen. Wagner advocated theatre as mythical music; he was devoted to dramatizing the ideal world. Conversely, Saxe-Meiningen aimed at producing lifelike pictorial illusions. Both of these men were among the first great directors. Saxe-Meiningen was instrumental in unifying theatrical production by using realistic costumes and sets and effective ensemble playing.

Rene Pixérécourt did for melodrama in France what Kotzbue had done for melodrama in Germany. (A melodrama is a serious play in which good and evil are clearly separated, characters are simple, action is full of sus-pense, a double ending rewards virtue and punishes evil, and plot and characterization are frequently reinforced by music and physical proper-ties.) Pixérécourt's melodramas paved the way for the rise of Romantic drama in France. In addition to Victor Hugo, Alexandre Dumas (père) and Alfred de Musset also wrote important Romantic plays. French Roman-ticism was ultimately modified toward Realism by the end of the nine-teenth century.

Eugène Scribe and Victorien Sardou contributed to the development of Realism (see chapter 15) in France by writing realistic plays that were tightly structured or well made. The great playwright of early Realism Henrik Ibsen was greatly influenced by these plays.

Similarly in England the Romantic movement advanced toward re-alism. W. C. Macready, Charles Kean, and other actors were leaders in the development of increasingly realistic acting in the nineteenth century. They also helped introduce reforms in staging and costuming, along with J. R. Planché, Madame Vestris, Charles Mathews the Elder, and Charles Mathews the Younger. Madam Vestris also introduced the first realistic *box set* in England. The great English actors during these times included Sarah Bernhardt, Henry Irving, and Ellen Tree.

Across the Atlantic Ocean, the new United States imitated English drama but produced some excellent actors and persons of the theatre such as Edwin Forrest, Edwin Booth, Clara Morris, Ada Rehan, and Joseph Jefferson III.

Acting in Romantic Plays and Melodramas

Nineteenth-century Romantic plays and melodramas are rarely performed in the theatre today. In present-day presentation of a Romantic drama, the style of acting should emphasize intense emotional expression; rhythmic, melodic, poetic vocal delivery in a highly elevated manner; and sweeping, flowing movements and gestures. Center stage should be used predominately, and the focus should be on the presentational mode. The overall impression of style should be an elevated version of the Elizabethan acting style.

If you are cast in a nineteenth-century melodrama (not to be mistaken for the kidded or mocked comic melodramas of cabaret theatre), your style of acting should employ the tenets of Realism described in chapter 15—in other words, lifelike character creation, predominately representational mode (except for asides), detailed pantomimic business, and natural speech and movement.

What is known as the beginning of modern drama and modern styles of acting was initiated in the late nineteenth and early twentieth centuries. The foundation of all current acting styles commences with a study of Realism and Naturalism.

Suggested Characters and Plays for Scene Work

Congreve, William

Millamant, Mirabell, Fainall, Mrs. Marwood
The Way of the World
Valentine, Miss Prue, Sir Sampson Legend, Ben, Angelica
Love for Love

Etherege, George

Dorimant, Bellinda, Lady Loveit, Sir Fopling Flutter
The Man of Mode

Dryden, John

Antony, Cleopatra
All for Love

Farquhar, George

Airwell, Archer, Bonniface, Cherry, Lady Bountiful, Dorinda, Sullen
The Beaux' Stratagem

Wycherley, William

Marjorie Pinchwife, Horner
The Country Wife
Manly, Olivia, Freeman, Widow Blackacre
The Plain Dealer

Vanbrugh, John

Sir John Brute, Lady Brute, Lady Fanciful
The Provok'd Wife

The Country Wife by William Wycherley. James Hooks as Dr. Quack, William Kelsay as Sir Jasper Fidget, Katherine Parks as Mrs. Squeamish, Mary Pat Quintin as Lady Fidget, and Michael Krause as Mr. Horner in "The China Scene" at the University of Missouri Summer Repertory Theatre. Note the accurate wing and drop scenery complete to spectator boxes over the stage. Directed by Larry D. Clark, scenery by Edward L. Gallagher, costumes by Linda Conaway, lighting by Steve Ross.

Gay, John

Macheath, Polly Peachum, Lucy Lockit
The Beggar's Opera

Goldsmith, Oliver

Kate Hardcastle, Marlowe, Tony Lumpkin
She Stoops to Conquer

Sheridan, Sir Richard

Sir Peter Teazle, Lady Teazle, Joseph Surface, Charles Surface, Maria, Lady Sneerwell
The School for Scandal

Mrs. Malaprop, Lydia Languish, Captain Jack Absolute
The Rivals

O'Keeffe, John

Twitch Rover, Amelia
Wild Oats
All characters
The Poor Soldier

Additional Suggested Characters and Plays for Scene Work

Goldoni, Carlo
> All characters
>> *The Servant of Two Masters*
>
> All characters
>> *Il Campiello*

Goethe, Johann Wolfgang von
> Goetz, Bishop of Bamberg
>> *Goetz von Berlichingen*
>
> Doctor Faust, Mephistopheles, Margaret
>> *Faust Part 1*

Schiller, Friedrich
> Mary Queen of Scots, Queen Elizabeth
>> *Mary Stuart*
>
> William Tell, Gessler
>> *William Tell*

Hugo, Victor
> Hernani, Dona Sol
>> *Hernani*

Dumas (fils), Alexander
> Marguerite Gautier, Armand Duval
>> *Camille*

Rostand, Edmund
> Cyrano de Bergerac, Roxanne, Chistian
>> *Cyrano de Bergerac*

de Musset, Alfred
> Camille, Perdican, Rosette
>> *No Trifling with Love*

Sardou, Victorien
> Cyprienne, Des Prunelles, Adhemar
>> *Let's Get a Divorce*

Buchner, Georg
> Danton, Robespierre
>> *Danton's Death*
>
> All characters
>> *Woyzeck*

Kotzebue, August
> The Stranger
>> *The Stranger*

Actor Checklist   Restoration Comedy

Voice	Exaggerated inflection; rapid but clear; smooth and polished line delivery; precise diction; clear articulation and effective vocal production.
Movement	Elevated; exaggerated; elegant when appropriate; controlled; well-executed use of bows, curtsies, and asides; predominately presentational; generally rapid tempo; highly artificial for most characters (such as the fop).
Gestures	Hand, head, facial dominate; clear; elevated; exaggerated, especially for fops.

Pantomimic Dramatization	Clear; inventive; selective; extensive and elaborate use of period props and costumes: female headgear, fans, staffs, handkerchiefs, half-masks, snuff, jewelry, makeup, and so on.
Character	Often one-dimensional; extra dimension usually comes from intelligence and not from emotion; rooted in social mores, conduct, and foibles, representative social facet clear; actor involvement somewhat detached or objective.
Emotion	Usually single obsession; clear; nonsentimental; scheming and cynical.
Ideas	Clear; satiric; witty; cynical.
Language	Brittle; witty; rhythmic; brilliant vocabulary; correct pronunciation.
Mood and Atmosphere	Clear in terms of satire, repartee, and wit; supportive of usually cynical and flirtatious-sexual situation; some serious undertone with certain lead characters.
Pace and Tempo	Generally rapid.
Special Techniques	Wit and language demand unusual vocal dexterity; unusual attention to movement in costume.

Selective Readings

Dobree, Bonamy. *Restoration Comedy, 1660–1720*. London: Oxford University Press, 1924.

———. *Restoration Tragedy, 1660–1720*. London: Oxford University Press, 1929.

Downer, Alan S. ''Nature to Advantage Dressed: Eighteenth Century Acting.'' *PMLA* (1943), 58:4 (part I), pp. 1002–37.

Fujimura, Thomas H. *Restoration Comedy of Wit*. Princeton, N.J.: Princeton University Press, 1952.

Furst, Lilian R. *Romanticism in Perspective*. New York: Humanities Press, 1969.

Gildon, Charles. *The Life of Mr. Thomas Betterton*. New York: A. M. Kelley, 1970.

Henshaw, N. ''Graphic Sources for a Modern Approach to Acting Restoration Comedy.'' *Educational Theatre Journal,* May 1968, pp. 157–70.

Krutch, Joseph W. *Comedy and Conscience after the Restoration*. New York: Russell & Russell, 1949.

Loftis, John, ed. *Restoration Drama, Modern Essays in Criticism*. London: Oxford University Press, 1966.

————, et al. *Revels History of Drama in English, Vol. 4:1660–1750.* New York: Barnes & Noble, 1976.

Lynch, James J. *Box, Pit and Gallery: Stage and Society in Johnson's London.* Berkeley: University of California Press, 1953.

MacCollum, John I., Jr. *The Restoration Stage.* New York: Houghton Mifflin Co., 1961.

Muir, Kenneth. *The Comedy of Manners.* London: Hutchinson University Library, 1970.

Oxenford, Lyn. *Design for Movement.* A textbook on stage movement. New York: Theatre Arts Books, 1952.

————. *Playing Period Plays.* London: J. G. Miller, 1957.

Palmer, J. L. *The Comedy of Manners.* New York: Russell & Russell, 1962.

Perry, Henry T. *Comic Spirit in Restoration Drama.* New York: Russell, 1962.

Wilcox, John. *The Relation of Molière to Restoration Comedy.* New York: Benjamin Blom, 1964.

Suggested Filmography

1. *The Beggar's Opera.* 1953. British. Playwright—John Gay. Director—Peter Brook. With Sir Laurence Olivier.
2. *Cyrano de Bergerac.* 1950. United Artists. English. Playwright—Rostand. Director—Michael Gordon. With Jose Ferrer and Mala Powers.
3. *Dangerous Liaisons.* 1988. From the play, *Les Liaisons Dangereuses* by Christopher Hampton. With Glenn Close and John Malkovich. While not set in the exact Restoration period, this film approximates the Restoration brittle acting style for dark comedy in very fine fashion. Directed by Stephen Frears.
4. *The Draughtsman's Contract.* 1982. British. Director—Peter Greenaway. With Janet Suzman and Anthony Higgins. Although not based on a play, this is an extraordinary example of wit and Restoration/Heroic Tragedy (serious drama).

Note

1. It should be noted that Sheridan and Goldsmith attempted to break with sentimentalism and create brittle comedy in the Restoration style, but were only partly successful. Nonetheless, as examples of eighteenth-century comedy (sometimes called *baroque* or ornate) in the Restoration *tradition,* their work ranks high.

Realism and Naturalism: Selectivity and Photographic Detail

15

Details are also the thing in the sphere of psychology. God preserve us from generalizations. Best of all, avoid depicting the hero's state of mind; you ought to try to make it clear from the hero's actions. It is not necessary to portray many active figures. The center of gravity should be two persons—he and she.

Anton Chekhov to his brother
Alexander from Ernest Simmons
Introduction to Russian Realism

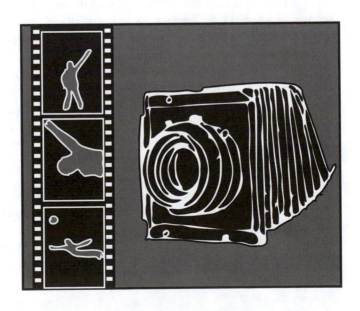

Overview of Realism

The movement toward Realism was allied with the origins of modern science. Instead of being based on emotional or mystic explanations, late nineteenth-century theatre was based on natural, rational explanation as evidenced and experienced through the five senses. The work of the philosopher August Comte (1798–1857) was a primary influence on realistic thought. His philosophy was based on ''positivism'' as the key to knowledge. Positivism was the examination of all apparent things, of all one could see. Evidence was based on precise observation and experimentation; events were understood in terms of cause and effect. When Charles Darwin published *On the Origin of the Species by Means of Natural Selection* in 1859, his advanced theories concerning the influence of heredity and environment on man's behavior gave tremendous impetus to the dramatic community. Man became one of many objects worthy of scientific study. The individual was part of an evolutionary movement whose hereditary traits and environmental conditions determine human existence and explain human character. The theory of evolution strengthened the theory of human progress—individual and collective improvement became inevitable.

The realists observed man and his environment primarily through the five senses. Playwrights consciously set out to abandon antiquated techniques such as formula plays, surface characterization, romantic subject matter, and scenic splendor in favor of duplication of contemporary life. Although realistic plays were well constructed, they were not overly predictable in terms of cause and effect. Characters were based on real-life, three-dimensional human beings. Plots were concerned with the problems of daily life—the environmental and social forces that encroached on man. Scenery mirrored contemporary environment in an attempt to express external realism. The playwright exercised careful selectivity and control in arranging events within a play. All action was motivated to achieve truth and believability in character portrayal. Although a character's actions were usually impelled by thoughts, feelings, and environmental conditions, realistic playwrights tended to emphasize outward action more than inner psychology. Dialogue was significantly more conversational than, for example, the formal dialogue in plays by Scribe or Sardou. However, there was a tendency in realistic plays to heighten conversation at moments of high emotion.

Henrik Ibsen was the most representative playwright of the realistic school. A native of Norway, Ibsen gave Realism stature by writing plays with lifelike dialogue, settings, costumes, and stage business. However, the term must be qualified when it is applied to Ibsen. He did not copy reality in explicit detail. Because he was not interested in the raw material of life in the manner of a factual recorder, he became both a creative artist and a re-creative artist. His material was carefully selected and organized into a pattern of refinement, omission, and intensification.

Ibsen's themes suggest man's unending conflict between duty to himself and duty to others. His characters constantly try to achieve individual integrity. Although external action is somewhat static, his dialogue is tight, dynamic, and full of hints and allusions. Ibsen had a tremendous capacity for conveying the unspoken thought with emotional and mental undercurrents. In his realistic plays, Ibsen abandoned the aside and the soliloquy. Expository material was interwoven in cause-and-effect sequences.

Ibsen was flexible enough to explore many types of plays including historical-romantic studies (*The Pretenders*), poetic drama (*Peer Gynt*), realistic or thesis dramas (*A Doll's House, The Wild Duck, Ghosts, Hedda Gabler*), and symbolic plays (*The Master Builder*). His historic-romantic plays are militant in tone, inspired by his yearning for a better man and a better world. His poetic dramas are episodic but impressive accounts of lofty ideals. Ibsen's realistic thesis or social-problem plays are perhaps most noteworthy for their convincing characters and dialogue, exciting and innovative social ideas, and realistic prose. His symbolic plays grope sensitively into mysticism. All of his plays blend art, morality, philosophy, and social considerations. Although Ibsen was basically a reformer and a fighter against the evils of society, his art has a warm feeling for life.

In England, the tenets of Ibsen's playwriting were emulated by Arthur Wing Pinero, Henry Arthur Jones, Sir James Barrie, John Galsworthy, and George Bernard Shaw. Shaw fused paradox and satire effectively. He had a devastating wit aimed at shattering established beliefs and false ideals. Shaw was a master of clever, brilliant ideas. Although he sometimes made his characters a mouthpiece for his own ideas, Shaw created vital characters who discovered themselves during a crisis. The message in a Shavian play rests on character development. Some of Shaw's most famous plays include *Major Barbara, Arms and the Man, Candida, The Devil's Disciple, Caesar and Cleopatra,* and *Man and Superman* (a combination of Romanticism and Realism).

The impact of Ibsen's realism was not felt specifically nor purely in all countries at the same time or in the same manner. Since most dramatic work in Europe was in the Romantic tradition, playwrights varied in immediate acceptance of realistic techniques.

In Ireland, the first effective realistic and poetic plays were the peasant dramas of Lady Gregory and the poet-playwright William Butler Yeats. In order to give Irish playwrights a "home," Lady Gregory and Yeats established the Abbey Theatre. Principal Abbey playwrights were John Millington Synge and, later, Sean O'Casey. The realism of Synge's modern dramas was infused with poetry shaped from Irish colloquial speech, Irish humor, and Celtic romanticism. Synge's realism was not inspired by that of Ibsen; it was unique because his poetic language was slightly elevated and the exhilaration of his characters was based firmly in the traditions of the Irish peasant class. *The Playboy of the Western World* and *Riders to the Sea* rank as two of the finest examples of early twentieth-century drama. Synge was a great realist/naturalist with a poetic flair.

In Hungary, Ferenc Molnar wrote several fine plays depicting the contemporary salon life of Budapest and early twentieth-century European society. His plays reveal verbal beauty, detailed characterizations, irony, light humor, and romantic plots (his nineteenth-century heritage). Chief among his works are *Liliom* (later adapted to the musical, *Carousel*) and *The Guardsman.*

In Russia, Nikolai Gogol introduced Realism to the stage. Gogol's most famous play was a satire on provincial corruption called *The Inspector General.* Although his character delineation was somewhat exaggerated and grotesque, Gogol was notable for having ushered in Realism to Russian drama at a time when other European countries were still struggling with Romanticism and melodrama. Ivan Turgenev (*A Month in the Country*) explored psychological realism further by portraying ordinary men with humor and understanding (Turgenev was actually a precursor of Naturalism). Alexander Ostrovsky's plays (such as *The Thunderstorm*) depicted Russian middle-class life in considerable detail. However, most Russian playwrights of early realistic drama sacrificed subtle characterization for external realism.

Overview of Naturalism

In 1873, Emile Zola proposed the first naturalistic doctrine in the preface to his play *Thérèse Raquin.* In his treatise, Zola stated his determination to base dramatic work on scientific methods of observation. Zola foresaw man formulating laws of human conduct based on observation, analysis, and classification of facts in a manner similar to that of scientists. *Naturalism* was a philosophical theory dating back to the sixteenth century that proliferated during the early nineteenth century. In Naturalism nature was

A scene from Nikolai Gogol's *The Inspector General.* Bob Balaban as Ossip at the Hartman Theatre, Stamford, Connecticut. Directed by Byron Ringland, scenery by Peter Harvey, costumes by Dona Granata, lighting by John McLain. (Photo by Dave Robbins.)

considered the first principle in the universe, even above God. During the eighteenth century, Rousseau used the term *naturalism* to describe his concept of a "return to nature." In the eighteenth century, advocates of the Age of Enlightenment also used the term as the basis for their spirit of inquiry. By the nineteenth century, Balzac, Flaubert, and the Goncourt brothers were already studying scientific methods. Zola's originality lay in the thoroughness of his scientific documentation and his choice of medical science as the inspiration for his literary work.

Zola's use of Naturalism was in rebellion against the sterotyped formula of morality and rhetoric fostered by the Romantic movement. In order to recapture truth in literature and drama, Zola attacked the conventions restricting the scope of the stage. He wanted to open the eyes of the public to the possibilities in new forms and new subjects. Zola prescribed lifelike scenery, costumes, and methods of acting. With the eye of a scientific observer, Zola wanted segments of life (*tranche de vie,* or slice of life) to be represented onstage in exact duplication, as in a photograph. Scenery had to express the inner spirit of the play as well as the

The Lower Depths by Maxim Gorky. Rebecca Nibley as Vasilissa and Victor Love as Vaska Pepel at the University of Wisconsin–Milwaukee. Directed by David Chambers, scenery by Bob McBroom, costumes by Maura Smalover. Photograph by Alan Magayne-Roshak.

external details of its milieu. Action was simplified and lifelike. Characters were psychologically motivated and physiologically correct in appearance and manner. Environment was the primary influence on characters. Naturalistic plays did not present the logic of facts, sensations, or sentiments. For Zola, there was no difference between truth in the theatre and truth in life. Spectators were "invisible" to the actors. Although the public was invited to the theatre, they were required only to "peek through the fourth wall" to watch *life,* not a play. In theory, it was therefore permissible for actors to stand with their backs to the audience and speak with slovenly diction. The correct attitude for naturalistic actors was to *live* the life of the characters on stage rather than to *play* the role. Zola strove to make the vocabulary of language different for each class. Since language had to fit the character and situation, crudity was appropriate in sordid scenes. The total effect of Zola's naturalism was an attempt to reproduce photographic detail on the stage.

Most naturalistic playwrights were preoccupied with human maladies. Among the foremost naturalistic playwrights (in addition to Zola) were

Henri Becque (*The Vultures* and *La Parisienne*), Gerhart Hauptmann (*The Weavers*), Arthur Schnitzler (*Anatol* and *La Ronde*), August Strindberg (*Miss Julie* and *The Father*), Anton Chekhov (*The Seagull, The Three Sisters, The Cherry Orchard,* and *Uncle Vanya*), Maxim Gorky (*The Lower Depths*), and Sean O'Casey (*The Plough and the Stars* and *Juno and the Paycock*).

Dissatisfaction with nineteenth-century theatre produced a growth of individual writers, directors, and scenic and lighting designers (electricity was then in use) dedicated to eliminating abuses on the stage—namely, the commercial managerial system, the "staginess" of productions, and the histrionic style of acting with its emphasis on star roles. After 1875, playwrights demanded characterization from actors beyond their technical repertoire. Nineteenth-century acting in the declamatory style was so solidly entrenched in Europe that it inevitably fell to the director and the scenic and lighting designers to nourish the realistic and naturalistic movements. Director André Antoine, founder of the *Théâtre Libre* (Free Theatre) in Paris, was the practical, innovative leader of the naturalistic movement, and Gordon Craig, Aldoph Appia, and Vsevolold Meyerhold were the leaders of innovative scenic and lighting design and staging, albeit much of it was in a nonrealistic style (see chapter 16).

Other new or little theatre movements occurred throughout Europe, paralleling Antoine's objectives (i.e., developing new writers and new acting styles). Otto Brahm's *Freie Buhne* in Germany, J. T. Grein's Independent Theatre in England, Lady Gregory's Abbey Theatre in Ireland, and, above all, Constantin Stanislavski's Moscow Art Theatre in Russia gave impetus to theatrical experimentation and innovation. Stanislavski developed a system of acting techniques which became the foundation of all modern acting theory.

The evolution of realistic acting continued to vacillate between representational and presentational concepts until the emergence of Stanislavski and his partner Vladimir Nemirovich-Danchenko. Stanislavski's acting system was influenced by the work of the actor Mikhail Shchepkin. Shchepkin discovered that a natural speaking tone resulted in realistic characterization. Together with Gogol, Shchepkin urged actors to identify with the character being portrayed, to take on his identity, and to strive for truth and naturalness in speech and bodily movement. Character believability was further heightened by accurate study of the background of the role. It was Shchepkin who gave Stanislavski the motto for the Moscow Art Theatre: There are no small parts, only small actors. Although the playwrights Ostrovsky and Turgenev continued to develop the realistic style of acting, Stanislavski saw that even in the 1890s, realistic acting was still based on able elocution. During the last decade of the nineteenth century, Stanislavski and Danchenko were influenced by the work of the Duke of Saxe-Meiningen, an innovative German director who is often considered to be the first director in the theatre and notable for his emphasis on natural ensemble acting.

The policies of the Moscow Art Theatre, as described by Stanislavski (the artistic director) and Danchenko (the administrator), focused on the production of plays of distinction by both Russian playwrights and foreign writers and on the subordination of individual acting to the intention of the playwright. Careful attention to detail in scenic design and realistic characterization were prime considerations. A new rehearsal concept in which the cast studied plays in thorough detail, supervised by the director, was established. Rigid discipline was enforced throughout the rehearsal period.

Stanislavski's early efforts at theatre reform were directed against the style of acting noted for its shouting, rapid tempo, and exaggerated gestures and actions. Except for the few attempts at Realism mentioned earlier, theatrical productions prior to this time were notoriously contrived and stereotyped. Repertory offerings included light farcical plays whose only appeal was the star in the lead role. Stanislavski's primary goals of reform were to discover a more realistic base for acting and to eliminate technical stage abuses. Early productions of the Moscow Art Theatre were more lifelike, perhaps even more realistic, than ordinary Realism—that is, superrealism or Naturalism. Stanislavski was dedicated to photographic duplication. Lighting and sound effects were essential to producing naturalistic sounds such as thunder, rain, wind, and ordinary sounds of daily life (e.g., birds singing, bells ringing, and dogs barking). Sound was used to reveal contrast or to heighten a significant moment. However, scenic detail, three-dimensional settings, and external facts were eventually *over*emphasized.

It was not until he worked on three plays by Maeterlinck (*The Blind, The Interior,* and *The Unbidden Guest*) that Stanislavski began to search for still newer forms of expression. Realizing that impressionist paintings and music usually produced fantastic and imaginative evocations of the mind and heart, he studied the works of modern painters, sculptors, and composers. This knowledge led Stanislavski to repudiate his former dependence on the scene designer. He realized that inner truth could not be achieved merely by the scenic atmosphere of a play. He made the key discovery that emotions and feelings come from the actor and his person.

The tenets of style encompassing Realism and Naturalism are contained within the techniques of acting described by Stanislavski.

In 1909, Stanislavski set down his refined principles of acting, and his acting system became the foundation for all realistic and naturalistic acting of the twentieth century. The most profound question probed by Stanislavski was, How can an actor achieve a creative mood that would favor inspiration?

Voice

Stanislavski did not neglect cultivation of the actor's external techniques. All his actors received vocal training for intonation, inflection, use of pause, and tempo-rhythm. Stanislavski believed that an actor should study singing in order to learn how to use the whole vocal scale. He treated the front of the actor's face as though it were a mask with resonators, and he stressed natural speaking using good breathing technique, clear articulation, and excellent projection. He believed in a disciplined vocal instrument and very expressive speech. Simplicity and clarity created precise patterns of speech, rooted in natural movement and emotion. Stanislavski treated *words* as the physical side of action and images in the mind as the psychological side of action. Perhaps the most important contribution Stanislavski made to stage speech was his explanation that there are reasons why characters say words. The actor's task is to make the author's words his own. Thus, dialogue must have purpose if words are to be meaningful and have impact. The actor then uses his craft through intonation, enunciation, and expression to color vocal delivery imaginatively. Stanislavski believed that mechanical memorization ruined believability and created artificial vocal delivery. Stanislavski often said, "Treasure the spoken word." He knew that energetic language and vocal expressiveness stirred emotions. A word becomes a verbal action when the action is motivated by purpose. Therefore, speech influences character and emotion. Stanislavski knew that actors should analyze their speeches in order to deliver them logically and convincingly. He believed that speaking was acting. Stanislavski also knew that verbal action depends upon physical action (which will be discussed later).

Exercise 1   Voice

1. Sing the vocal scale repeatedly until it becomes instinctive. You should be capable of using the scale in a modified manner when speaking as well as when singing.
2. Think of the front of your face as a mask with resonators connecting the mouth and nose. Imagine you are in a canyon calling back and forth to your own echo. Call or sing such expressions as *Helloooooooooo, Farewellllllllll,* and *Where are Youuuuuuu.* With conscious effort you should be able to actually feel vibrations in the resonating areas of your face.

3. Study the speeches by Nora and Tusenbach given at the beginning of this chapter. Determine the purpose or motivation for each idea in the speech and, if possible, for each word. When you have determined purpose, deliver the speech using imaginative, colorful intonation, pauses, and natural expressiveness. Finally, permit natural gestures to accompany your vocal delivery.

4. In your own words, paraphrase the ideas contained within the speeches by Nora and Tusenbach at the beginning of this chapter. Improvise the speeches in your own words. Then return to the actual text, which should be richer and clearer to you.

Movement

Training the body in movement was an important part of the Stanislavski acting system. His actors worked for complete, graceful control of all physical activity. Stanislavski opposed the artificial mannerisms and mechanical gestures of most of the preceding acting styles. He believed that gestures should relate to inner experience. Stanislavski insisted upon movement that was motivated, honest, and logical. He stressed that actors must practice every day just as must musicians and singers. Both voice and body must be trained to the point at which they instantly express correct, external activity linked to and motivated by inner experience.

The significance of external form and physical detail was directly tied to correct costuming. Stanislavski recognized that costumes and properties were not extraneous or mere support items. They were rather an integral part of character, tied to motivation, action, and emotion.

Onstage, an actor must be physically free, attain muscular control and relaxation, and have limitless concentration.

Stanislavski believed in dance training for actors because he considered it important in increasing physical dexterity of both actors and musical theatre performers. Movement should be simple, vital, and natural. Movement is an actor's most intense means of expression.

An actor's whole physical being represents the character being interpreted. Stanislavski taught that an actor should always be ''in character,'' should not recognize the audience, and should concentrate on producing an ensemble effect in production. Personalization was in effect the foundation for physical activity in the Stanislavski system. That is, after study and practice, an actor's person united with the role until they *appeared* to be one and the same. Great art hides art. Stanislavski knew that the organic totality of an actor's personality and physical being was always at work in the art of role creation.

Exercise 2   Movement

1. Center your body.
2. Select music from Brahms, Debussy, Copland, Ravel, or Stravinsky and as the music plays interpret the moods and rhythms of the music through improvised movement. In some instances the movement can become modern dance activity.
3. Sit down before a group. Conversationally and naturally relate an interesting personal experience. Animate your story with instinctive natural gestures, particularly of the face, hands, and upper portions of the body. When you have completed the story, discuss the gestures you have used. Listen carefully to any criticism concerning arbitrary, meaningless, or repetitive gestures. Relate another personal story and attempt to use more expressive, artistic, disciplined gestures without losing the natural, spontaneous, inner-motivated behavior.
4. Sit silently and listen to every sound you can distinguish. Create a movement, walk, dance, or pantomime that reflects the activity and/or mood of the sound that motivates your activity; for example, the ringing of a bell might cause you to hop and tremble with joy or sorrow.

Character and Emotion

In his search to discover the inner truth of human feeling and experience, *Stanislavski urged his actors to personalize and display character motivation and emotion simply and naturally.* In addition to this role creation technique, Stanislavski suggested heavy reliance on intuition. In time, Stanislavski discovered that most of his actors were continuing to ''act'' rather than to behave naturally. The intuitive method, combined with background material from the play, produced only surface character. The actor was executing the appropriate walk, emotional state, and rhythm of speech, but the depth of true inner character was still missing. It remained for the tremendous influence of Anton Chekhov to bring that deep inner truth to the productions of the Moscow Art Theatre. Chekhov's plays required actors to use an extra dimension in character portrayal. The complexity of the writing demanded that actors seek the truth of their inner life and then equalize that reality with their role. In seeking to liberate the deeper individuality of the actor, Stanislavski rose to the task Chekhov presented. Stanislavski helped his actors free their innermost feelings, moods, thoughts, and experiences. As you learned in Part I, one of the best techniques of role creation involves actor personalization. Stanislavski's actors strove to achieve expression of an inner image by awakening the subconscious from which flowed the outer image. The roots of the personalization theory of acting are imbedded in that striving.

A scene from *The Cherry Orchard* by Anton Chekhov, at the Juilliard School, New York. Directed by the late Alan Schneider. (Photo by Louisa Johnson.)

One of the first steps in Stanislavski's process of using the actor's person as the foundation for role creation is the technique known as the "Magic If." Stanislavski thought that actors must believe in the possibility of events in their own life before they could believe in events onstage. He saw the value of transforming a character's aim into an actor's aim. An actor says to himself, "If I were the character *in this situation,* what would I do?" Providing the answer to the Magic If enables him to react to the unreal life onstage as if it were real. (Note: Stanislavski did not say to ask yourself, "What would I do if I were the character?" He said, "If I were the character *in this situation,* what would I do?" The former can lead to artificial "acting"; the latter can lead to present- and future-oriented *activity.*) Stanislavski's point concerning the Magic If and personalization is clear: Always and forever, when you are on stage, you must play yourself. The *person* is at base in any role you play—*your* person.

Stanislavski believed the next step in role creation was to examine the given circumstances of a play including time and place of action, director's interpretation, setting, lighting, and sound effects.

Stanislavski also stressed concentration as the key to dynamic, believable performance onstage. Concentration leads to truthful, believable, relaxed stage activity, which in turn leads to what Stanislavski called "communion" or interaction with other people. Both physical communion and psychological communion are necessary to accomplish action that is both realistic and naturalistic.

An important aspect of communion involves "adaptation" or adjustment. An actor must overcome many obstacles to achieve his goal, finding ways to adapt or adjust his activity or action to accomplish his goal. The actor asks: What must I do? Why must I do it? and How can I do it? Both personal adaptation and character adaptation are involved in acting. For example, if you are a woman playing a love scene with a man several inches shorter than you, the need for physical adaptation is obvious. The actors and director must find an adjustment to the problem, probably by seating both persons for the love scene. Similar, but more complex, characterization may demand that you sob convulsively. You must find a way to adapt to the demand and accomplish the behavior.

Finally, the actor focuses upon tempo-rhythm in execution of all aspects of a role. Correct speed and varying intensity of activity are identified and rehearsed. The tempo-rhythm is tied to the emotional and mood disposition of both character and actor in conjunction with the speed of speaking and moving.

Stanlislavski knew that the foremost method of expressing the truthful emotional life of a character was through observation, imagination, and use of the senses. An actor recalls and draws attention to each encountered object to discover its living substance. This method is known as affective memory or emotion memory, a process by which the actor selects emotions from his living experiences analogous to those of his character and utilizes duplication of emotional sensations within the role. Emotion recall leads to inspiration whereby an actor uses the best within himself and carries it onstage. The use of emotion recall varies according to the necessities of a play. In any event, when emotions are created in this manner onstage, they are usually alive and vital. (However, it should be noted that late in his life, Stanislavski turned away from use of this technique.)

Stanislavski believed in thorough role analysis prior to onstage performance. The tenets of role analysis correspond closely to Stanislavski's concept of role analysis. Central to Stanislavski's theory was identifying what he called "the Super-Objective" and "the Through Line of Actions." The Super-Objective was the main idea or final goal of each performance. Some theatre artists call the Super-Objective the "spine" of the role. The Through Line of Actions is a logical mental line running through a role, which an actor can trace in his mind. The Through Line of Actions guides the actor toward accomplishment of his Super-Objective. For example, all of the Through Lines of Actions by Willy Loman in *Death of a Salesman* lead to the Super-Objective of winning Biff's love again. (The Super-Objective is the same as the *MF,* or Motivating Force, discussed in Part I of this book.)

Exercise 3   Character and Emotion

1. The main exercise technique employed by Stanislavski in the practice of his theories focused on improvisation. Define the circumstances before performing actions. In the following, circumstances are defined for you. Using those circumstances, improvise what *you* would do *if* you were in each situation.

   a. You are in a small elevator when it becomes lodged between floors. What do you do?

   b. You arrive at the home of a civic leader on the wrong night for a banquet. What do you do?

   c. You receive word of the death of a beloved family member. What do you do?

   d. You are walking home late at night along a dark street. You think someone is following you. You learn you are in a blind alley. What do you do?

   e. You are alone on your first solo flight as a pilot when you learn you have forgotten your maps, your radio is out, and your gas is low. What do you do?

   f. You are waiting for a message concerning an operation performed on a beloved family member. What do you do?

   g. Listen carefully to all sounds. React to each sound individually.

   h. Treat the room as though it were a sunken submarine incapable of surfacing. What do you do?

   i. You are in a cell awaiting execution. What do you do?

   j. You are a criminal lawyer interrogating a prisoner about a murder. Relate to one another.

   k. You are proposing marriage to someone. Relate to one another.

   l. You are meeting a blind date. What do you do?

   m. You are in a hurry, but you are at the rear of a supermarket line. What do you do?

   n. You are waiting to meet a truant officer after having skipped school for a week. What do you do?

   o. An alarm wakes you and you discover you are one hour late for an appointment. Establish the correct tempo-rhythm for what you do.

   p. You are alone on the beach at sunset. Establish the correct tempo-rhythm for what you do.

2. Review each of the 16 circumstances in number 1. Define your Super-Objective, or spine, for each circumstance and state it as a desire using the action verb "want"; for example, "I want to escape the elevator through the small trapdoor in the ceiling."

3. Define a "Through Line of Actions" for each of the circumstances in number 1. For example (*a*) I stand on the iron handrail in the elevator; (*b*) I push open the trapdoor; (*c*) I pull myself through the tiny trapdoor; (*d*) I shimmy up the cable to the floor above; (*e*) I force the door open to the hallway or I pound on the door for help; and so on.
4. Attempt to relate the given circumstances in number 1 to specific instances in plays written by Chekhov, Ibsen, and Strindberg.

The influence of Stanislavski has been continued through the work of such disciples and pupils as Eugene Vakhtangov, Richard Boleslavsky, Michael Chekhov, Lee Strasberg, Sonia Moore, and many others, particularly actors who study or have studied at the famous Actor's Studio in New York. The Actor's Studio generally follows nine basic steps:

1. The coach starts a session by announcing that it is beginning— an automatic signal for total silence from the observers. A tape recorder is turned on; all sessions are taped. A large clock is always close to the coach; each actor (or actors if working as a team) receive fifty minutes when they work.
2. Total silence prevails as the actor prepares—*whatever* time is needed for relaxing and concentrating is provided (the time used is part of the fifty minutes). The Studio members believe that discipline is essential, and the greatest test of it is both the actor's preparation time and the control required by others to observe it.
3. The scene is performed without interruption.
4. The actor speaks first at the conclusion of the scene (no one ever applauds because it would be a violation of rehearsal/coaching principles).
5. The actor explains the goal in selecting the scene; then the actor explains the specific, single intention for doing the scene that particular time. He explains exactly what he was trying to accomplish.
6. Observers may then comment on what was seen and heard relative to the stated intention.
7. The coach then asks questions.
8. A general discussion ensues.
9. The coach summarizes with a brief critique and advises on what might be followed as a next rehearsal step.

Actors also select scenes to work on to sharpen their skills between jobs. No actors are students in the usual sense of that word; all are working professionals who use the Studio to investigate, experiment, seek help, and sustain their craft; risks can be taken and mistakes can safely be made. Members are all proven professionals who have been invited into membership or who have auditioned successfully. A half dozen or so new members are also added each year from several hundred applications and many auditions. (Note: The Actor's Studio should not be confused with the Strasberg Institute. The latter is a professional training school for students, utilizing standard admission procedures and tuition fees. The Actor's Studio is reserved as a laboratory for the established professional with membership granted solely by audition and/or invitation.)

A word of caution: Do not create the notion that a realistic or naturalistic acting style can be achieved *solely* by performing character intentions in the manner of Stanislavski's *internal* approach to acting. Locate and use late nineteenth-century and early twentieth-century customs, habits, and activities to determine *how* character intentions are achieved. Use your personal experiences to personalize the manner or style of playing a given psychological intention for the characters under study from Ibsen, Chekhov, Strindberg, and the like.

While Realism and Naturalism (and the tenets of Stanislavski) remain the foundation of most twentieth-century acting styles, a few other important styles remain to be examined.

Suggested Characters and Plays for Scene Work

Ibsen, Henrik

Hedda Gabler, Eilert Lovborg, Judge Brack, Miss Tesman
Hedda Gabler
Bernick, Mrs. Bernick
Pillars of Society
Nora Helmer, Torvald, Mrs. Linde
A Doll's House
Dr. Stockman, Mrs. Stockman
An Enemy of the People
Mrs. Alving, Oswald
Ghosts
Gregers, Hialmar, Gina, Hedvig, Old Ekdal
The Wild Duck

Shaw, George Bernard

Gloria, Valentine
You Never Can Tell
John Tanner, Ann Whitfield
Man and Superman
Barbara, Undershaft
Major Barbara
Dick Dudgeon, Reverend Anderson, Mrs. Anderson
The Devil's Disciple

Synge, John M.

Maurya, Nora, Cathleen, Bartley
Riders to the Sea
Christopher, Pegeen
Playboy of the Western World

Hedda Gabler by Henrik Ibsen. Susannah York and Roxanne Hart at the Roundabout Theatre, New York City. Gene Feist and Michael Fried, producing directors.

O'Casey, Sean

Fluther, Mrs. Gogan, Nora
The Plough and the Stars
Juno, Joxer, Boyle
Juno and the Paycock

Turgenev, Ivan

Natalya, Vera, Adam, Alexey
A Month in the Country

Gogol, Nikolai

Khlestakov, Osip, Anton, Anna, Marya
The Inspector General

Zola, Emile

Thérèse Raquin, Laurent
Thérèse Raquin

Chekhov, Anton

Masha, Olga, Irina, Natasha, Kulygin, Vershinin, Tusenbach
The Three Sisters
Nina, Trigorin, Treplev, Irina
The Seagull
Madman Renevsky, Lopahin, Anya, Varya, Gaev, Trofimov, Firs
The Cherry Orchard
Yelena, Sonia, Serebryakov, Uncle Vanya, Ostrov
Uncle Vanya

Strindberg, August

Miss Julie, Jean
Mis Julie
Laura, The Captain
The Father

Gorky, Maxim
   Luka, The Baron, The Actor,
Satin, Vassilisa, Natasha
     The Lower Depths

Molnar, Ferenc
   Liliom
     Liliom
   All characters
     The Guardsman

Actor Checklist   Realism and Naturalism

Voice	Lifelike, more precise articulation and effective vocal production in Realism; more vocal pointing used in Realism; emphasis on dialects; unusual use of silence and pauses; conversational mode, but more heightened in Realism; use of full vocal scale; expressive speech; motivated speech; intonation and imaginative coloring.
Movement	Motivated by thoughts, feelings, and speech; total and controlled body response; considerable physical interaction with others; some selective movement imposed in Realism, seemingly none in Naturalism; all stage areas used; all body positions used; totally representational.
Gestures	Related to inner experience; natural and spontaneous; full use of the entire body; lifelike; more selective in Realism.
Pantomimic Dramatization	Costuming and properties integrally related; extremely inventive; detailed in Naturalism; more selective in Realism; lifelike; motivated; closely tied to environment and scenery, especially in Naturalism.
Character	Rooted in inner psychology and believable human emotion; multidimensional; tied to environment, particularly in Naturalism; subjective, internal use of observation, imagination, senses, and personal experience; highly motivated, particularly in Naturalism; Super-Objective clear; ensemble important.
Emotion	Complex; rooted in human psychology; use of affective or emotional memory; motivated; closely tied to physical action and speech; audience identification and empathy strong.

Ideas	Strong social orientation in Realism; strong human orientation in Naturalism; related to experiences in daily living, problems of environment, and heredity.
Language	Lifelike prose; often rich in symbolism and imagery; more selective in Realism.
Mood and Atmosphere	Closely tied to character, situation, and environment; not superimposed for theatrical purposes; mixed and varied; lifelike.
Pace and Tempo	Unusually varied.
Special Techniques	Full use of Stanislavski system: (1) personalization, (2) Magic If, (3) given circumstances, (4) concentration, (5) tempo-rhythm, (6) observation, (7) imagination, (8) the senses: affective memory or emotion memory, (9) role analysis: Super-Objective and Through Line of Actions (*MF* clear).

Selective Readings

Cole, Toby. *Acting: A Handbook of the Stanislavski Method.* New York: Crown Publishers, 1949.

Durbach, Errol., ed. *Ibsen and the Theatre: The Dramatist in Production.* New York: New York University Press, 1980.

Edwards, Christine. *The Stanislavski Heritage.* New York: New York University Press, 1965.

Emeljanow, Victor., ed. *Chekhov: The Critical Heritage.* Boston: Routledge & Keegan Paul, 1981.

Gorchakov, N. M. *The Directorial Lessons of K. S. Stanislavski.* Moscow: Iskusstvo, 1950.

———. *The Vakhtangov School of Stage Art.* Moscow: 1960. Translated by G. Ivanov-Mumjier.

Hapgood, Elizabeth R., ed. and trans. *Stanislavski's Legacy.* New York: Theatre Arts Books, 1958.

Hethman, Robert H., ed. *Strasberg at the Actor's Studio.* New York: The Viking Press, 1965.

Houghton, Norris. *Moscow Rehearsals: An Account of Methods of Production in the Soviet Theatre.* New York: Harcourt Brace Jovanovich, 1936.

———. *Return Engagement: A Postscript to "Moscow Rehearsals."* New York: Holt, Rinehart, and Winston, 1962.

Hull, Lorrie. *Strasberg's Method.* Woodbridge, Conn.: Ox Bow Press, 1988.

Lewis, Robert. *Method or Madness?* New York: Samuel French, 1958.

Magarshack, David. *Chekhov the Dramatist.* New York: Hill and Wang, 1950.

Marowitz, Charles. *The Method as Means.* London: Herbert Jenkins, 1961.

———. *Stanislavski and the Method.* New York: Citadel Press, 1964.

Moore, Sonia. *The Stanislavski System.* New York: Viking Press, 1974.

Munk, Erica, ed. *Stanislavski and America.* New York: Hill & Wang, 1966.

Norvell, Lee. ''Stanislavski Revisited.'' *Educational Theatre Journal,* March 1962, pp. 29–37.

Stanislavski, Constantin. *Actor's Handbook,* 1963; *An Actor Prepares,* 1936; *Building a Character,* 1949; *Creating a Role,* 1961; *My Life in Art,* 1952. Translated by Elizabeth R. Hapgood. New York: Theatre Arts Books.

Valency, Maurice. *The Flower and the Castle.* New York: Macmillan Co., 1963. (About Ibsen and Strindberg.)

Willis, Ronald. ''The American Lab Theatre.'' *Tulane Drama Review,* Fall 1964, pp. 112–16.

Suggested Filmography

1. *Caesar and Cleopatra.* 1945. U.A. Playwright—G. B. Shaw. Director—Gabriel Pascal. With Claude Rains, Vivien Leigh.
2. *A Doll's House.* 1973. Playwright—Henrik Ibsen. Director—Joseph Losey. With Jane Fonda.
3. *An Enemy of the People.* 1978. English. Playwright—Ibsen. Based on the adaptation by Arthur Miller. With Steve McQueen.
4. *Hedda.* 1975. (*From Hedda Gabler*). Playwright—Ibsen. Director—Trevor Nunn. With Glenda Jackson.
5. *The Inspector General.* 1949. Warners. Playwright—Nikolai Gogol. Director—Henry Koster. With Danny Kaye.
6. *Juno and the Paycock.* 1930. British. Playwright—Sean O'Casey. Director—Alfred Hitchcock.
7. *The Power of Darkness.* 1922. German film. Director—Conrad Wiene. With Players of the Moscow Art Theatre.
8. *Riders to the Sea.* 1935. MGM. Playwright—J. M. Synge. Director—B. D. Hurst.
9. *The Sea Gull.* 1968. Warners. Playwright—Anton Chekhov. Director—Sidney Lumet.
10. *The Three Sisters.* 1970. British. Playwright—Chekhov. Director—Laurence Olivier. With Olivier, Joan Plowright.

Early Twentieth-Century Nonrealism: Distortion— A New Reality

16

Scene: The steward's box of velodrome during a bicycle race. Jewish gentlemen, stewards, come and go. They are all alike; little animated figures in dinner jackets, with silk hats tilted back and binoculars slung in leather cases. Whistling, catcalls and a restless hum from the crowded tiers of spectators unseen, off right. Music. All the action takes place on the platform.

Stage Direction   Scene Five *From Morn to Midnight* by George Kaiser

If life is a dream, then a drama is a dream of dream, even though you have employed it as reality.

Instructor   *The Isle of the Dead* by August Strindberg

Overview of Nonrealism

By 1900, the naturalistic movement had reached its peak and given way to nonrealistic forms and styles. Many European playwrights turned away from Realism and Naturalism and adopted techniques of symbolic and nonrealistic drama. In his later years, Ibsen wrote plays such as *The Master Builder, Rosmersholm, John Gabriel Borkman,* and *When We Dead Awaken* that used symbols and abstractions in an integral way. Gerhart Hauptmann, from Germany, turned from Naturalism (*The Weavers*) to Symbolism. Hauptmann's *The Sunken Bell* is a highly successful play in the symbolic style. Strindberg abandoned Realism around the turn of the century. Although his later plays were forerunners of Eclecticism in which at least three styles—Realism, Naturalism, and Expressionism—were combined, Strindberg's later dramatic work utilized Expressionistic techniques.

Maurice Maeterlinck, from Belgium, favored symbolistic technique in all of his plays. *The Intruder, The Blind, The Blue Bird,* and *Pelléas and Melisande* are his best-known works. Maeterlinck espoused the belief that most dramatic moments onstage should be static and silent, with thought, introspection, mystery, and intuition revealing the secrets of existence. His plays are famous for sound interspersed with silence, frequent vocal repetition, and dreamlike color combinations in lighting. The plots and characters in Maeterlinck's plays are not based on realistic circumstances. His characters live on another plane—on a mystical level where they communicate with a ''higher world.'' In a world beyond reality, characters appear to move through a dream in which personification and symbolism take precedence.

It is tempting, if not totally accurate, to think of Maeterlinck as a kind of Impressionistic dramatist in the tradition of Impressionistic painting. That is, as an example, the artist Renoir painted people and nature with a gentle stroke, slightly blurred at the edges, as though life had been caught in a static reflection, remembered as a soft and gentle impression left lingering in the mind and senses. (See Renoir's famous painting of *Monet Working in His Garden in Argenteuil,* 1873.) Plays by Maeterlinck contain this same feeling of a gentle, slightly blurred, static quality (see *Pelléas and Melisande*).

During the 1890s, Alfred Jarry, from France, wrote *Ubu Roi,* a play that had far-reaching impact on playwrights of the twentieth century. Because of his extreme dependency on Symbolism and caricature distortion, Jarry was in a sense an early Surrealist and Absurdist.[1]

The Symbolists reacted violently against the popular notion of a writer's scientific duty to propound social problems in political terms. The basic tenet of Symbolism stresses the autonomy of art, measured entirely in terms of aesthetic standards. Authors used symbols to transcend what was normally considered ''realistic'' in everyday life. They hoped that the symbols would take them beyond the truth, which heretofore had been expressed only directly and explicitly (as in Realism). Characters were created in poetic terms. Ideas were expressed in sophisticated form and term, as opposed to the naturalistic simplicity of, for example, Maxim Gorky. Note that while Gorky also deploys symbols in his play *The Lower Depths,* and Chekhov does the same in his naturalistic plays, the form, structure, environment, and characters are very lifelike in essence and behavior, unlike that of the Symbolists (e.g., Maeterlinck as an example) who created an abstract rather than a real world. Symbolists firmly believed that literature should not be used as a weapon for social reform. (Conversely, most Expressionists desired social reform.)

The Symbolists delved deeply into the world of the subconscious mind. Existence of the subconscious human mind has been thought probable since ancient times. In explaining the subconscious, ancient men spoke of Pandora's box. According to this legend, the god Mercury left a box in the cave of Pandora with a warning not to open it. Curiosity got the better of Pandora. She opened the box and allowed all the evils and sufferings of the world to escape. According to mythology, if forces of the subconscious mind were given free expression, universal chaos would result.

However, there is another aspect of subconsciousness. Pandora's box also contained the spirit of hope that sustains and uplifts mankind. The subconscious is a reservoir of individual and collective wisdom, just as Pandora's box promised ''all gifts'' to those who possessed it. It is possible to take all that we have seen and heard from our subconsciousness and bring it into harmony with our consciousness.

The most direct knowledge of subconsciousness comes from the study of dreams. Symbolists and other nonrealists of the twentieth century were particularly influenced by dreams. Although Sigmund Freud provided the definitive modern analysis of dreams in the nineteenth century, the ancients also recognized the power of the subconscious mind. Alexander the Great was always accompanied by men versed in dream interpretation. On the night before he lay siege to the city of Tyre, he dreamed of a satyr dancing in victorious triumph. The sages foretold that Alexander would take the city, and Tyre fell before the Macedonians as was predicted.

Artemidorus lived during the time of Emperor Hadrian (A.D. 76–138). His theory of dreams was modern in tone. According to Artemidorus, a dream ''happens in that instant when the affections are so vehement that they ascend up to the brain during our sleep and meet with the more watchful spirits.'' Thus, Artemidorus recognized the presence of conflict in dreams, anticipating Freud's modern theories.

Prior to Artemidorus, Plato stated, ''In all of us, even in good men, there is a lawless, wild beast nature, which peers out in sleep.''

A fourth-century writer, Synesius of Cyrene, emphasized a value in dreaming beyond that of providing a safety valve for man's animal nature. He remarked, ''We do not sleep merely to live, but to learn to live well.''

When we sleep, we escape from the outer world. Dreaming proves that while we sleep our mind is active. Our mind reacts in a specific way while we sleep. It creates strange events from both reality and fantasy. Although we forget most dreams soon after waking, other dreams remain with us for a long time.

Freud's psychological theory of dreams focused on wish fulfillment, that is, a wish appearing in a dream travels from the subconscious mind (i.e., the *id*) to the conscious mind (i.e., the *ego*). Since the id constantly demands satisfaction from the ego in terms of fulfilling its wishes, a dream often presents a conflict situation. Since the subconscious operates differently from the conscious, perception of the subconscious alters perception of the conscious and distortion in the conscious mind arises. Material is condensed and displaced in illogical patterns and structures.

Expressionism was and remains a loosely used term, and confusion often arises as to what exactly the term means. Expressionism had its roots in a German political movement. It was philosophically oriented against mass industrialization and dehumanized mechanization. Its predominate methodology was to transform nature rather than imitate it. The result of the transformation was often distortion. Thus, robots replace people in *R.U.R.* by Josef and Karel Capek. Expressionism as a movement began with artists such as Edvard Munch and Oskar Kokoschka. As early as 1892 Munch was on exhibit in Germany as a leading Expressionist. Kokoschka would follow suit early in the 1900s, before turning to landscape work. Kokoschka also wrote plays of political importance. These artists turned observed reality to distorted reality in order to make both political and social points. Their art was not merely an imitation of reality, but a transformation of it.

In literature, Franz Kafka and James Joyce developed a style of Expressionism through the technique of ''stream of consciousness'' writing. The Expressionists, like the Cubists in art, tried to depict a conceptualization of the mind's total understanding of what it grasps. Cubism is the total understanding of the two-dimensional plane. Expressionists in theatre attempt this when they show how a simple object may take on gigantic proportions because the viewer sees it as such (e.g., Mr. Zero's view of the adding machine and the Judge's stand in Elmer Rice's *The Adding Machine*).

Dramatic artists became increasingly disenchanted with scientific study of man and his environment. Since the material of science must have a cultural base to give it human significance, many German writers perceived man and his value system as a reflection of a mechanical, contrived, stifling, intellectually oppressive society. Georg Kaiser was a leader in Germany's influential Expressionistic drama. (See *From Morn to Midnight, Gas I, Gas II,* and *The Coral.*) As noted earlier, the Swedish playwright Strindberg was one of the first major authors to traverse the confines of Naturalism by exploring symbolistic and expressionistic techniques in several of his later plays. In the preface to his *A Dream Play,* written in 1911, Strindberg said he wanted to follow the pattern of dreams in which anything seemed possible, in which time and space had no reality. In other words, he began to explore the subconscious mind through the forces of the conscious mind in the Freudian tradition. Strindberg believed that by using imagination in combination with memory, fantasy, absurdity, and improvisation a dramatist could create new patterns of existence. Characterization was not to be based in reality. Instead, characters split, doubled and multiplied, vanished and reappeared in a dramatic structure held together by the consciousness of the Dreamer (i.e., the central character who often represented the author). Strindberg advocated a new dramatic form based on artistic subjectivity as opposed to Naturalism, which was based on objectivity. Strindberg's dream world was also created from an imaginative "soul." His characters were never fixed and changed according to his subjective, introspective whims. Strindberg was devoted to interpreting life using spiritual methods and to discovering the secrets of the subconscious mind. His most famous plays utilized the transformation techniques of Expressionistic concepts (e.g., see *To Damascus* [a trilogy], *A Dream Play,* and *The Ghost Sonata*—all variations on the mind of a dreamer).

In Expressionism, fantasy and symbolism are combined, as well as fragments of Realism and Naturalism (as are the dream sequences of the human mind). A playwright's subjectivity is necessarily affected by his emotional, political, philosophical, and aesthetic experiences that in turn affect his view of the world. Hence, distortion in stage conceptualization occurs. Characters are more or less representative of states of mind, comparable to dreams, deliriums, or opinions, in which appearance, time, and space lose continuity. A playwright, then, "objectifies the subjective"—

Scene from *A Dream Play* by August Strindberg. Directed by Philip Benson, scenery design by Thad Torp, scenic projections by Hal Howe, lighting design by David Thayer, costumes by Margaret Hall, at the University of Iowa.

that is, he puts onstage the happenings inside the head, in the mind. Because in expressionistic plays fantasy and reality alternate in remarkable elusiveness, characters *at times* appear to be robots or dream figures and at other times to be real (the appearance of robotlike characters are reflections of a mechanized society). In expressionistic plays, people are usually not bound by traditions of duty, morality, society, or family. Man is not represented as an individual nor classified in a specific role. Characters often have generalized names such as Mother, Worker, and so on. The playwright transcends the individual to reveal all of mankind, or the playwright emphasizes human values and polarizes an individual at odds with a collective entity (see German Expressionism). Expressionism was consciously primitive and simplified in order to penetrate man's universality.

Expressionism and its techniques as applied to art spread throughout central Europe and beyond after 1912. In utilizing expressionistic techniques, playwrights aligned themselves with contemporary painters such as Munch and Kokoschka, as well as Emile Nolde and Paul Klee. In music, Expressionism was fostered by such composers as Arnold Schoenberg and Alban Berg. Following a war with France (Franco-Prussian War) and facing the probability of another war, artists (of theatre, music, literature,

A scene from *Spring's Awakening* by Frank Wedekind, at the Juilliard School, New York. Directed by Liviu Ciulei.

and art) experienced the aftereffects of revolt on social and political values. In addition to Kaiser, several great expressionistic playwrights emerged, such as Walter Hasenclever (*The Son, The Seduction*), Ernst Toller (*Man and the Masses*), Franz Wedekind (*Spring's Awakening*), and the Capek brothers, Josef and Karel (*R.U.R., The World We Live In,* or *The Insect Comedy*). By using fluid scenes, condensation of reality, situations and characters abstracted by symbolism, intensified distortion, illogical patterns, and lyricism, these authors wrote Expressionist plays. Generally, language was compressed into a staccato or telegram style. Juxtaposed against these abstractions was occasional interpolation of long monologues. Continuity of action was lost in dream sequences.

Some expressionistic plays have one or two acts with large numbers of scenes, and in other plays acts are missing altogether in favor of many scenes, or tableaux. Sometimes physical action in expressionistic plays is so dominant that language becomes unnecessary (when this occurs, the actor must focus on pantomimic dramatization).

In many plays women and men were social equals. A woman served as a comrade or friend to a man. She loved with complete understanding. To the Expressionist, love was absolute, a way to escape the restrictions and compromises of the world. Sexual passion was not usually a major theme. Since Expressionism depicted the worthiness of mankind, characters were drawn with pathos. They also had a definite social point of view, which usually represented the view of the author.

Expressionistic plays require kaleidoscopic outdoor and indoor settings. Scenic units and props are symbolic; for example, in *A Dream Play* note the scenic transformation of the flower bud on the roof that opens into a gigantic chrysanthemum (usually accomplished onstage by lighting or slide projection). Settings are used to support the main thought of the play. For example, in *Gas I* and *Gas II* by George Kaiser, spacious concrete domes with massive girders and wire apparatus, fanning out from a central platform, suggest the functional industrial architecture of an age of mass production and mechanization. Little or no naturalistic detail is included. Light and shadow contrast frequently to create spectacle (i.e., to create visual wonder and excitement). Music and sound effects are integrated much like music and sound in a film. A ''total theatre'' approach is used—that is, balanced integration of all theatrical elements.

As the twentieth century began, Stanislavski's system was the dominant acting style. He had opened his studio workshop in 1905 and invited Meyerhold back to experiment with nonrealistic styles, realizing that one approach could not work for every play. Stanislavski became interested in Hindu philosophy, especially the Toga system of abstract meditation and mental concentration. At the end of 1914, Stanislavski explored further the sphere of the subconscious to discover other methods of stimulating activity. He subsequently conceptualized and wrote his theory of emotion memory. Meyerhold helped ''modernize'' Stanislavski's style of acting. Uncomfortable with a theatre designed to mirror life, Meyerhold advocated a presentational theatre experience whereby actors and audiences encountered one another with mutual recognition. Meyerhold labeled his acting theories ''biomechanics'' (see discussion that follows).

To perform expressionistic drama, approach your interpretation of character with the techniques of Stanislavski in order to provide a human base. However, when the human elements of character give way to nonrealistic and dehumanized elements, Meyerhold's technique of biomechanics may be used to great advantage. Biomechanics was an idea focused on efficiency and economy of means. Finding new forms in an industrial society resulted in the external reflex action of biomechanics. The economic necessities in Russia after the revolution resulted in the inexpensive scenic design known as constructivism. On such a set, movement became superior to speech in that ''gesture'' could often communicate more than dialogue. (Meyerhold was particularly famous for staging a Lovborg-Hedda scene in Ibsen's *Hedda Gabler* in which Meyerhold used a hot, flaming punch rather than a cold liquid to help depict the ''fire'' and intensity of Hedda in the scene, thereby revealing the action better than through mere dialogue.) Biomechanics were kinetic and often mechanical, utilizing gymnastics, circus movement, ballet, dance, and acrobatics. Such mechanics were usually superimposed upon the actor by a strong director. Meyerhold believed that such activity could best be performed on platforms, ramps, trapezes, cylinders, and scaffolding (e.g., the ''constructivism'' just noted).

However, there is far more to biomechanics than mere gymnastics and dance. With proper training, the external reflex action can trigger emotional/psychological states in actors with a new efficiency and economy—reflective of a new society.

The acting style was highly theatrical and, for the most part, in a new direction from the work of Meyerhold's mentor, Stanislavski. Meyerhold rejected psychological Realism in favor of the science of biomechanics. He believed that movement was superior to speech. He also borrowed heavily from Asian acting style and staging techniques. (Asian acting is discussed in chapter 17.) Under Meyerhold, actors studied in three phases: a period of movement, a static period of posing, and a so-called realistic period related to lifelike mimicry. Meyerhold was devoted to grotesque satire. Despite this devotion, he retained some of the influence of Stanislavski in his actor coaching, allowing truthful human feeling to be expressed when needed.

Voice

Although three major nonrealistic styles are discussed in this chapter (Symbolism, Expressionism, and biomechanics), the major focus is on Expressionism because it was most influential on the work of the twentieth century.

Vocal work in symbolist drama primarily utilizes the tenets of Stanislavski and Realism, with heightened use of silence and static intonation. Also, in some passages in symbolic plays, poetic lyricism is necessary.

The dialogue in expressionistic plays modulates between realistic language, nonrealistic, staccato language, and lengthy, at times, poetic monologue (poetic in imagery though usually written in prose).

The key quality of expressionistic language is its clipped repartee mixed with staccato sounds. Generally, linguistic or literary conventions are disregarded and the language is concise and direct. Articles are often omitted, verbs are usually separated and forged into strange union, and nouns are frequently arranged in a series of lines. Alliteration is used abundantly, and continuous repetition of one sound is frequent. Crescendos heighten the impact of theme. As a result, your speaking is rhythmic and intense, rather than natural and fluid. When the script calls for dehumanized behavior, you may chant and intone or shout and bark to produce noise rather than words. Vocal sounds and noise have direct emotional impact on other characters and the audience. You may lapse into spiritual ecstasy; suddenly you may burst into wild screaming. For example, in the plays of the German playwright Hasenclever, wild noise in combination with telegram-style language is often used. At times the sound is just short of a yell, other times it is a lyrically ecstatic cry, or it may be simply a wild, piercing yell. Verse is frequently used to increase the emotional intensity of the play and to heighten the mysticism and the imagination of both participant and viewer. The playwright often creates fables in order to transcend the material world and enter the realm of the imagination; for example, people become robots or insects.

To deliver expressionistic language, you need wide vocal range, flexible vocal quality, and varied vocal rhythmic patterns. The staccato or vocal telegram segments require exceptional vocal clarity and emotional intensity. Rhythmic variety and control are equally important to all your vocal and physical work in this style, especially in the robot and dream segments.

Exercise 1 Voice—Early Twentieth-Century Nonrealism

1. Practice the following speech aloud. In the speech, staccato, expressionistic dialogue is emphasized, with articles omitted, words separated by dashes—all in a machine-gun-like manner. The effect should be somewhat mechanical and dehumanized.

   This Lady from Florence—who claims to come from Florence—has a vision like that ever visited you in your cage before? Furs—perfume! The fragrance lingers—you breathe adventure. Superbly staged. Italy . . . enchantment—fairy-tale—Riviera—Mentone—Prodighera—Nice—Monte Carlo—where oranges blossom, fraud blooms too.

   Scene One *From Morn to Midnight* Georg Kaiser

2. Practice the following speech aloud. The speech emphasizes the lyric monologue also found in expressionistic, symbolic, and nonrealistic drama. The effect may be somewhat ethereal, human, but elevated to a dream quality.

The two passages in Exercise 1 are from *From Morn to Midnight* by Georg Kaiser. In *Introduction to Drama* edited by Robert C. Roby and Barry Ulanov, McGraw-Hill Book Company. Reprinted with permission of Robert C. Roby and Barry Ulanov.

Why did I hesitate? Why take the road? Whither am I bound? From first to last you sit there, naked bone. From morn to midnight, I rage in a circle . . . and now your beckoning finger points the way . . . whether?

Scene Seven   *From Morn to Midnight*   Georg Kaiser

3. Invent or imitate a variety of nonhuman sounds, such as those used by insects, birds, and animals. Practice these sounds and cries as intermittent vocal effects within the speeches of appropriate plays selected from the list at the end of this chapter.

Movement

Movement serves to represent ideas of most realistic plays and less frequently the actor's personal motivation or the character's motivation. Movement helps define character relationships; movement also helps clarify emotional and symbolic attitudes. For example, expressionistic plays require you to fill stage space with pantomimic dramatization and curious dances as others speak or during long periods of silence. At times you perform theatrical acrobatics (as called for in Michel de Ghelderode's *Christophe Colomb* and *Pantagleize*). Movement is often enhanced by strange lighting and music. Around you the "drift of dream" or the "mechanics of routine" prevails in an essentially naked environment.

The key problem in nonrealistic movement is "to leave much of your real world behind"—that world of logical, organized action relatively free from chaos and surging passion. A nonrealistic play carries you into a world in which reality and dream abstractions mingle. Action is often only symbolic stereotype resulting from the nightmares and mental distortions/transformations of the playwright. Actions are fragmentary and disconnected and take place within symbolic forms or open spaces. Characters often wear symbolic masks and makeup in order to generalize the concept of mankind (exemplified in Eugene O'Neill's *The Great God Brown*). Frequently the realistic base of movement is dehumanized and distorted. In the manner of a marionette, movements are either slow and ephemeral (dreamlike) or mechanical and robotlike. Gestures are graceful, free, and fluid or abrupt, studied, and stilted. As you enter the world of distortion and transformation, conventional logic disappears. Nonetheless, your movement must retain some semblance of realism because realism is part of a dream, and a dream is in part true to observed, experienced reality. Yet, the overall projection of nonrealistic movement (especially expressionistic movement) must be distorted, transformed, and incongruous with everyday life.

Meyerhold's biomechanics work extremely well for nonrealistic acting. Imaginative gestures, gymnastic and acrobatic activity reinforce the mechanical aspects of movement. Ballet and dance are effective for ephemeral dream movement.

Exercise 2   Movement—Twentieth-Century Nonrealism

Following is a list of exercises that will enable you to practice nonrealistic movement.

1. Construct a facial mask that typifies a stereotype attitude, emotion, or character (possibly you can purchase a mask from a party shop). Wear the mask and study it in a mirror. Then practice movement that exemplifies the countenance of the mask. Explore many types of physical action, for example, move in slow motion, move rapidly across the room, move mechanically, move grotesquely, and so on.
2. Imagine you are a puppet. Move according to the strings controlling your arms, legs, head, back, and torso.
3. Imagine you are an insect. Move according to the type of insect you choose to be.
4. Imagine you are a robot. Move according to how a robot behaves.
5. Imagine you are any kind of modern machine (for example, an adding machine, a typewriter, a washing machine, a telephone, and so on). Move according to the actions of the machine.
6. Imagine you are a snowflake, a cloud, rain, lightning, wind, a leaf, a feather, or any similarly lightweight or fragile thing. Move according to the activity of the object in motion.
7. Invent and practice imaginative gestures, gymnastics, circus tricks, acrobatics, ballet movements, and expressive dance activity for application to speeches selected from the plays listed at the end of this chapter.

Character and Emotion

To perform early twentieth-century expressionistic and nonrealistic styles, use Stanislavski's character premise that acting is like living, and then counter and balance the style by using Meyerhold's biomechanics. At times believability in role creation is needed in expressionistic and other nonrealistic acting styles, while at other times a formalized or mechanical design and shape are needed to accomplish some of the actions and movements of characters. The actor and director have the important task of careful script analysis to determine which factor is operative at any given moment (e.g., Is it Stanislavski's realism? Is it Meyerhold's biomechanics?). Combined properly, realism and biomechanics define character and emotion in expressionistic and nonrealistic acting styles. This mix produces a range of character and emotion complexity from simplistic to multidimensional. For example, the mix of realism and biomechanics can be applied clearly and effectively in Kaiser's *From Morn to Midnight*. The Teller (or the Cashier as he is sometimes called) is the central character. In part I, scene 1, the Teller is totally immersed in mechanical routine. Kaiser provided over twenty-four stage directions for the Teller without one word of dialogue. Most of the stage directions involve counting money or rapping on the Teller's window ledge. Analysis quickly reveals how dehumanized the Teller's life in the bank is. Finally, at the end of scene 1, the Teller chokes out the words, ''Fetch—glass of water!'' The Teller is little more than a robot in the assembly line of the banking business. In this scene, highly formalized robot action and speaking dictate the acting style.

However, in scene 3, the Teller is alone in a snow-covered field near a single tree. As the sun casts bluish shadows on the snow, the Teller begins a long monologue in which he explores the change in his life now that he has stolen money and run away. As the scene and speech progress, a storm develops. The Teller is engulfed in a dreamlike trance, his eyes scanning the field. He murmurs, ''snow, snow, sun, silence.'' His words and movements glide into the ethereal formality of slow motion. As the wind and storm increase, the dream becomes a nightmare. The tree takes on the shape of a human skeleton with grinning jaws. In dream and nightmare fashion, the Teller converses with the tree. In this scene, highly formalized dream movement and speaking dictate the acting style, contrasting vividly with the earlier robot or mechanical style. Of course, both of these formalized elements are constantly contrasted with the real or human element at the base of the character, that of a man with a home, a mother, a wife, daughters, a job, and so on. As the play moves toward its conclusion, the Teller becomes increasingly humanized, discarding his robot and dream natures. By the final scene of the play, the Teller has achieved self-understanding as well as understanding of the world he lives in. No longer a robot or a dreamer, he sees himself and the world clearly. In this scene, the Teller must be performed with genuine warmth and naturalness; the best of Stanislavski realism can be applied here to enhance audience identification and empathy with the pathetic, martyred Teller. Realistic acting should prevail throughout his confession speech. Then, as the play concludes with his death, the audience both observes and feels the loss of a sacrificial human being.

The journey of the Teller provides a solid example of the mixture of styles necessary for successful work with character and emotion in expressionistic acting. Careful role and play analysis determine when to use Realism and when to use biomechanics (either as the unreality of a robot or as a dream).

Exercise 3   Character and Emotion—Early Twentieth-Century Nonrealism

1. Perform the following brief improvisations, first as a mechanical robot, second as a sleepwalker midst a dream or nightmare, third as any insect of your choice, and fourth as any modern machine of your choice. Be certain to define the circumstances prior to performing the improvisation. Keep each of the four phases of the improvisation under five minutes.

   a. A woman serves breakfast to her husband.
   b. A bank teller receives money from a customer.
   c. A woman pleads with her dead son to lay down in his grave and be still.
   d. A man and a woman hoard food by piling it in a cellar.
   e. A man stands lost on a street corner on Madison Avenue, New York City, as people rush by.
   f. An accountant adds columns of figures as his boss observes him.
   g. A man lost in a thick jungle thinks the trees are horrifying figures of fear.

2. Repeat the seven improvisations from number 1 in a natural, believable, realistic style. Finally, perform them with selective use of both realistic and nonrealistic character and emotional behavior.

In a lighter vein, nonrealistic acting techniques also assist with presenting comic fantasies, such as the popular *Peter Pan* by Sir James M. Barrie. While fundamental realism carries most of the action in this delightful fantasy, the techniques described in this chapter prove applicable to segments in *Peter Pan* dealing with the dog, Nana, the crocodile, and the antics of Captain Hook, the Indians, and the pirates. Such acting techniques are also well utilized in many children's theatre plays and fantasies, such as *Reynard the Fox, Winnie the Pooh, The Great Cross Country Race,* and others.

A clear understanding of nonrealistic acting techniques is vital if you are to make the playwright's philosophic premise clear. The universality of these styles usually rests with the playwright's emphasis on human values, on love, and on spiritual brotherhood. Understanding these styles and the stylistic writing techniques of early twentieth-century nonrealists, the actor applies a mix of realistic and biomechanic acting techniques to fulfill the intentions of the author.

While so-called pure Expressionism and similar nonrealistic movements in theatre disappeared by the mid-1920s, their influence on writing, design, and acting style has continued. When combined with Stanislav-ski's system of Realism and Naturalism, the styles of the nonrealists led to the unique innovations of Bertolt Brecht and the Absurdists that finally culminated in the contemporary Eclectic theatre.

Suggested Characters and Plays for Scene Work

Stringberg, August

Father Indra, Indra's daughter, Officer, Lawyer
> *A Dream Play*

Hummel, The Student, The Milkmaid, The Lady in Black, The Mummy
> *The Ghost Sonata*

Kaiser, Georg

Gentleman in White, The Clerk, The Engineer, The Billionaire's Son
> *Gas Part I*

Cashier, Salvation Lass, The Lady, The Son
> *From Morn to Midnight*

Shaw, Irwin

Bess, Schelling, Joan, Levy, Julia, Morgan, Katherine, Driscoll, Martha, Webster
> *Bury the Dead*

Rice, Elmer

Mr. Zero, Mrs. Zero, Daisy, Shrdlu
> *The Adding Machine*

O'Neill, Eugene

Brutus Jones, Henry Smithers, The Little Formless Fears
> *The Emperor Jones*

Yank, Mildred Douglas, Paddy
> *The Hairy Ape*

Dion Anthony, Margaret, Lillian Brown, Cybel
> *The Great God Brown*

Capek, Karel

Harry Domin, Sulla, Marius
> *R.U.R.*

Capek, Karel and Josef

Parasite, Chrysalis, Vagrant, Mr. Beetle, Mrs. Beetle, Fly, Larvae
> *The World We Live In (The Insect Play)*

Maeterlinck, Maurice

Pelléas Golaud, Melisande
> *Pelléas and Melisande*

Boy, Girl, Fairy, Light, Night
> *The Blue Bird*

Jarry, Alfred

Ubu Roi (King Turd)
> *Ubu Roi*

Wedekind, Frank

Melchoir, Wendla, Moritz
> *Spring's Awakening*

Toller, Ernst

The Woman, Nameless One
> *Man and the Masses*

Connelly, Marc, and George S. Kaufman

Composer, Girl
> *Beggar on Horseback*

Barrie, Sir James M.

Peter Pan, Wendy, Nana, Captain Hook, John
> *Peter Pan*

(Also see the many children's theatre plays and fantasies utilizing nonrealistic and nonhuman characters and devices.)

Actor Checklist   Early Twentieth-Century Nonrealism

Voice	Extensive range; lyrical when appropriate; staccato when appropriate; extensive use of pause and silence; varied rhythms; when appropriate, extensive use of chant, intonation, yells.
Movement	Motivated by idea, social function, and theme; when appropriate, distortion through robotlike, puppetlike dehumanization; when appropriate, distortion through slow and ephemeral dream quality; mix of presentational and representational mode; varied.
Gestures	Graceful, free, fluid, as appropriate; or abrupt, studied, stilted as appropriate; more selective in dehumanized moments; full use of entire body.
Pantomimic Dramatization	Use of masks; Asian techniques; acrobatics, strange dances; gymnastics; extremely inventive.
Character	Human reality base; distorted through dehumanization when appropriate, for example, mechanical and dreamlike; symbolic, clear social universality; combination of personalization and role identification and biomechanic formalism; when appropriate, analogous to inaminate objects, machines, animals, insects, and so on.
Emotion	Simplistic in dehumanized moments; complex in human moments; closely tied to social, thematic concepts.
Ideas	Strong philosophical and social orientation against machine age and modern technology; antiscientific; oriented to the common masses.
Language	Mix of prose and verse; mix of staccato and telegramlike dialogue and lyrical monologue.
Mood and Atmosphere	Closely tied to idea and social theme; generally serious; mix of reality and fantasy.
Pace and Tempo	Unusually varied.
Special Techniques	Careful analysis necessary to combine Stanislavski realism and Meyerhold biomechanics; unusual flexibility in physical activity.

Selective Readings

Arnold, Paul. "The Artaud Experiment." *Tulane Drama Review,* Winter 1963.

Artaud, Antonin. *The Theatre and Its Double.* Translated by Mary C. Richards. New York, Grove Press, 1958.

Balakian, Anna E. *Surrealism: The Road to the Absolute.* rev. ed. New York: E. P. Dutton & Co., 1959.

Benedikt, Michael, and Wellwarth, George, eds. *Modern French Theatre: The Avant-Garde, Dada, and Surrealism.* New York: E. P. Dutton and Co., 1964.

Braun, Edward, ed. *Meyerhold on Theatre.* New York: Hill & Wang, 1969.

Breton, Andre. *What Is Surrealism?* London: Faber & Faber, Ltd., 1936.

Brockett, Oscar G., and Findlay, Robert R. *Century of Innovation: A History of European and American Theatre and Drama Since 1870.* Englewood Cliffs, N.J.: Prentice-Hall, 1973.

Chiari, Joseph. *Symbolism from Poe to Mallarme.* 2d ed. New York: Gordian, 1970.

Kenworthy, B. J. *Georg Kaiser.* London: Oxford University Press, 1957.

Patterson, Michael. *The Revolution in German Theatre.* Boston: Routledge & Kegan Paul, 1981.

Roose-Evans, James. *Experimental Theatre: From Stanislavski to Today.* rev. ed. New York: Universe, 1973.

Schmidt, Paul, ed. *Meyerhold at Work.* Translated by Paul Schmidt, Ilya Levin, and Vern McGee. Austin: University of Texas Press, 1980.

Willett, John, *Expressionism.* New York: McGraw-Hill, Inc., 1970.

Suggested Filmography

1. *The Adding Machine.* 1969. British. Playwright—Elmer Rice. With Milo O'Shea, Phillis Diller.
2. *Brazil.* 1985. British. Director—Terry Gilliam (of *Monty Python*). With Robert DeNiro, Jonathan Pryce, Michael Palin (also of *Monty Python*). Though not drawn from a play, this film is a textbook of Expressionistic techniques, adapted to the 1980s.
3. *The Cabinet of Dr. Caligari.* 1919. German. Silent. Director—Robert Wiene. With Conrad Veidt (later of *Casablanca,* as the evil Nazi). While not based upon a play, this film *defines* Expressionism as used in drama and performance. Its production design is still influential today. Available on video.
4. *The Dance of Death.* 1968. Based upon Strindberg's play. Directed by David Giles. With Laurence Olivier.

5. *The Emperor Jones.* 1933. U.A. Playwright—Eugene O'Neill. Director—Dudley Murphy. With Paul Robeson.
6. *The Hairy Ape.* 1944. U.A. Playwright—O'Neill. With Wm. Bendix, Susan Hayward.
7. *The Long Voyage Home.* 1940. United Artists. Director—John Ford. With John Wayne. Adapted from Eugene O'Neill's sea plays: *Bound East for Cardiff, In the Zone, The Long Voyage Home,* and *Moon of the Caribbees.* Noteworthy for use of dream-like, expressionistic techniques rather than the expected strict naturalism.
8. *Worm in the Bud.* 1970. Based upon Wedekind's *Spring's Awakening.*

Note

1. In 1917 a movement known as Dadaism (*dada* means "hobby horse" in French) proposed to free the plastic and graphic arts, as well as the verbal arts, from traditional ways of seeing and feeling. The Dadaists took their lead from the nihilistic works of Tzaraz. The work was political, revealing disillusion with World War I, traditional conventions and aesthetics. Dada stresses the unpredictable. Dadaism was followed in the 1920s by a movement called Surrealism. Its leader, Guillaume Apollinaire, coined the term *Surrealism* in the preface to his play *The Breasts of Tireias* (subtitled "Drama Surrealisti"). Dadaism and Surrealism promised to free the mind of rational control by exposing the subconscious mind of man. The literature and plays provided audiences with vague scenery, fragmentary and unmotivated characters, minimal conscious activity, disjointed events, and in general a chaotic universe. These philosophical forerunners of the Absurd movement preached a new psychology based on combining the dreaming state with the waking state. The goal was to find a new reality, a kind of *sur* ("above") reality.

Brecht and Epic Style: Didacticism 17

MOTHER COURAGE   I won't have my war all spoiled for me! It destroys the weak, does it? Well, what does peace do for 'em? Huh?
(She sings her song)
So cheer up, boys, the rose is fading
When victory comes you may be dead
A war is just the same as trading
But not with cheese—with steel and lead!

    Christians, awake! The winter's
        gone!
The snows depart, the dead sleep on.
And though you may not long survive
Get out of bed and look alive!

   Mother Courage by Bertolt Brecht

. . . don't show him too much
But show something. And let him observe
That this is not magic but
Work, my friends.

              Bertolt Brecht
      from Kenneth Tynan, *Curtains*

Overview of Brecht Epic Theatre—From Illusion to Fact and Social Action

It is told that shortly after the death of Bertolt Brecht in 1956, the late Lotte Lenya, a principal actress in the Berliner Ensemble, was speaking in Iowa. According to the story of this incident, she related a personal account about Brecht to a group of university students. Lotte was having great difficulty understanding Brecht's acting theories as they applied to a role she was playing in one of his plays. Upon asking Brecht how she was to interpret her role to achieve a performance faithful to his Epic theories, Brecht supposedly patted her reassuringly on the shoulder and said she should simply "follow her instincts" and "go about the business of acting." This was Brecht's way of admitting that his famous theories can be taken only so far, that ultimately traditional acting craft must also be part of the work necessary to present his plays effectively. In other words, there is a vast distinction between Brecht's theories and Brecht's practice.

Since 1956, the ideas of Brecht have revolutionized playwriting, production techniques, and acting methodology. Ironically Brecht's theatre concepts had far-reaching impact only after his death. Brecht wrote his first play (*Baal*) in 1918 and formulated his writing style during the 1920s (*A Man is a Man* and *The Threepenny Opera*). When the Nazis began their rise to power in 1933, Brecht left Germany and settled in Scandinavia. While in exile, he wrote several major works: *The Private Life of the Master Race, Mother Courage, Galileo, The Resistible Rise of Arturo Ui,* and *The Good Woman of Setzuan.* Later, he left the northern countries of Europe for the United States, making his home in Santa Monica, California until the end of World War II. One of Brecht's most famous plays was written during this time, *The Caucasian Chalk Circle.* Although Brecht had become a convert to Marxism, he did not return to the Eastern Sector of Berlin immediately after the war. He spent some time in Switzerland in 1947, finally settling in East Berlin in 1948. After his self-imposed exile, the name and work of Bertolt Brecht found acceptance and acclaim throughout Europe, the United States, and England.

German theatre during the 1920s received its inspiration from the director Erwin Piscator. Upon founding the First Epic Proletarian Theatre, Piscator formed an alliance with Brecht. Both men were interested in treating subjects in strictly intellectual, didactic terms. They opposed the traditional late nineteenth-century and early twentieth-century focus on Realism, Naturalism, and orientation toward "suspension of disbelief" with its emotional element and its escape-into-make-believe quality. Piscator and Brecht favored a social activist theatre in which the audience

Photo of *Galileo* by
Bertolt Brecht. Lype
O'Dell as Galileo, Martin
Molson as Federzoni,
Marshall Borden as
Andrea Sarti, and Arthur
Inman as Little Monk.
Directed by Leonard
Leone, scenery by
Richard Spear, costumes
by Robert Pusilo, lighting
by Gary M. Witt.

remained aware that they were in a theatre absorbing messages and ideas.
They documented plays by prefacing scenes with electronically or mechanically projected captions explaining themes and exhorting action. The
expressionistic technique of constructing a series of disjointed, episodic
scenes was used as a desirable method for abolishing suspense, which was
an emotional and undesirable characteristic of traditional theatre. Music
was used to neutralize emotion rather than to intensify it. Atmospheric
lighting was rejected in favor of general illumination. Actors wore
everyday dress; property items were used as blatant theatre props to assist
in making an idea clear rather than in reinforcing an emotional "reality."
Scenery was constructivistic in design, using stairs, levels, scaffolding,
treadmills, and revolving stages. Films, used as background scenery, projected images of places and people from a variety of historical periods
and subjects on screens, all for the purpose of better explaining present

social circumstances (this technique, later known as *historification,* is explained in detail later in this chapter). Piscator dominated the Berlin theatre of the 1920s and provided an important function by creating a milieu for Brecht's plays.

However, before the 1920s ended, Piscator and Brecht ended their collaboration. Although both men sought enlightenment and education of the masses, the means of achieving that end became a source of contention between them. The young Brecht felt the only true means of achieving social action in the theatre was elimination of all emotion from the stage. Piscator did not want to banish emotion completely; instead, he tried to correlate fictional dramatic story and real contemporary world (e.g., surrounding the play with contemporary slide projections and films from real contemporary society). However, the tempo of the times in Germany (i.e., the concentrated rise of Fascism) proved to Brecht that Epic Theatre had to heighten and intensify didacticism in order to change the social, economic, and political conditions of the country. Piscator's desire to combine traditional emotionalism and didacticism was seen by Brecht as a weakening of their work. Brecht began to explore the pragmatics of didacticism and materialism. Brecht hoped to unify the thinking of his audience members and provoke them into strong, direct social action.

The Epic play presents historical subject matter from the viewpoint of a single storyteller. Sections of dialogue and narration are interspersed throughout the play. Changes in time and place are frequent, and time is bridged by a sentence or a brief passage. In Epic Theatre the sweep of a specific historical period is presented similar to the manner in which Homer wrote his poetic narration, *The Iliad.* Since Epic plays narrate or report many experiences, audiences have little opportunity to identify with the action onstage. Few Brechtian characters gain audience empathy. (Although the Epic actor consciously demonstrates, suggests, and describes behavior, rather than realistically create the inner truth of a role, Piscator would not have denied that emotion is an integral element of characterization. As Lotte Lenya's story indicates, in later years Brecht came to agree!) To counteract emotion onstage, Epic Theatre provides a narrator whose primary function is to *observe* the action and *report* events. The actors, in conjunction with the narrator, attempt to arouse the capacity for social action in an audience. The actors propose arguments, hoping to force decisions involving change in social conditions. To futher clarify the didactic elements of the play, Epic staging often includes use of general illumination of both the stage and the auditorium, elimination of act curtains, use of blatant scene-shifting with revolves, and use of slide and film projections. The main thesis in Epic Theatre is that human beings can be altered, are capable of change; from moment to moment, man makes many decisions affecting social and economic circumstances.

By the late 1920s, in his theoretical writing Brecht began to explore and expand his concept of Epic Theatre. He also wrote poems, aphorisms, stories, essays, polemics, and novels. However, his greatest achievements were his forty plays and adaptations. In 1948, Brecht published his theoretical writings. Chief among this work was "Small Organum for the Theatre." Thereafter, he turned from the concept of Epic Theatre to theatre oriented more toward didacticism. Although most of Brecht's theories may be categorized under the term *Epic,* his plays tend to transcend the limitations of this label. His plays are a rich mixture of Realism and Expressionism embellished by new and special techniques.

The Brechtian era initiated a change in drama and theatrical production. Brecht viewed the old dramatic theatre as a rigid structure that presented fixed, unchangeable events. Historical subjects were treated in historical terms. Past and present remained separated. Audiences were accustomed to watching events that mirrored their own emotional or psychological makeup, and their sensibilities had been lulled into acceptance of and passivity toward the old order of events. Brecht did not intend to pacify audiences; his plays were meant to arouse, shock, and "make strange" (i.e., alienate audiences by making them *think* and, hopefully, *act* to change society).

The subject matter of Brecht's plays is always based on history. He emphasizes the past in order to place the present in perspective. Brecht believed an audience should see the present through the past. In this manner an audience can view both present and past objectively, unemotionally, and with detachment. The present, then, offers a spectator alternatives for positive action. Brecht labeled this philosophy or technique "historification," a concept dependent on psychological behaviorism. Analysis is possible at any given moment by the thrust of a man's action in a particular circumstance. The primary subject of Brecht's plays is the relationship between men. Instead of watching modern man relate to the present, we study his behavior as he reacts to the past. Or the process is reversed and we watch historic figures react to the present (e.g., St. Joan in a Chicago stockyard, Hitler in an American gangster environment, and so on). The didactic lesson of historification can be likened to a Medieval morality play or to the biblical style of writing in parables. In effect, historification is a kind of propaganda made palatable by quality theatricalism.

An integral element of the process of historification is the concept of *verfremdungseffekt* or *alienation.* The literal translation of *alienation* is "to make strange" (to make actions strange). Objectivity is implied in the theory of alienation. An audience does not identify or empathize with strange events that take place in a blatantly theatrical way. Such events take precedence over character and emotional depth. To this end Brecht employed a number of shock-making theatrical devices: visible theatre mechanics; scenery changed in view of the audience; musicians participating in stage events; fragmentary, practical sets designed only *to indicate* the place of the scene. Piscator's theatre set the tone for Brechtian production by using multiple treadmills rotating in opposite directions, lifts to hoist actors, and screens to project documentary films. (Documentary films usually confirm or contradict what the characters say by showing *real*-life figures in support of or in contrast to *created* characters onstage.) Films show similar events simultaneously in different places, thereby revealing the world in flux. The Epic scenic design can be easily constructed and does not impede the action of the story or the flow of actors onstage. The set is often lighted in flat, white light, and no attempt is made to represent different moods or shades of meaning. Illusion is frequently assaulted by the open use of visual mechanics on the stage.

Brecht also used music as a means to further objectify stage action. He used dissonant music to aid in communicating the text. In Brecht's plays, music helps to eliminate meaning by delineating moral attitude. Songs comment on the action; they become means of arousing social consciousness.

Brecht used satire, comic dance, and mime in his plays for both theatrical diversion and didactic purposes. His plays were studded with satiric and farcical elements in the tradition of the witty fool and the circus clown—laughter tinged with irony, sadness, pratfalls, and jokes. Brecht deliberately added comedy to his plays to reveal the ludicrous nature of man's helplessness in a corrupt capitalist world. (It was also fun and entertaining!) Shocking and strange devices were used at every turn: for example, long presentational songs with dissonant music (*The Caucasian Chalk Circle*); signs from the ceiling proclaiming War Is Evil (*Mother Courage*); a man standing in a 1930 business suit speaking with a Chicago accent as a motion picture reveals Hitler speaking in the same manner (*The Resistible Rise of Arturo Ui*); an American flier surrounded by Chinese coolies (*The Good Woman of Setzuan*); unmasked peasants surrounded by masked tyrants (*The Caucasian Chalk Circle*); an actor throwing away a moustache and costume to speak as himself rather than as a character (at the final moments of *The Resistible Rise of Arturo Ui*).

The virtuosity of Brecht's Epic Theatre is allied to ancient Asiatic theatre (mainly of India, Indonesia, China, and Japan).

Early Indian plays were primarily dance and music set to plays written in Sanskrit. Later Indian plays were very romantic and highly symbolic—for example, Kalidasa's *Shakuntala*.

Indonesia was famous for its shadow puppet plays and its dance drama.

Mainland China produced two types of drama, Southern drama and Northern drama. Today, the Peking Opera is the center for classical Chinese drama, a highly symbolic combination of dance and music oriented toward civil and military stories.

Japanese drama has been the most influential of the Eastern dramas. Japan has produced three major theatrical forms: Noh plays, puppet theatre, and Kabuki dramas. Noh is essentially dance drama whose plays are brief and deal with gods, warriors, women, spirits, and demons. The actors are all male. Japan's puppet theatre is internationally famous and centers around a group called Bunraku. Kabuki is the most flexible and most popular Japanese drama. The three types of Kabuki drama are historical and domestic plays and dance dramas. Kabuki plays are inordinately long, running as much as five or more hours. The material is both comic and serious. The American occupation of Japan produced a new kind of theatre called Shingeki, in which Western plays are adapted to the Japanese language.

Acting is the key to all Asian dramatic forms. The performer, whether a dancer, singer, or actor, uses highly complex symbolic systematic gestures emanating from every part of the body. Asian audiences recognize and immediately understand the system. Asian acting emphasizes body control and discipline, focusing primarily on movement, gesture, pantomimic dramatization, mood, and use of intricate masks, costumes, and makeup. Character and language are subordinate to the theatrical elements just listed. However, speaking, chanting, and singing are nonetheless important. The vocal work combines with the musical accompaniment of the drama and requires unusually clear, precise diction. Character is primarily symbolic and far less complex and psychological than in Western drama. The presentational mode dominates in Asian acting. The overall effect is colorful and blatantly theatrical. Brecht found this effect appealing because Asian acting style provided practical models for his acting theories. Of particular importance to Brecht was the disciplined physical prowess of Asian actors. Movement is graceful, forceful, and rhythmic. Basically the Chinese use three types of walking, each distinguished by prescribed movements:

1. The roll-walk, in which the hips rotate as the feet move carefully from the ball of the foot onto the heel
2. The flat-walk, in which there is no hip movement and the entire foot lands flat at each step
3. The kick-walk, a goose step in which the lower leg is thrust forward at each step

Music is an integral part of Asian theatre. However, it is used for supportive purposes rather than for independent value. Whereas Brecht wanted music to stand as an independent element in the drama, in Asian theatre it is used to create mood and to reinforce thought.

The total theatrical effect of Asian theatre is substantially less didactic than Brecht's theatre. In spite of his admiration for it, Brecht found Asian theatre too hypnotic. However, he enthusiastically favored the transparent power and grace of Chinese acting techniques. Brecht discovered a well of social communication within the mimetic and gestural expression of the Chinese theatre. He soon discovered that his actors could clarify and define social relationships if they performed in a detached manner, as though observing their own actions. Thus, both performer and audience became observers. This is the identifying characteristic of Brecht's theatre.

Voice

One of the most striking features of Brecht's plays is the language. Brecht wrote "colloquial poetry," which has sensual simplicity. His poetry contains melancholy, tenderness, sadness, malice, wit, lyricism, logic, and paradox. When an actor first encounters the plays of Brecht, he may continually make the mistake of fighting the theory that "factual statements claiming reason over emotion" must dominate textual analysis. The language of Brecht is filled with poetry and emotion. The songs (generally set to music by Kurt Weill) are the epitome of Brecht's poetic diction.

Vocal work in Brecht's plays is a selective combination of believable human speech and overtly theatrical, detached, or even dehumanized speech. In other words, both Realism and nonrealism are at work in the Epic plays of Brecht. His is not a pure form. Elements of Realism, Naturalism, Symbolism, and Expressionism can be identified in his scripts. As a result, your voice must be pliant, flexible, and lively to achieve subtle

The Caucasian Chalk Circle by Bertolt Brecht. Don Blakely (seated) as Azdak, Barbara Meek as The Governor's Wife, David Falk as The Governor's Son, and Phyllis Somerville as Grusha at the Hilberry Theatre, Wayne State University. English version by Eric Bentley. Music score by Herbert Pilhofer. Directed by Leonard Leone. Scenery by Timothy R. Dewart. Costumes by Judith Haugen. Lighting by Gary M. Witt. Musical direction by Alvin H. Yungton.

variations of meaning, as well as overt variation of style. Constant attention should be paid to vowels and consonants. National and regional dialects are common in Brechtian plays and must be handled perfectly. Class distinctions are also written carefully into the language. The voice must be used economically. When characterization is multidimensional, as for Grusha in *The Caucasian Chalk Circle,* vocal nuances should reflect the best of Stanislavski's realistic vocal training. On the other hand, when the speech is mechanical and theatrical, as for the Iron Soldiers in *The Caucasian Chalk Circle,* vocal work should reflect the best of the nonreal expressionistic techniques. A large vocal range is of aid to an actor in Brecht's Epic plays. When they are appropriate, dissonant singing, chanting, and intonation in the expressionistic and Asian manners are valuable assets. Occasionally, lyrical passages require harmonious, pleasant vocal delivery. Sometimes, with very little transition, such passages are followed by disconnected, dissonant, strange-sounding segments. A disciplined, fully trained vocal mechanism is essential for effective delivery of Brecht's plays.

Gestures are fluid, full, mimetic, and descriptive, and their action and attitude are also symbolic. For example, to indicate a door opened forcefully, an actor raises both hands in front of him and then separates them violently. Some other prescribed gestures are these:

1. An action to repulse, in which one arm is thrust forcefully sideways
2. An action of resolution, in which one arm is thrust forcefully high above the head and the other arm is thrust down and backward at the side
3. An action to conceal, in which the back of the hand is placed across the eyes
4. An action for weeping, in which the fingers are moved up and down in the conceal position

All of these and other important gestures used in the Asian theatre are accentuated by manipulation of *watersleeves* worn at the wrists of most costumes. Watersleeves are long, dangling scarflike draperies that create lovely, flowing images during movement. (The feet are as important as the hands to gesture. In fact, every part of the body is used for precise, meaningful communication.)

Asian drama, like that of Spain and England, has always made interesting use of fans on stage. A distinct "language" of the fan has developed over the centuries, with subtle variations between countries. The essence of "fan language" on stage may follow these suggested guidelines:

With handle to lips:	kiss me.
Carrying in the right hand in front of face:	follow me.
Carrying in the left hand:	desirous of acquaintance.
Placing it on left ear:	you have changed.
Twirling it in left hand:	I wish to get rid of you.
Drawing across forehead:	we are watched.
Carrying in right hand:	you are too willing.
Drawing across cheek:	I love you.
Drawing through hand:	I hate you.
Twirling in right hand:	I love another.
Closing it:	I wish to speak to you.
Drawing across eyes:	I am sorry.
Letting it rest on right cheek:	yes.
Letting it rest on left cheek:	no.
Open and shut:	you are cruel.

Dropping:	we are friends.
Fanning slowly:	I am married.
Fanning fast:	I am engaged.
Open wide:	wait for me.

In Asian theatre, action is enhanced by vocalization. Emotion is indicated by symbolic body gestures coupled with either dissonant or lyrical vocal qualities. At times, the voice is clipped, staccato, or monotone. The depth of the emotion is indicated by ascending or descending emphasis on the combined effect of body and vocal elements. Diction is always precise and clear.

Exercise 1   Voice—Brecht Epic Theatre

Practice the speech from *Mother Courage* given at the beginning of this chapter, emphasizing the following techniques.

1. Believable, human, realistic delivery
2. A variety of regional and national dialects (e.g., British, Japanese, Italian, Irish, Swedish, and American Southern)
3. A variety of class distinctions (e.g., British royalty, common Cockney, American Midwestern middle class, Southern hillbilly, and so on)
4. Robot or mechanical
5. Dreamlike ephemeral
6. Singing, chanting, and intonation
7. Opposite emotional values from those that *seem* apparent in the speech.

NOTE: Both men and women should practice this speech. Actresses may impersonate male roles, and vice versa.

Movement

Movement, gesture, and pantomimic dramatization in Brecht again require combining several kinds of techniques, namely, realistic, biomechanical, expressionistic, and Asian. Careful script analysis by you and your director will lead you to the correct determination of which to employ and when. Such variety of movement necessitates a totally trained body, a body whose muscles must remain loose and flexible for maximum control. Acrobatics, dance, mime, imaginative gestures, and gymnastic training are highly effective in acting Brecht.

Exercise 2   Movement—Brecht Epic Theatre

1. Again using the speech from *Mother Courage* appearing at the beginning of this chapter, invent movement, gestures, and pantomimic dramatization to accommodate each of the vocal deliveries used in all seven of the techniques in foregoing Exercise 1.

2. Practice the following Asian techniques of movement described in this chapter:
   a. The roll-walk
   b. The flat-walk
   c. The kick-walk
   d. The gesture to repulse
   e. The gesture of resolution
   f. The gesture to conceal
   g. The gesture for weeping
   h. The fluid mixture and combination of all these techniques, a–g.

Exercise 3   The Fan—Brecht Epic Theatre

Practice all the "fan language" descriptions listed under *Asian Influence on Brecht*. If possible, attach makeshift watersleeves to your wrists when performing.

Character and Emotion

Except when creating key three-dimensional roles such as Grusha in *The Caucasian Chalk Circle* and Mother Courage in the play of the same name, you usually will not create complex characterization. A certain objectivity or detachment in performance reveals the *actor* as well as the *character*. In theory, most of Brecht's characters do not grow or develop onstage (in practice, growth sometimes takes place in spite of Brecht and his theory). You often encounter your audience directly and honestly; similarly, you often encounter your fellow actors in the same manner. The play and the acting are not disguised by illusion. Your objective is to provoke examination of social issues and raise questions for the viewers. You must frequently increase the spectator's awareness of being in the theatre by revealing your total consciousness in performing your role. In theory, your audience will then concentrate on ideas and action, rather than on emotion and character. (In practice, audiences still seem to respond best to emotion and character in Brecht, rather than to ideas.)

In his plays, Brecht provides you with devices to enhance the concept of alienation such as overt prologue, epilogue, narration, direct address, reference to the author, episodic scene progress, and didactic trial argument. Brecht also outlined a series of specific acting techniques related to character and emotion, which can help you discover how to accomplish some of his theory.

1. Perform with an awareness of being watched.
2. Look at the floor and openly calculate movement.
3. Separate vocalization from gesture (in other words, make vocal and physical timing strange and disconnected).

4. Remain uninvolved with other actors, physically and emotionally.
5. Stand and move in a simple, loosely held together group (removed from your colleagues, you are free to change the course of action and make independent decisions).
6. In order to better instruct your audience, freely acknowledge their diversity by speaking to the various collective units as well as to individuals within the units. For example, isolate a group of businessmen by focusing your eyes on the group, and then focus on each member in turn within the group. Similarly, recognize other groups and then each individual within a group until you have contacted the entire audience.
7. Address the audience directly from center stage in full-front presentational fashion.
8. Speak your lines as if they were a quotation and in the manner of delivering a speech in the third person.
9. Occasionally speak stage directions aloud to intensify unemotional acting.
10. Be critical of your character, as though all of your actions had occurred in the past.
11. Change roles with other actors during rehearsals and even during performances to purify and conceptualize ideas and to remain unattached to any role.
12. Stand in front of a mirror and meticulously study your movements and gestures.
13. Employ robot, mechanical, dreamlike, and other nonrealistic techniques.
14. Utilize an acting style absolutely opposite to what you normally would use for the scene in order to create fresh values; for example, do a modern war scene in the style of Restoration comedy.

Total attention to the concept of alienation can produce theatre generally free from emotional, empathic response from viewers. Do not strive for feeling and passion. Express excitement in terms of symbolism and ritual. Emotional portrayal is decorously exemplified and economically projected (for example, to indicate disdain or aloofness, simply turn your back on other actors). The emotional response of your audience need not correspond to the economic emotions of the character portrayed (for example, a spectator may laugh when you are angry). One of the most effective means of heightening alienation in Brecht Epic Theatre is to follow the Asian example of using white makeup on your face. For example, a curtain opens to reveal you sitting on the stage. Your body is completely still; you rest your head in your hands. Slowly, with much ceremony, your head comes up, revealing a stark white face and traces of the makeup on your hands. No one in the audience misses the point. You are an actor in a theatre! All subsequent action should be tied to that theatrical beginning, even if you later remove the makeup.

In Brecht Epic Theatre, emotional power over an audience is frequently muted, leaving the actors and characters free to perform thought-provoking action. To protect the intellectual content of his plays, Brecht also uses some expressionistic techniques involving robot or mechanical and dreamlike action. Characters frequently and suddenly burst into song or formal commentary. Characters often become grotesque and unreal (e.g., Hitler as a marionette in *The Resistible Rise of Arturo Ui*). With practice and experience, you can adjust to these unusual techniques and provide the appropriate response—such as ''dropping character'' and singing a song that has nothing to do with the emotion of action and everything to do with the intellectual message or performing in a dehumanized, robot manner as for The Iron Soldiers in *The Caucasian Chalk Circle*.

Exercise 3   Character and Emotion—Brecht Epic Theatre
1. Using a scene from *The Caucasian Chalk Circle,* practice the fourteen techniques for character and emotion previously described.
2. Practice the scene again with only selected items from the fourteen techniques, appropriately combining realistic, biomechanical, expressionistic, and Asian techniques.
3. Perform the scene in a totally realistic, natural, believable style. Finally, orchestrate the scene from this reality base with selected use of ''Epic techniques.''

In concluding the discussion of Brecht's acting theories, we must caution that, paradoxically, any totally faithful application of Brecht's theories to his or other Epic plays (see the work of Peter Weiss, Rolf Hochhuth, and Max Frisch, for example) is doomed to almost certain failure. Audiences have generally rejected rigid use of alienating and didactic techniques.

The problem is how to reconcile Brecht's theory with Epic plays and sustain audience interest. Edward Payson Call, an American director, has provided one of the keys to solving this problem. His analysis and directing of highly successful productions of Brecht plays have captivated audiences. Call uses Brechtian acting theory with discretion and pinpoint selectivity. Apart from Brecht's Epic theories and some use of expressionistic, biomechanical, and Asian techniques, Call permits certain actors in key roles to perform in a traditional, realistic style, creating emotion

Rebecca Renfroe in a scene from *The Threepenny Opera* by Bertolt Brecht, music by Kurt Weill, at the College Conservatory of Music, Cincinnati, Ohio. Directed by William Shorr. (Photo by Sandy Underwood.)

and empathy (again, Grusha in *The Caucasian Chalk Circle* and Mother Courage must be played this way). As a result, the eclectic *mix* of the Epic, the nonreal and the real, creates palatable Brecht onstage and also imparts the appropriate didacticism. Perhaps Brecht's advice to Lotte Lenya (given at the beginning of this chapter) best guides your acting: *Once aware of and rehearsed in the Epic techniques, follow your instincts and play the role without worrying about the theory.* Brecht's plays probably present adequate opportunity to achieve his intention without inordinate application of all his acting theories.

Suggested Characters and Plays for Scene Work

Brecht, Bertolt

Azdak, Grusha, The Ironshirt, Ludovica, The Governor's Wife
   The Caucasian Chalk Circle
Shen Te/Shui Ta, Mr. Shu Fu
   The Good Woman of Setzuan
Arturo Ui, Givola, Roma, Dogsborough, Docdaisy
   The Resistible Rise of Arturo Ui
Galileo, Andrea
   Galileo

Mother Courage, Swiss Cheese, Catherine, Eilif, Yvette
   Mother Courage
Polly, Macheath, Peachum, Lucy
   The Threepenny Opera
Joan
   St. Joan of the Stockyards
Any role
   A Man's a Man
Any role
   The Private Life of the Master Race

See also the list of characters and plays at the end of chapter 19 for playwrights influenced by Brecht Epic Theatre, such as Weiss, Hochhuth, and Frisch.

Actor Checklist   Brecht Epic Theatre

Voice	Selective combination of human and dehumanized; pliant, flexible; lively; unusual attention to vowels and consonants; national and regional dialects; class distinction; dissonant singing, chanting, intonation, and lyrical, as appropriate.
Movement	Appropriate mix of realistic, biomechanical, expressionistic, Asian; loose and flexible muscle control; some use of acrobatics, dance, mime, and gymnastics; ranges from graceful to forceful; mix of presentational and representational mode.
Gestures	Varied; at times full use of entire body; highly inventive; at times use of specific Asian techniques; descriptive; fluid; isolated body gestures.
Pantomimic Dramatization	Unusual use of mask, makeup, music, costume, particularly for Asian; highly inventive; theatrical; rhythmic.
Character	Combination of real and nonreal; combination of historical and fictional; ranges from simple to complex; oriented toward social issues and themes; clear; controlled; realized with a mix of alienation devices and human behavior; diversified and theatrical.
Ideas	Unusually important; clear; didactic; socially, politically, and philosophically oriented; directed to the masses.
Emotion	Ranges from simple to complex; ranges from human to nonhuman; ranges from full empathy to no empathy.
Language	Colloquial-poetic; sensual simplicity; diversified; unusual use of songs.
Mood and Atmosphere	Clear; controlled; tied to idea, social, and political purpose; combination of real and nonreal; combination of serious and comic.
Pace and Tempo	Unusually varied.
Special Technique	Selective use of alienation devices and Asian techniques; unusual vocal and physical flexibility; unique character and emotional analysis and execution.

Selective Readings

Brecht, Bertolt. *Brecht on Theatre*. Translated by John Willett. New York: Hill & Wang, 1964.

Esslin, Martin. *Brecht: The Man and His Work*. rev. ed. New York: Doubleday & Co., 1971.

Gray, Ronald. *Brecht*. New York: Grove Press, 1961.

Innes, C. D. *Erwin Piscator's Political Theatre*. New York: Cambridge University Press, 1972.

Ley-Piscator, Maria. *The Piscator Experiment: The Political Theatre*. New York: James H. Heineman, Inc., 1976.

Munk, Erica. ed. *Stanislavski and America*. New York: Hill & Wang, 1966. See Eric Bentley article, "Stanislavski and Brecht," pp. 116–23.

Needle, Jan, and Thomson, Peter. *Brecht*. Chicago: University of Chicago Press, 1981.

Weideli, Walter. *The Art of Bertolt Brecht*. New York: New York University Press, 1963.

Willett, John. *The Theatre of Bertolt Brecht*. New York: New Directions Pub. Corp., 1959.

———. *Erwin Piscator*. New York: 1979.

Suggested Filmography

1. *Galileo*. 1975. British-Canadian. American Film Theatre. Playwright—Bertolt Brecht. With Topol, Edward Fox.
2. *The Threepenny Opera*. 1962. Playwright—Brecht. With Curt Jurgens, Sammy Davis, Jr.
3. *Woyzeck*. 1978. German. Playwright—Georg Buchner. Director—Werner Herzog. With Klaus Kinski.

Absurd: Beyond Reason   18

. . . We are here as on a darkling plain,
Swept with confused alarms of struggle and flight
Where ignorant armies clash by night.

> Matthew Arnold
> from James H. Clancy,
> ''Beyond Despair:
> A New Drama of Ideas,''
> in Morris Freedman,
> *Essays in Modern Drama*

ORATOR   He faces the rows of empty chairs; he makes the invisible crowd understand that he is deaf and dumb; he makes the signs of a deaf-mute; desperate efforts to make himself understood; then he coughs, groans, and utters the gutteral sounds of a mute: He, mme, mm, mn. Je, gou, hou, hou. Heu, heu, go, fou, gueue.

> *The Chairs* by Eugene Ionesco

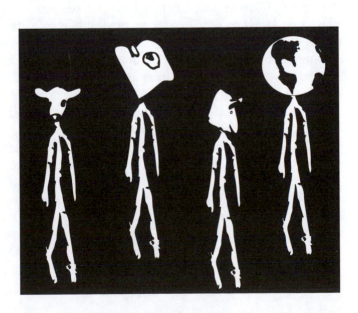

Overview of the Existential, the Absurd

Originating in the philosophical ideas of Existentialism as expounded by the great French philosopher-author Jean-Paul Sartre (1905–1980), this genre burst impressively upon the theatre world in the early 1950s in the work of such playwrights as Beckett, Eugene Ionesco, and Jean Genet. The genre made a steady, pure contribution to world theatre for more than ten years, and its influence continues to the present day. (Some of the ideas found in the essays, novels, and plays of the French writer Albert Camus, 1913–1960, are also valuable in understanding the philosophy inherent in most existential, Absurd plays, although Camus essentially rejected the label of existentialist.)

How considered Absurd? In what way, Absurd? What does the word mean in the context of drama and acting?

The answers to these questions begin with examination of *Existentialism* as employed by one of the main precursors of Absurd drama, Jean-Paul Sartre. Other forerunners of the Absurd include Alfred Jarry (discussed in chapter 16) and Luigi Pirandello (1867–1936). Jarry often distorted human character to the level of cartoon figures to make a negative point concerning existence. Pirandello was an Italian dramatist who emphasized that truth was a matter of personal viewpoint. Pirandello's plays, such as *Six Characters in Search of an Author, Right You Are,* and *Masks,* depict grotesque conflict between illusion and reality.

Existentialism refers to a particular view of the nature of man's existence. The existentialist believes that man starts life with nothing. His life is made up of acts; through the process of acting, man becomes conscious of his original nothingness. By choosing to act, man passes into the arena of human responsibility that makes him the creator of his own existence. However, the existence inevitably ends with death. Man returns to his original state of nothingness. This existential notion eliminates the Western concept of man's exalted nature. Life becomes meaningless and useless—a condition that is in essence "absurd." Man's only freedom in this condition is the exercise of his conscious mind. However, consciousness means conflict—between man's awareness of the absurdity of his existence and his need for justification of his human action.

The Sartrian existentialist sees man as adrift in the world. There is no God or religion; man is a quirk of environmental accident and development, "absurdly" (meaning unreasonably) thrust into special consciousness beyond his animal relatives due to the persecuting factors of mind and voice (e.g., thinking and speaking). What man is left with is the tedious condition of waiting to die, whereby he evaporates into nothingness in an empty or meaningless universe. However, if man can recognize and accept the simultaneous existence of his absurdity and his responsibility to give himself definition through choice and action, *there may be hope.*

The chief twentieth-century exponents of existential philosophy were the late Jean-Paul Sartre and the late Albert Camus (albeit Camus denied the label and albeit Sartre and Camus differed on their precise view of human existence). Sartre, a playwright as well as a novelist, dramatized existential man struggling to cope with a meaningless world. Orestes, in *The Flies,* acts as a free man devoid of emotional attachments in a corrupt world. Although Orestes takes full and, in his view, courageous responsibility for his actions, freedom serves only to isolate him. Absurdity again triumphs. Meaningful existence is only as valuable as man views it to be in light of the demands he places on himself. Since God does not exist (if He did exist, the world would not be in chaos), values are created on the basis of individual decision alone. Most of Sartre's plays focus on a character faced with moral choices or struggles (e.g., *The Flies* and *No Exit*).

Camus's characters are usually repulsed by their existence and violently attack their world (e.g., *Caligula*). The importance of Camus as a playwright rests on his rejection of a didactic premise for his plays in favor of presenting the world as a chasm of frantic, aimless activity. Camus was the first writer to use the term *absurd* in describing the senselessness of the human condition. (See his *Myth of Sisyphus* for a full definition and discussion of his concept of the word *absurd.*) By abandoning the rational approach to life, the existential man must attempt to find values in a world devoid of values; he must attempt to find order in a world gone mad (as opposed to Brecht, whose characters do not accept absurdity but rather look to social change for a more purposeful, rational world).

The nonrealistic theatre movements and the work of Brecht were well-known by Sartre and Camus. These movements had considerable influence upon their *theatrical* thinking.

Another important influence on the Theatre of the Absurd came from Antonin Artaud (1895–1948), a French theatrical genius whose work began in the 1920s. His theatre experimentations proposed to cure the ills of the traditional Western theatre, which he believed were deadening the lives of its members as well as of its audiences. Artaud described theatre in terms of ritual and myth, expecting the audience to experience trance and inspiration. His work attempted psychologically to remove the audience from the present to a primitive past by eliminating words and reliance upon script. Influenced by the Balinese dances and Eastern theatre, Artaud bore witness to a theatre of mystifying spectacle where words had no power and language became incantation. Artaud felt that the Western theatre was a slave to words, to text, and to realistic imitation. Instead, he wanted the Western theatre to utilize aspects of the Eastern theatre and create a shock force that would jar audiences from the complacent conditions of everyday life. Artaud used mechanical devices to create visible and audible frenzy. Light, sound, and physical movement and dance were used to tyrannize or assault the sensibilities of the audience. The overall effect was similar to the impact of Asian theatre wherein gestures, signs, postures, and sounds were compressed and symbolized.

Artaud called his dramatic theory the Theatre of Cruelty. He saw life and theatre as a "double," one reflecting the other. In his concept of *cruelty,* a bloodless state was implied. Artaud defined cruelty as a psychological purging of man's soul, freeing him from the bondage of logical and verbal experience. To effect a reevaluation of our lives, Artaud used shocking, violent, and often pornographic techniques to stimulate a vision that reached beyond ordinary reality. He wanted the subconscious mind to probe the mysteries of existence. The idea of cruelty was comparable to the high priest (actor) disrupting the logical response of the congregation (audience) to subject them ruthlessly to emotional and primitive response.

Absurd plays depict man tyrannized by nonman, by the intractable universe. Life is a "waiting period" that is at best painful and monotonous. For escape, man is left routine and fantasy. In the concept of good and evil, each cancels the other out—nothing is absolute—everything is relative. The Absurdists frequently obliterate the distinction between human and nonhuman (for example, men and animals are interchangeable, speech is often disconnected and noncommunicative). References to God's abandoning man to isolation and alienation are frequent. There are no more Western myths or illusions about an Omnipresent Being holding sway over man. Without hope, time and space are meaningless references. Within the concept of time, everything has happened before. Man can only perpetuate the art of game playing to pass the insidious factor of time. Idle songs may be sung, dances danced, jokes exchanged—violence, sex, and simple hygiene may take on hedonistic excess—inanimate objects may take on life and inordinate significance. If man is strong enough to face reality, he is left to the only certain escape, namely, death via what may be man's only possibility for a heroic act—suicide—through willful choice.

The Absurdists force us to look over the precipice into the abyss defined by the existentialists. We may reach that precipice through our subconsciousness and our dreams. We may doubt our reality, our traditional and usually abstract values such as love, family, art, science, occupation, religion, education, and so on. These are narrow confines and are rendered meaningless and beyond communicative possibility. An occasional laugh is the most convenient relief from living in such fantasy (and perhaps more meaningful than any of the traditional values). Pain comes with the knowledge that a vast difference separates what we are from what we might be.

How do the existential Absurdists justify the creation of art (plays) if they philosophically view all activity as ultimately meaningless? The playwright invariably justifies the writing as being merely *his* particular fantasy, *his* escape, and thereby *validates* the philosophy. Ask him to explain his philosophy and he may reply, "The forceps of birth lead directly to the shovel of death." To the Absurdist, the surgeon becomes the grave digger merely by exchanging instruments. In between birth and death is only an absurd or unreasonable existence, voided forever by the only certain end of any living existence: death in an eternal anonymity. Paradoxically, while the Absurdist view of life seems negative (chaotic, disintegrated, and despairing), he may find hope in man's effort to abandon his illusions and confront the truth of his existence. Recognizing his limitations gives man strength to go beyond reality and confront the intangible—a test of ultimate reality. In 1968 the challenging intellectual and emotional impact of these plays reached its zenith when the Nobel Prize was awarded to Samuel Beckett. His "forceps-grave digger" image stands as one of the clearest symbols of the entire Absurdist movement in theatre.

Now that the viewpoint of existential Absurd drama has been briefly clarified, it is easy to sympathize with the plight of the actor playing the role of Didi. To perform a role in one of these plays, you should retain a sense of humor and adhere to your life values. It is distracting and pointless (possibly even dangerous) to become overinvolved in existential philosophy, especially if you find yourself agreeing with that philosophy. Your task is to understand the point of view and then, as always, turn to the vital work of creating your role honestly, truthfully, and in the appropriate style.

In *The Theatre of the Absurd,* Martin Esslin, the acknowledged leading critic of Absurd Theatre, discusses the leading playwrights of the Absurdist movement. Chief among them are Eugene Ionesco (1912–), Samuel Beckett (1906–89), and Jean Genet (1910–86). It is enlightening to consider the fact that most of the "Absurdist" playwrights (i.e., Ionesco, Beckett, and Genet in particular) were *not* involved with theatre when they developed their ideas about life, man, and existence. In fact, they revolted against theatre and its conventions (such as Ionesco calling his scripts "antiplays"). Sartre and Camus had based their revolt on a philosophical tenet; Beckett, Genet, and others revolted as much against traditional theatre techniques as they did against traditional philosophic premises.

While Harold Pinter (1930–), Edward Albee (1928–), Tom Stoppard (1938–), and others have also been considered Absurdists by some critics, they are perhaps better classified as contemporary Eclectics. As previously noted, Ionesco called his plays "antiplays"—plays lacking traditional action, characters, and dialogue. His plays are emersed in fantastic hallucination, secret desires, and pulverizing fears. On the surface, Ionesco's plays resemble light comedies; further examination reveals serious social implication aligned with existential thought. Ionesco usually uses a conventional middle-class drawing room for his setting and conventional clichés for his dialogue (taken from a language primer). The result is a "put-on" with serious intent. Characters are carried away by words, changing identity, and farcical activity (such as having no head, as in *The Leader,* or laying eggs, as in *The Future Is in Eggs*). In *The Bald Soprano,* the banalities of their clichéd dialogue serve to make two middle-class British families appear mad. In *Rhinoceros,* a man seems to change into a rhinoceros. The images created by Ionesco are immediate and strange, comparable to those experienced in a dream or by primitive man. Images evolve with the irrational but compulsive logic of a dream. A corpse grows in a bedroom and Ionesco makes it seem perfectly normal (e.g., *Amedée*). Human beings are displaced by the proliferation of objects (e.g., furniture in *The Tenants;* chairs in *The Chairs*). Displacement such as this is a common occurrence in our lives. Do not material possessions often govern our thoughts and actions? In these plays everything appears to make sense, yet paradoxically is beyond reason. Nightmares are staged in the most unpredictable, irrational, abrupt manner. Dialogue is rendered meaningless by use of countless puns, speech inversions, sonic associations, non sequiturs, purposeless nouns, and so on.

Yet, beneath the structure of the game playing, the automatized language, the mimetic action, and the farcical antics smolders a curious disenchantment. Ionesco sees the individual consciousness isolated in an absurd universe. His characters are generally clowns and marionettes who ape man. The mechanical forces inhibiting man only provoke our laughter, making us nostalgic for the human element.

Early in the 1950s, Samuel Beckett, who was Irish, began to publish frequently in Paris. *Malloy, Malone Dies, The Unnamable,* and *Waiting for Godot,* all originally written in French, were published between 1950

Waiting for Godot by Samuel Beckett; The Acting Company on Tour for the John F. Kennedy Center for the Performing Arts. Directed by the late Alan Schneider for the twenty-fifth anniversary production of *Waiting for Godot.* Photo by Martha Swope.

and 1952. Sixteen remarkable years later, Beckett was awarded the Nobel Prize for Literature—a prize that recognized the man as a renowned playwright and the Absurd movement as a major force in the world of literature. Early in the Absurd movement, Beckett was usually associated with Ionesco, a fact that severely limited the importance of Beckett. For Ionesco, absurdity meant uproarious farce; for Beckett, absurdity meant a life lived in isolation and despair. Hence, Beckett's vision of the world is not as irrational and unpredictable as is the world depicted by Ionesco. Beckett's unique contribution to the Absurd movement is his view that man's absurdity is simply an outgrowth of his self-conscious condition. As man approaches the end of the game (i.e., life), he remains, above all, rational and precise. The best man can do is pass the waiting time as painlessly as possible. He can plot his life and calculate his actions, making himself ''sane'' by repetitious patter and vaudeville calamities (e.g., pratfalls and collapsing trousers). This is both the worst and the best that can befall man. The best that man can hope for! The comic and tragic merge in Beckett's plays (*Endgame, Happy Days, Krapp's Last Tape, Play*). Any line spoken in a Beckett play can provoke either reaction. Actions, characters, dialogue, and business are a tragicomic commentary on the infinite complexities of our daily lives.

Jean Genet was primarily interested in exploring the spatial and optical possibilities of the theatre. His plays are renderings of ceremonies and rituals created to depict a universe in the throes of annihilation. In this sense they are reflective of an influence from Artaud. For Genet, the theatre is the ultimate exorcist of man's fantasies. Characters are reflections of something other than themselves, prisoners of their own imagination (e.g., *The Balcony* and *The Maids*). What appears to be truth is simply an illusion. The real meaning of life lies in the opposite of what is expected: black is white, white is black; evil is good, good is evil; the criminal is virtuous, the virtuous is criminal (*The Blacks*). Again, we see the relation to Artaud and his concept of the theatre and its double, the theatre and life, the theatre and cruelty. Ritual is the means devised to perpetuate some semblance of order in a chaotic universe. In keeping with the Absurdist concept of purposeless existence, Genet heightens and grotesquely shapes his so-called order and puts it on display. As members of the audience, we are confronted by our own image in shattered glass—an image distorted and horrifying. According to Genet, we wear black suits, yellow shoes, excessive makeup, clashing and gaudy colors; we wear patched garments and incorrect masks (we are black, not white; we are white, not black—what is *color?*). We use highly artificial language, often eloquent and poetic; yet we steal from the language of the gutter. We curse and scream. No action onstage justifies our outcast existence. We are all alienated, although we pretend not to be. Agree with it or not, Genet presents a highly effective treatise on the decadence of the individual isolated in society doomed to a meaningless death.

Voice

It is interesting that words and language in Absurd plays are frequently considered part of the spectacle. That is, words are frequently used as sound and noise (therefore, spectacle) rather than for purposes of logical communication. In a way, words are transparent, revealing only immediate meaning. Language seems to "participate" in the theatrical activity, similar to properties and scenery. On the surface, speech is frequently confusing and nonsensical. However, you should play against the emptiness of the stereotyped language. In other words, you must speak the words with energy, variety, and certainty, even when they seem to be meaningless. Silences and pauses are vital in handling language in Absurd plays. Your vocal tools must function exceptionally well to vary your speech patterns, vocal rhythms, and speaking-singing range. Language is often redundant and monotonous. As a result, many audience members reject the material if actors are not especially effective at providing vocal variety to alleviate the monotony. (Of course, you must be selective in providing variety because if it is overdone, you may violate the philosophical intention of the playwright who has deliberately established the tedium of the language.) Careful script analysis by you and your director will clarify whether to apply realistic or nonrealistic vocal techniques.

Exercise 1   Voice—Absurd

1. Select one of the longer speeches by Estragon or Vladimir in a scene from *Waiting for Godot* (the speeches work effectively for both men and women). Practice the speech applying the following techniques:
   a. As realistic prose
   b. As nonsense gibberish through use of strange pauses, inflections, intonations, and so on
   c. As an ephemeral dream
   d. As a mechanical robot
   e. As a didactic message
   f. As primitive, ruthless rage
   g. As philosophic reflection

   Finally, practice the speech with an appropriate mix of any or all of the foregoing techniques. (Ionesco's *The Bald Soprano* or any of his other plays are also particularly well suited to this exercise.)
2. Study and observe the traditional rituals practiced by various churches, lodges, clubs, social organizations, judicial systems, and so on. Select facets of these rituals to use in performing the language of the ritualistic segments in plays by Genet, Beckett, Ionesco, and others of the Absurd style. (For example, the use of incense, candles, and gavels can provide interesting, valid activity for use with many speeches in plays by these authors.)

Movement

Absurd plays are unusually antiliterary and frequently nonverbal because they are linked to ritualistic ceremony, circus activity, and routines and techniques used by commedia dell'arte, itinerant jugglers, mime troupes, music hall burlesques, acrobatics, and silent films (including those of Buster Keaton, Charlie Chaplin, the Keystone Cops, Laurel and Hardy, and the Marx Brothers). In all of these activities complex physical dexterity and precise timing are stressed (the timing is even more important when coordinated with dialogue and sounds). These activities are closely tied to what we think of as popular entertainment, that is, visual escape entertainment, which is often used as a device to pass time. Hence, these activities relate closely to the philosophical premise of the material (e.g., meaningless routine and the passing of hours, days, weeks, months, and years). Your body should be relaxed, disciplined, and nimble.

Exercise 2 Movement—Absurd

1. Everyone become involved in silently arranging twenty chairs in the room. Once arranged, completely rearrange them. Continue rearranging them for a full five minutes.
2. After five minutes of number 1, relieve the monotony by performing a variety of the following activities. Interchange activities at will, always being certain that between each activity you return to some rearrangement of the chairs.
   a. Remove your shoes, shake them out, put them on again.
   b. Practice a soft-shoe shuffle.
   c. Practice juggling two or more objects.
   d. Practice a series of gymnastic or acrobatic exercises.
   e. Rearrange the chairs in the speeded-up tempo of a silent film being run at fast speed.
   f. Vary your tempo in all of these activities by using mechanical robot movement, ephemeral dreamlike movement, Epic alienation techniques, and primitive assault techniques.
3. Return to the rituals studied and practiced in Exercise 1. Perform them pantomimically, void of all dialogue and sound.

Character and Emotion

Character and emotion in Absurd plays range from one-dimensional and lack of feeling to multidimensional and sensitive feeling. For example, Berenger in Ionesco's *Rhinoceros* is a full-dimensional, human characterization that permits the use of Stanislavski's techniques. On the other hand, the characters in Ionesco's *The Bald Soprano* are fundamentally one-dimensional stereotypes. Berenger passes through a gamut of emotion, whereas *Soprano's* characters seem relatively free of feeling. In view of the fact that Absurd characters frequently seem involved in pointless activity devoid of traditional plot action, it is best not to ask, What has happened in the past? and What comes next? but rather, What is happening *now?* Neither the actor nor the audience can rely on cause and effect and logical sequence of motivated action. We can only be amused or shocked by the often grotesque nature of the spontaneous movement.

Most characters in Absurd plays are based on realism. However, at some point in the play the authors usually distort reality by dehumanization or by having inanimate objects take on life. Absurdist playwrights utilize many of the alienating techniques of Epic Theatre. In fact, some critics believe Absurdist playwrights are more effective alienists than was Brecht (by use of the proliferation of objects, changes in identity, and repetition of language and action).

Absurd material also lends itself well to the primitive assault techniques of Artaud. For example, Absurd characters assault the sensibilities of an audience by such activity as "urinating" onstage and crudely masticating food (see Beckett's *Krapp's Last Tape*). An actor can perform these activities alternately as realistic behavior or as ritualistic behavior. The latter is germane to Artaud's intentions. For example, peeling and eating a piece of fruit can be performed as primitive man's discovery of nourishment.

At times, the nonrealistic distortion of robot and ephemeral dreamlike behavior can also be used effectively in Absurd theatre. For example, Lucky and Pozzo in *Waiting for Godot* seem almost to be dehumanized robots of power and slavery. In the same play, Didi and Gogo (Vladimir and Estragon) speak of living in a dream. In these moments the actors can permit the characters to react as in a dream state.

Line-by-line textual analysis will help you find the correct style and mood and provide the appropriate interpretation. Absurdist playwrights have a tendency to carry poetry, farce, dialogue, and cabaret activity to excess. When a conflict exists between realistic and nonrealistic characterization and emotion, you are usually well advised to play the humor arising from the incongruity. It is this safety valve of humor that makes the Absurd character palatable to most audiences. At such moments you generally need not rely upon the realistic techniques of Stanislavski for motivation or probe for deep emotion. Simply perform the immediate action.

Creating Absurd characters and emotion requires acute awareness of your own personality and physical and mental resources. The Absurd acting style is a sensitive combination of several preceding styles (e.g., Realism, Naturalism, Expressionism, and Epic, plus vaudeville humor). Its execution necessitates using an inordinate amount of your own personality traits and your own behavioral habits and routines. Once again, personalization is the key to success—ability to skillfully observe your world, sensitive and active perception of your own sensory equipment, vivid imagination, and active knowledge of how your body rhythms fluctuate as you pass the time or engage in routine life activities.

Above all, understand the intentions of the playwright. Do not lose yourself in the interchangeable nature of his vision of the universe. The last and the next moment onstage are unimportant in light of the question, What is happening *now?* Your task is to penetrate both the internal and external realities of action *moment by moment.*

Exercise 3   Character and Emotion

1. Select a monologue from a character of your choice from one of the Absurd plays given in the list at the end of this chapter. Perform the monologue after analysis, incorporating the types of character and emotion just discussed (e.g., realistic, expressionistic, Epic, and cabaret or vaudeville). Your character and emotion should range from multidimensional and real to simplistic and nonreal. For the purpose of the exercise, do not hesitate to superimpose some of these stylistic techniques for the sake of practice. However, you should note that an effective mix of styles cannot usually be accomplished in a single monologue (an exception might be Lucky's unique monologue from *Waiting for Godot*).

2. Using the famous monologue by Lucky from Act One of *Waiting For Godot,* create and perform a series of rituals that help reveal the complex character and emotion revealed by Lucky in this ideal personification of the Absurd effectively dramatized.

In the 1960s the Absurd movement splintered. The final style for our examination is the natural extension of the combination of techniques used in Absurd drama. Playwrights ranging from Eugene O'Neill at the beginning of the twentieth century to such contemporary artists as Harold Pinter intermingle the stylistic considerations prevalent in the last ninety or more years. Our remaining study is of the proliferation of eclectic, stylistic acting techniques.

Suggested Characters and Plays for Scene Work

Camus, Albert

Caligula, Caesonia, Scipio
Caligula

Sartre, Jean-Paul

Goetz, Heinrich, Nasti, Tetzel, Hilda, Cathrine
The Devil and the Good Lord
Kean, Soloman, Anna, Amy, Eleana
Kean
Estelle, Inez, Garcin
No Exit

Orestes, Electra, Aegistheus, Clytemnestra
The Flies

Jarry, Alfred

Ubu Roi
Ubu Roi

Pirandello, Luigi

Mother, Father, Stepdaughter, Son
Six Characters in Search of an Author

Beckett, Samuel

Vladamir, Estragon, Lucky, Pozzo
Waiting for Godot
Krapp
Krapp's Last Tape
Winnie, Willy
Happy Days
Nagg, Nell, Hamm, Clove
Endgame

Ionesco, Eugene

Mr. Smith, Mrs. Smith, Mr.
Martin, Mrs. Martin, The Firechief
The Bald Soprano
Old Man, Old Woman
The Chairs

Pupil, Professor
The Lesson
Berenger, Daisy, Jean
Rhinoceros

Genet, Jean

Claire, Solange
The Maids
Green Eyes, Maurice, Lafranc
Deathwatch
The Bishop, Irma, The Chief of
Police, The Judge
The Balcony
Archibald, Deodatus, Adelaide,
Newport News, Augusta, Felicity,
Diouf
The Blacks

The playwrights included in this list were early leaders of Absurd drama. Later and related dramatists are discussed in chapter 19.

Actor Checklist   Absurd

Voice	Words, sound, and noise as spectacle; energy; variety; certainty; unusual use of silence and pause; rhythmic; monotone; wide range; combination of real and nonreal techniques.
Movement	Mix of realistic, nonrealistic, ritualistic, circus, commedia, acrobatics, silent films; dexterity and precise timing; muscles relaxed; disciplined and nimble; vaudeville and dance activity; balance of presentational and representational mode.
Gestures	Inventive; disciplined; fluid; considerably oriented to hands and feet.
Pantomimic Dramatization	Inventive as appropriate to routine behavior of life, combined with theatrical and entertainment techniques; see Movement.
Character	Combination of multidimensional and complex with stereotype and simplistic; heavily oriented to action of the moment; real to nonreal.
Emotion	Same combination as described for Character; special use of primitive, ritualistic Artaud techniques.
Ideas	Clear and usually relevant to Existentialism.

Language	Part of theatrical spectacle; often illogical; often immediate meaning only; often stereotyped and clichéd; combination ranging from prose to lyric poetry; philosophical—usually Existentialism.
Mood and Atmosphere	Extremely varied; at times, moment-to-moment combination of serious and comic.
Pace and Tempo	Generally used in consistently fast or consistently slow tempo.
Special Techniques	Cabaret or vaudeville activity; soft-shoe and tap dancing, pratfalls, tumbling, juggling, magic, balancing, sight gags, and slapstick.

Selective Readings

Abel, Lionel. *Metatheatre.* New York: Hill and Wang, 1963.

Artaud, Antonin. *The Theatre and Its Double.* Translated by Mary Caroline Richards. New York: Grove Press, 1958.

Barnard, G. C. *Samuel Beckett: A New Approach.* New York: Dodd, Mead & Co., 1960.

Brustein, Robert. *The Theatre of Revolt: An Approach to Modern Drama.* Boston: Little, Brown and Co., 1964.

Chiari, Joseph. *The Contemporary French Theatre: The Flight from Naturalism.* London: Barrie and Rockliff, 1958.

Cohn, Ruby, ed. *Casebook on Waiting for Godot.* New York: Grove Press, 1967.

———. *Just Play: Beckett's Theatre.* Princeton, N.J.: Princeton University Press, 1979.

Esslin, Martin. *Absurd Drama.* London: Penguin Books, 1965.

———. *The Theatre of the Absurd.* rev. ed. Garden City, N.J.: Doubleday & Co., 1969.

Foreman, Richard, et al. *The Theatre of Images.* Edited by Bonnie Maranca. New York: Drama Book Specialists, 1977.

Grossvogel, David. *Brecht, Ionesco, Beckett, Genet: Four Playwrights and a Postscript.* Ithaca: Cornell University Press, 1962.

Guicharnaud, Jacques. *Modern French Theatre from Giraudoux to Beckett.* New Haven, Conn.: Yale University Press, 1961.

Innes, Christopher. *Holy Theatre: Ritual and the Avant Garde.* New York: Cambridge University Press, 1981.

Killinger, John. *World in Collapse: The Vision of Absurd Drama.* New York: Dell Publishing Co., 1971.

Kostelanetz, Richard. *The Theatre of Mixed Means.* New York: The Dial Press, Inc., 1968.

Ragusa, Olga. *Pirandello: An Approach to His Theatre.* New York: Columbia University Press, 1980.

Styan, J. L. *The Dark Comedy: The Development of Modern Comic Tragedy.* Cambridge: The University Press, 1962.

Valency, Maurice. *The End of the World: An Introduction to Contemporary Drama.* New York, 1980.

Suggested Filmography

1. *A Very Handy Man.* 1966. Pirandello.
2. *The Balcony.* 1963. Continental. Playwright—Genet. Director—Joseph Strick. With Shelley Winters and Peter Falk.
3. *The Maids.* 1975. British-Canadian. American Film Theatre. Playwright—Jean Genet. Director—Christopher Miles. With Glenda Jackson.
4. *Rhinoceros.* 1974. American Film Theatre. Playwright—Eugene Ionesco. With Zero Mostel, Gene Wilder.

Eclectic: Intermingling

. . . conglomerations of past and present stages of civilizations, bits from books and newspapers, scraps of humanity, rags and tatters of fine clothing, patched together. . . .

August Strindberg
discussing plays and characters in
Preface to Miss Julie

I can sum up none of my plays. I can describe none of them, except to say: That is what happened. That is what they said. That is what they did.

Harold Pinter
from a speech by Harold Pinter
at The University of Hamburg,
June 4, 1970

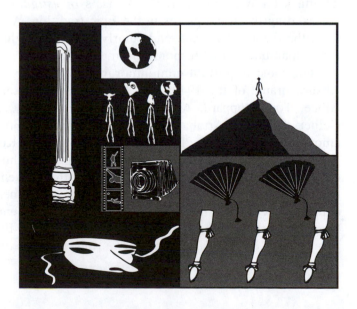

Overview of Eclectic

Theatre in the Western Hemisphere in the 1960s, 1970s, and 1980s was somewhat diffused. The mixing of styles that followed the nonrealistic movements were embellished by new contributions from Brecht and the Absurdists. However, in those three decades, playwrights generally wrote various styles to produce an extremely Eclectic drama and, as a result, an extremely Eclectic style of acting. *Eclectic* refers to material drawn from several sources, much as just described by Strindberg. The result is plays that are difficult to categorize or label. As Pinter noted at the beginning of this chapter, often the plays cannot be summed up or described. They merely happen.

What are the results of the eclectic intermix of Realism, nonrealism, Brecht Epic Theatre, and Absurd drama? Several groupings of dramatists need to be discussed.

The most important playwrights influenced by Brecht Epic Theatre include Max Frisch, Rolf Hochhuth, and Peter Weiss. Each of these authors used history as the basis for interpretation of the present. Also, dramatic structure, use of music, and other staging techniques in their plays clearly illustrate Epic influence. However, each author modifies that influence and creates fresh theatrical experience that is best categorized as Eclectic. Also, they tend to use less Asian material, although Frisch does use the technique in *The Chinese Wall*. Also their plays have more emotional content and less focus on didacticism. *The Firebugs* is one of the most important plays by Frisch. *The Deputy* by Hochhuth is a modern landmark of controversy because of its attack on the Catholic church and Pope Pius XII. Hochhuth's *Soldiers* is similarly controversial because of its attack on Winston Churchill. Weiss's *Investigation* and *Marat/Sade* are exciting theatrical pieces in the Epic tradition. Again, Weiss differs from the theory of Brecht, particularly in premises that elicit emotional rather than intellectual response from an audience.

The most important contemporary playwrights influenced by the Absurd drama of the 1940s and 1950s include Harold Pinter, Edward Albee, Tom Stoppard, Arthur Kopit, David Storey, Boris Vian, Jack Gelber, Fernando Arrabal, Jack Richardson, and Francois Billetdoux, among others. Of these, Pinter, Albee, Stoppard, and Kopit are frequently produced in the United States. Each of these playwrights has written plays directly in the Absurd vein but perhaps with an even greater sense of humor than the early European leaders of the movement. Some of these authors have also written plays that are distinctly entrenched in other forms and styles such as Realism, Symbolism, and Epic. For example, Albee's *Zoo Story, The Sandbox, The American Dream,* and *Tiny Alice* are Absurdist, but *Who's Afraid of Virginia Woolf?* is closely related to Realism and Symbolism. Kopit's *Oh, Dad, Poor Dad* is Absurdist, but *Indians* is in the Epic manner. Stoppard's plays are the most consistently Absurdist but have fresh, contemporary humor. Storey's plays are considerably more realistic than Absurd.

Pinter's plays are especially unique in use of character, environment, language, and silence. In Pinter's plays, characters handle the menace of the unknown and unspoken with comic fright. Unable to come to grips with reality, they dwell miserably in a room that becomes their entire world. Settings have only realistic overtones; conversations begin with comic realism. With varying rhythm, comedy reveals the hidden menace that threatens the characters. The colloquial pattern of London speech degenerates into repetition, staccato rhythm, and finally, silence. Minds wander through vague recollection with no certainty about what happened or what is happening (*Old Times* and *No Man's Land*). In his early plays, the menacing quality climaxes in violent action (such as when Bert Hudd attacks a blind Negro in *The Room*). After *The Caretaker* and *The Birthday Party,* Pinter used sex as the prime force in the breakdown of an individual (e.g., *The Homecoming, Old Times* and *Betrayal*).

In contrast to Pinter, Albee uses vicious comic dialogue to reveal the serious-tragic aspect of human experience. Albee's serious drama does not grow out of the comedy (as does Pinter's). The serious intent of Albee's characters, their motivation, and their underlying justification force action to be immediately serious, although occasionally sentimental. Albee's biting, satirical, highly intense dialogue leaps at an audience (e.g., *Who's Afraid of Virginia Woolf?*). Recently, he has written plays in the manner of the Eclectic playwrights who mix several styles (e.g., *A Delicate Balance, All Over, Seascape, Tiny Alice, Malcolm, The Ballad of the Sad Cafe, Everything in the Garden, Listening, Counting the Ways,* and *The Lady From Dubuque*).

Both Pinter and Albee reject the Absurd label. They consider their plays to be highly personal forms of symbolic Realism and basically comic.

Earlier in the century, Eugene O'Neill, James Thurber, George S. Kaufman, Moss Hart, and Thornton Wilder wrote plays in such a variety of styles that in an overall view of their work they may best be called Eclectic. American authors such as Sherwood Anderson, Elmer Rice, Paul Green, Carson McCullers, Mary Chase, William Saroyan, and others have contributed a generally Eclectic drama whose roots are in realism with branches in nonrealism. In France, Jean Cocteau and Jean Giraudoux did much the same thing, with some effort at a return to Classicism. Maxwell

Anderson, T. S. Eliot, Christopher Fry, Federico García Lorca, Archibald MacLeish, and others led the way into modern poetic verse drama.

Perhaps O'Neill, the late Tennessee Williams, Arthur Miller, Albee, Lanford Wilson, and Sam Shepard may be considered the most successful, popular, and lasting American dramatists of this century. (In recent years, such playwrights as David Mamet, David Rabe, August Wilson, Tina Howe, Marsha Norman, Beth Henley, Caryl Churchill, and others also reveal potential as writers with lasting or universal appeal—however, for purposes of this discussion, the focus goes to O'Neill, Williams, Miller, Albee, Lanford Wilson, and Shepard among the American playwrights.) The plays of these six playwrights combine many styles that draw material from many sources. Because of this, it is difficult to place their work in an overall category. For example, Miller's *Death of a Salesman* and Williams's *The Glass Menagerie* exemplify detailed Naturalism mixed with Expressionism. At times, pure stylistic form was used principally by O'Neill. For example, O'Neill's *Lazarus Laughed* is Epic in nature; *The Hairy Ape, The Great God Brown,* and *Emperor Jones* are all Expressionism; *Beyond the Horizon* is Realism; *Long Day's Journey into Night* is Naturalism; *Mourning Becomes Electra* is based on the classical Greek *Oresteia;* and *Strange Interlude* is an intermix of several styles. O'Neill's canon of plays envelops a mixture of forms and styles probably unparalleled in dramatic history. Most of the plays of O'Neill, Williams, Miller, Albee, Lanford Wilson, and Shepard permit the Naturalism approach to character creation as determined by role analysis, personalization, and Stanislavski techniques. Nonetheless, the varied Eclectic influence of the nonrealists on these authors at times obligates an actor to draw from other style sources ranging from Absurd techniques to Epic and Expressionism techniques. For example, such plays as Miller's *The Creation of The World and Other Business* and *After the Fall,* Williams's *Camino Real* and *The Milk Train Doesn't Stop Here Anymore,* Albee's *Tiny Alice* and *Seascape,* Lanford Wilson's *The Rimers of Eldritch* and *The Mound Builders,* and Shepard's *Operation Sidewinder, The Tooth of Crime* and *Seduced* all require a combination of acting styles dependent upon careful analysis. Accordingly, an actor is best trained to handle the Eclectic body of work offered by these six great American authors *after* training in all the other major twentieth-century acting styles.

In recent years, the motivation of many of the new Eclectic theatre artists was primarily nonverbal. They created basically out of improvisational techniques and modern dance under the direction of an artist-leader rather than of a director. The artist-leader differed from a director in that the artist-leader was often a creative performer onstage with the actors, rather than a backstage re-creative interpreter who assists actors. Much of the Eclectic theatrical expression centered on group efforts. The groups were closely united by common goals and strong social and political commitments. Their goal was a total theatre activity aimed at bringing the masses into the theatre again.

Artaud championed the concept of total theatre, which correlates with Eclectic theatre. This concept became highly influential in theatre movements of the 1960s and beyond. Artaud believed that theatre should be an interplay and synthesis of music, movement, voice, scenery, and lighting—a convergence of the arts as sensory modalities, transmitting information through integrated effects. The controlling factor in this theatre was the emotional ordering of what is often called "multimedia scenography." Artaud's theatre was nonliterary and emphasized dance, sound, and light as the primary expressions of language. Movement

Buried Child by Sam Shepard, at the Circle Repertory Company, New York City; Marshall W. Mason, artistic director. Photograph by Gerry Goodstein.

became highly stylized, similar to ancient hieroglyphic writings in which one sign (e.g., gesture or movement) combined many different meanings in a single prealphabetical symbol or emblem. Ideally, the space where a performer worked was unlimited and thereby no restrictions were placed. Marshall McLuhan, the late modern media theorist, saw this theatre as a "retribalization" of culture that focused on participation, tactility, and sculptural values. Artaud wanted a return to an archaic, primitive, ceremonial mode of expression. He wished to rediscover the "other" or intangible meaning of our existence, the deeper perceptions of the sensory and abstract. Artaud was too far ahead of his time to have significant impact. His was a theatre of the future—a theatre of dynamic forms and colors, filled with chaotic but expressive movement (e.g., jugglers, dancers, and gymnasts). Thirty years early, Artaud established the foundation for the Eclectic theatre of the 1960s and beyond.

The artist-leader attempted to elicit a group expression with didactic purposes (social, political, and religious) in the Brechtian tradition. As a result, the improvisational actor of the sixties became a performer of tasks rather than a creator of roles. The performer's own personality provided some characterization—but impersonation in much of this theatre activity was a dead issue. The goal was a compatible group effort in a highly charged theatrical presentation. Actual audience participation in the theatrical event was encouraged by some groups. Note that Brecht did not desire audience participation in the theatre event itself. He and Artaud wanted audiences to think and proceed to social action after the event.

Starting in the 1960s and continuing into the 1980s, there was a tremendous upsurge in Eclectic theatrical innovation in an attempt to explore new dramatic expressions in which the written word was reexamined and reshaped. The innovation also produced a new kind of actor, playwright, director, and scene designer, as well as a new kind of audience. The world of the sixties, seventies, and eighties evolved in flux, changing and adapting to a new society whose ethics and values produced a new liberalism in social, political, and cultural patterns. The new dramatists rejected many of the concepts of Realism and Naturalism, particularly in stage scenery and environment. Since Realism and Naturalism perpetuated the traditional social order in which humanity was emphasized and man's quest for freedom repressed, they were not harmonious with the political atmosphere of the times. Theatre innovators of the sixties and early seventies shared the Absurdist playwrights' distrust of the written word, of language, of dialogue. They limited the meaning and structure of words, and they communicated ideas with imprecision and inaccuracy. Late in the seventies, a trend returned toward traditional literary and scripted plays. In the eighties, a vast blend of theatre activity burgeoned, including revivals of earlier plays, productions of standard, realistic plays, performances of experimental plays, and productions of innovative works such as *Sweeney Todd; Evita;* the multihour "canvas" of the adapted Charles Dickens piece *Nicholas Nickleby;* the late Michael Bennett's musical success *Dream Girls;* and Kopit's musical based on a Felini film, *Nine.* Bennett's *A Chorus Line* established new box office records for length of run on Broadway. Extravagant musicals continued to dominate the New York City theatre scene, such as *Cats, Starlight Express, Les Miserables, The Phantom of the Opera,* and *Jerome Robbins' Broadway.* The more significant work in comedy continued to come from Neil Simon, with his autobiographical trilogy *Brighton Beach Memoirs, Biloxi Blues,* and *Broadway Bound.* Among the leading writers of serious drama, major contributions were made by August Wilson, whose plays concerned with the black experience in America (such as *Fences* and *The Piano Lesson*) created a lasting impact.

Voice

It is obvious that vocal training for the Eclectic drama of the late twentieth century requires a totally trained mechanism. The intermingling of styles requires extensive range, effortless articulation and effective vocal production, and flexible variation.

Exercise 1 Voice—Eclectic
1. Create an improvisation based on a job interview. Define your circumstances clearly. Perform the improvisation in three different ways.
   a. With no human speech, relying solely on sounds and noises
   b. With no human speech, relying solely on gibberish, which unlike sounds and noises, includes use of consonants and vowels
   c. Using human speech with good range, articulation, projection, and variety
2. Select a song from a modern musical of your choice and within your vocal range and acting type. Prepare and practice the song without and with musical accompaniment. (Ideally, use a pianist to accompany you.)

Movement

Eclectic drama in the late twentieth century has been unusually oriented toward movement and physical, nonverbal activity. The experimental groups of the 1960s were particularly outstanding for their focus on movement. These troupes went so far as to eliminate standard theatrical environment, frequently leaving the performer with only his body as the means of communication. It follows that the contemporary actor working in Eclectic drama must possess a totally trained physical apparatus. In today's theatre, dance training is almost a necessity. Academic and professional training centers also stress fencing, weight training, gymnastics, acrobatics, mime, Asian techniques (such as those found in the Tai Chi Chuan system of movement), the Laban theory of movement (a system of spatial movement), and improvisational games and the Suzuki System.

Exercise 2   Movement—Eclectic

1. Imagine that you are encased in a transparent ice cube.[1] Explore the confines of your rigidly defined space. Perform this exploration with every part of your body. Be aware that the area is extremely cold. Eventually permit your body heat to melt the cube and free you.

(a)

Nicholas Nickleby by Charles Dickens, adapted by David Edgar.
(*a*) Christopher Benjamin and Roger Rees in the Royal Shakespeare Company production. Directed by Trevor Nunn and John Caird and assisted by Leon Rubin; scenery by John Napier and Dermot Hayes, costumes by John Napier, lighting by David Hersey, music by Stephen Oliver. Photographs by Chris Davies, London. (*b*) Lila Kaye, Jule Peasgood, John McEmery, Vincent Crummley, and Roger Rees.

(b)

2. Select several interesting photographs of people in unusual physical positions. Practice moving from an aligned standing position into the physical positions shown in the photographs. From each position, move into another unusual physical position that evolves naturally from your sense of the space you occupy.
3. Position your body in an unusual way, for example, in a squatting position. Explore kinesthetic movement patterns emanating from particular parts of your body. Begin with extensive arm activity, varying movement in direction and tempo. Continue the kinesthetic experience with movement of the head. Continue the exercise by altering the position while using movement from other parts of the body; for example, recline upon your back, lift your legs in the air, and explore space with them.
4. Create an improvisation related to the Garden of Eden. Define your circumstances. Perform the improvisation without language, using movement and sound as the sole means of telling the story.
5. Select a solo and a group dance number from a modern musical play. Prepare and practice the number with musical accompaniment of some sort, ideally with a pianist and drummer.

Character and Emotion

In acting the contemporary Eclectic style of drama, careful textual analysis is necessary. Actors must play the realistic elements when character demands it, perform Brechtian techniques in Epic and intellectual segments, utilize Absurd stand-up cabaret or vaudeville humor at moments, use Artaud assault techniques when appropriate, use improvisation when required, combine nonrealistic and realistic techniques, and generally work with the fundamental of effective personalization. In other words, character and emotion in Eclectic drama range from simplistic to multidimensional, from stereotype to uniquely individual.

As Joseph Chaikin has noted, ''When working on character, it isn't enough just to imitate. What a person says is not as important as where he sees from.''

The contemporary actor should be familiar with and capable of using techniques ranging from Stanislavski to Brecht to Artaud to Grotowski to Chaikin to Tommy Tune to Hal Prince. The actor should understand human emotion and know when and how to use it or restrict it. The contemporary actor is often called upon to be playwright, director, and performer. In other words, full personalization is at work. It is probably to the credit of contemporary theatre with its Eclectic base that the art of the actor in terms of character, emotion, movement, and voice seems to be moving to the forefront of dramatic activity. Also, much of the drama in recent years requires skill in audience participation techniques, use of partial or full nudity, use of abusive, profane language, and heightened sexual activity. The so-called Power Plays are examples of such drama (see *The Drama Review,* vol. 14, no. 4, September 1970). Much of this activity carried into film acting in the 1970s and 1980s.

Exercise 3   Character and Emotion—Eclectic

1. Review the character and emotion exercises given in chapters 10 through 18.
2. Create an improvisation whose setting is a cocktail party. Define your circumstances clearly. Begin the cocktail party in a human form. Slowly, begin to change from being human to being nonhuman. Continue the improvisation until the last nonhuman has left the party.
3. Two people perform an improvisation in which there are two clearly defined characters (e.g., an impolite salesman and an irate customer). At various points throughout the improvisation, your instructor or director will call for reversal of roles. Attempt to change roles easily and smoothly in the improvisation.
4. Four people perform an improvisation in which there are four clearly defined characters involved in a specific activity (e.g., four neighborhood women getting ready for a Fourth of July party). When the director so indicates, change acting styles in the following sequence:
   a. Realism
   b. Expressionism
   c. Epic
   d. Absurd
5. Prepare a song and dance from a contemporary musical play in which you must *act* the song and dance, creating believable character and emotion. It may prove helpful to review the instructions in chapter 8 related to "Musical Theatre Auditions."
6. Practice "cold reading" from the many and varied scenes from plays included at the end of this chapter.

The contemporary theatre offers a continually expanding experience for actors. The demands imposed upon the actor are astonishing. The actor should not only study the role (à la Stanislavski), but also identify psychical and physical attributes common to both the character and the actor's personality. Further, he should learn how to work "detached," as in Brecht, often combining all these techniques in one Eclectic, complex performance. The excitement generated by contemporary acting evolves around the attempt to extend a character into life in an organic structure. It is an ongoing experiment. The search to discover an ultimate medium for playing the impulses of a character and yet make that character functional for the stage takes an extraordinary degree of intelligence, discipline, and concentration.

At this point, it may justifiably be asked: What does the contemporary dramatic scene mean in terms of the growth and development of an actor? Where is the training to take place? What is the specific training? And how does the actor train for a theatre in which audience participation is sometimes an integral part of the action onstage?

If university theatre departments, studio schools, and repertory workshops and training programs do not provide the necessary courses in textual analysis, dance, movement, voice, and improvisational techniques, if actors must still fight the concept of the master director who demands complete control in all areas of production and training, we can then only direct actors toward a new way of *thinking* about contemporary acting. Perhaps traditional *conceptions* (too often stereotyped) can be altered to encompass what acting in the theatre *should* be—*an important and respected art.*

Suggested Characters and Plays for Scene Work

Wilde, Oscar

Algernon, Cecily, Gwendelon, John Worthing, Lady Bracknell
The Importance of Being Earnest

Pinter, Harold

Bert, Rose, Mr. Kidd, Mr. Sands, Mrs. Sands
The Room
Max, Sam, Lenny, Joey, Teddy, Ruth
The Homecoming
Sarah, Richard
The Lover
All characters
Other Places
Anna, Kate, Deeley
Old Times
Mich, Aston, Davies
The Caretaker
Meg, Stanley, Petey, Lulu, Goldberg, McCann
The Birthday Party
All characters
No Man's Land
Jerry, Emma, Robert
Betrayal
All characters
The Hothouse

Stoppard, Tom

Rosencrantz, Guildenstern, The Player
Rosencrantz and Guildenstern Are Dead
Moon, Birdboot, Felicity, Cynthia, Hound
The Real Inspector Hound
George, Dorothy, Archie, Bones, Crouch
Jumpers
Henry Carr
Travesties
All characters
Dirty Linen and
New-Found-Land
All characters
Night and Day
All characters
Undiscovered Country
The Real Thing

Bolt, Robert

Sir Thomas More, Henry VIII
A Man for All Seasons
Mary, Elizabeth
Vivat! Vivat! Regina!

Anouilh, Jean
> Becket, Henry
> *Becket*
> Antigone, Creon
> *Antigone*
> All characters
> *Hurlyburly*

Feiffer, Jules
> Patsy, Marjorie, Carol, Alfred,
> Reverend Dupas
> *Little Murders*
> All characters
> *Knock, Knock*

Storey, David
> Harry, Jack, Marjorie, Cathleen
> *Home*
> The Athletes
> *The Changing Room*
> Ewbank, Claire, Maurice, Kay,
> Marshall
> *The Contractor*

Valdez, Luis
> All characters
> *Zoot Suit*

Stein, Joseph
> Tevye, Motel, Golde
> *Fiddler on the Roof*

Barry, Julian
> Lenny
> *Lenny*

Frisch, Max
> Biedermann, Babette, Sepp, Will
> *The Firebugs*
> The Contemporary, The Maskers
> *The Chinese Wall*

Durrenmatt, Friedrich
> Claire, Anton, Teacher
> *The Visit*
> Newton, Einstein, Mobiles
> *The Physicists*

Hochhuth, Rolf
> Father Riccardo, Gerstein, Pope
> Pius XII
> *The Deputy*
> Churchill, Dorland, Bell, Helen
> *Soldiers*

Weiss, Peter
> DeSade, Marat, Charlotte
> *Marat/Sade*
> All characters
> *The Investigation*

Ayckbourn, Alan
> Jane, Sidney, Ronald, Marion,
> Eva, Geoffrey
> *Absurd Person Singular*
> All characters
> *The Norman Conquests*
> All characters
> *How the Other Half Loves*
> All characters
> *Bedroom Farce*
> All characters
> *Absent Friends*
> *Woman in Mind*

Macleish, Archibald
> Zuss, Nickles, J. B., Sarah
> *J. B.*

Wilson, Lanford
> The People, The Residents
> *The Hot L Baltimore*
> Prof. Howe, Cynthia, Kirsten,
> D. K. Eriksen, Dan and Jean
> Loggins, Chad
> *The Mound Builders*
> All characters
> *The Fifth of July*
> Sally, Matt
> *Talley's Folly*
> All characters
> *A Tale Told*
> All characters
> *Balm in Gilead*
> All characters
> *The Rimers of Eldritch*

All characters
The Gingham Dog
All characters
Lemon Sky
All characters
Angels Fall
Talley & Son
Burn This

Hopkins, John

Julian, David, Alan, Jacqueline
Find Your Way Home

Shaffer, Peter

All characters
Equus
Antonio Salieri, Wolfgang
Amadeus Mozart, Constanze
Weber
Amadeus

van Itallie, Jean-Claude

Applicants, Interviewers
Interview
Hal, Susan, George
T.V.
Motel-Keeper, Man, Woman
Motel
The Group
The Serpent
All characters
Struck Dumb
(co-authored with Joseph
Chaikin)

Lawrence, Jerome, and Robert E. Lee

All major characters
Inherit the Wind
All major characters
First Monday in October
All characters
The Gang's All Here
Jabberwock
The Night Thoreau Spent in Jail
Only in America

Shange, Ntozake

All characters
*For Colored Girls Who Have
Considered Suicide When the
Rainbow is Enuf*

Jones, LeRoi (Imamu Amiri Baraka)

Clay, Lula
Dutchman
Grace, Walker, Easley
The Slave

Hanley, William

Glas, Randell, Rosie
*Slow Dance on the Killing
Ground*

Baldwin, James

Richard, Meridian, Lyle, Parnell,
Juanita
Blues for Mister Charlie

Gordone, Charles

Johnny, Gabe, Cora, Shanty,
Sweets
No Place to Be Somebody

Mason, Judi A.

All characters
Livin' Fat

Bullins, Ed

All characters
The Electronic Nigger
All characters
Goin' A Buffalo

Sherwood, Robert

Abe, Ann
Abe Lincoln in Illinois

Allen, Woody

Allan, Nancy, Bogart, Sharon,
Vanessa, Linda, Dick, Gina,
Barbara
Play It Again, Sam
All characters
Don't Drink the Water
All characters
The Floating Light Bulb

Ribman, Ronald
Fredrich, Richard, Miss Mudurga, Joseph
Cold Storage
All characters
Sweet Table at the Richelieu

Gray, Simon
All characters
Butley
Simon, Dave, Stephen, Jeff, Davina, Wood, Beth
Otherwise Engaged
All characters
Quartermaine's Terms
The Common Pursuit

Pinero, Miguel
Juan, Longshoe, Clark, Cupcakes, Ice, El Raheen, Blanca, Mr. Nett, Gypsy, Omar, Paco, Mr. Brown, Sgt. Morrison, Capt. Allard
Short Eyes

Athayde, Roberto
Miss Margarida, Student-Actor
Miss Margarida's Way

Coburn, D. L.
All characters
The Gin Game

Friel, Brian
Gar (Private and Public), Madge
Philadelphia, Here I Come!

Shaffer, Anthony
Bartholomew, Stenning, Elizabeth, Millie
Murderer

Milo, Andrew
Sleuth

Parnell, Robert
Stephen Hurt, Christine, William, Liz
Sorrows of Stephen
All characters
Romance Language

Clark, Brian
Ken Harrison, Dr. Emerson, Dr. Scott, Mrs. Byle, Nurse
Whose Life Is It, Anyway?

Pomerance, Bernard
Frederick, Treves, John Merrick, Mrs. Kendal
The Elephant Man

Davis, Bill C.
Father, Tim Farley, Mark Dolson
Mass Appeal
All characters
Wrestlers

Noonan, John Ford
Maude, Hannah
A Couple's White Chicks Sitting Around Talking

Cryer, Gretchen and Nancy Ford
All characters
I'm Getting My Act Together and Taking It on the Road

Sherman, Martin
All characters
Bent

Norman, Marsha
All characters
Getting Out
Jessie, Thelma
'Night, Mother

Giovanni, Paul
All characters
The Crucifier of Blood

Deane, Hamilton and John L. Balderston
All characters
Dracula

Fugard, Athol
All characters
Blood Knot

All characters
A Lesson from Aloes

All characters
Master Harold and the Boys
Hello and Goodbye
Boesman and Lena
Sizwe Bansi Is Dead and *The Island* (with John Kani and Winston Ntshona)
Statements After an Arrest Under the Immortality Act
A Place with the Pigs
The Road to Mecca

Doctorow, E. L.

Edgar, Joan
Drinks Before Dinner

Thompson, Ernest

Norman, Ethel, Charlie, Chelsea, Billy Rae
On Golden Pond
The West Side Waltz

Hirson, Roger O. and Stephen Schwartz

Pippin, Charles, Fastrada, Berthe, Catherine, Leading Player
Pippin

Jacobs, Jim and Warren Casey

All characters
Grease

Simon, Neil, Burt Bacharach, and Hal David

(based on a screenplay by Billy Wilder)
All characters
Promises, Promises

Simon, Neil, Marvin Hamlisch, and Carole Bayer Sager

All characters
They're Playing Our Song

Furth, George and Stephen Sondheim

All characters
Company

Kirkwood, James, Marvin Hamlisch, Nicholas Dante, and Edward Kleban

All characters
A Chorus Line

Wheeler, Hugh and Stephen Sondheim

(based on a version of *Sweeney Todd* by Christopher Bond)
All characters
Sweeney Todd
A Little Night Music

Edgar, David (adapter; based on the book by Charles Dickens)

All characters
The Life & Adventures of Nicholas Nickleby

Eyen, Tom and Henry Krieger

All characters
Dream Girls

Sondheim, Stephen and James Lapine

George and Dot
Sunday in the Park with George
Into the Woods

Webber, Andrew Lloyd

All characters
Cats (based on a book by T. S. Eliot)
Joseph and the Amazing Technicolor Dreamcoat
Jesus Christ Superstar
Evita (with Tim Rice)
Song and Dance
Starlight Express

Brenton, Howard and David Hare

All characters
Pravda

Hare, David

All characters
Plenty

Hampton, Christopher
　All characters
　　Les Liaison Dangeruses

Glowacki, Janusz
　All characters
　　Cinders
　　Hunting Cockroaches

Wolfe, George C.
　All characters
　　The Colored Museum

Churchill, Caryl
　All characters
　　Top Girls
　　Fen
　　Cloud 9

Fo, Dario
　All characters
　　*Accidental Death of an
　　Anarchist*

Barnes, Peter
　All characters
　　Red Noses

Fornes, Maria Irene
　All characters
　　Abingdon Square

Weidman, John and Stephen Sondheim
　All characters
　　Pacific Overtures

Hwang, David Henry
　All characters
　　M. Butterfly

Ashman, Howard
　All characters
　　The Little Shop of Horrors

Barry, P. J.
　All characters
　　The Octette Bridge Club

Bishop, John
　All characters
　　The Trip Back Down
　　*Musical Comedy Murders of
　　1940*

Bogosian, Eric
　All characters
　　Talk Radio

Brady, Michael
　All characters
　　To Gillian on Her 37th Birthday

Bramble, Mark
　All characters
　　Barnum

Byrne, John
　All characters
　　The Slab Boys

Chambers, Jane
　All characters
　　Blue Fish Cove

Collins, Kathleen
　All characters
　　Brothers

DeLillo, Don
　All characters
　　The Day Room

DiFusco, John, et al.
　All characters
　　Tracers

Diggs, Elizabeth
　All characters
　　Close Ties

Frayn, Michael
　All characters
　　Benefactors
　　Noises Off
　　Wild Hone (based on
　　Chekhov)

Fuller, Charles
　All characters
　　Zooman and the Sign
　　Soldier's Play

Gonzales, Gloria
　All characters
　　Curtains

Gray, Amlin
　All characters
　　How I Got That Story

Griffin, Susan
　All characters
　　Voices

Hanff, Helen
　All characters
　　84 Charing Cross Road

Harling, Robert
　All characters
　　Steel Magnolias

Harwood, Ronald
　All characters
　　The Dresser

Hauptman, William and Roger Miller
　All characters
　　Big River

Heifner, Jack
　All characters
　　Vanities

Hoffman, William
　All characters
　　As Is

Holmes, Rupert
　All characters
　　The Mystery of Edwin Drood

Jacker, Corrine
　All characters
　　Harry Outside
　　My Life

Kesselman, Wendy
　All characters
　　My Sister in This House

King, Larry L.
　All characters
　　The Night Hank Williams Died

Larson, Larry and Levi Lee
　All characters
　　The Illuminati

Luce, William
　Emily Dickinson
　　The Belle of Amherst

McIntyre, Dennis
　All characters
　　Split Second

Myers, Patrick
　Taylor, Harold
　　K2

Miller, Alan
　All characters
　　The Fox

Miller, Terry
　All characters
　　*The Miss Hamford Beauty
　　Pageant and Battle of the Bands*

Moon, Gerald
　All characters
　　Corpse

Nelson, Richard
　All characters
　　Principia Scriptoriae

Nichols, Peter
　All characters
　　Joe Egg
　　Passion

Pape, Ralph
　All characters
　　Say Goodnight, Gracie

Orton, Joe
  All characters
    Loot
    What the Butler Saw

Overmyer, Eric
  All characters
    On the Verge

Pielmeier, John
  All characters
    Agnes of God

Reynolds, Jonathan
  All characters
    Geniuses

Rimmer, David
  All characters
    Album

Roman, Lawrence
  All characters
    Alone Together

Ross, Judith
  All characters
    An Almost Perfect Person

Sackler, Howard
  All characters
    The Great White Hope

Sanchez-Scott, Milcha
  All characters
    Roosters

Taylor, C. P.
  All characters
    And A Nightingale Sang

Uhry, Alfred
  Daisy, Hokey
    Driving Miss Daisy

Vidal, Gore
  All characters
    An Evening with Richard Nixon

Wagner, Jane
  Trudy
    The Search for Signs of
    Intelligent Life in the Universe

Whitemore, Hugh
  All characters
    Pack of Lies
    Breaking the Code

Lebow, Barbara
  All characters
    A Shayna Maidel

Griffin, Tom
  All characters
    The Boys Next Door

Actor Checklist   Eclectic

Voice	Extensive range; effortless articulation and projection; flexible variation; intermix of many stylistic techniques.
Movement	Total body as communicator; dance, mime, gymnastic, acrobatic, Asian, Tai Chi Chuan, Laban, Suzuki System; spatial activity, improvisational; mix of presentational and representational mode; combination of many stylistic techniques.
Gesture	Inventive; varied; flexible.

Pantomimic Dramatization	Inventive; varied; flexible; improvisational theatre; limited use of objects, properties, and costumes.
Character	Ranges from stereotype to uniquely individual and multidimensional; intermingling of many stylistic techniques; at times includes audience contact, nudity, and profanity.
Emotion	Ranges from simplistic to complex; ranges from human to void.
Ideas	Usually complex; oriented heavily to social and political activity; at times extremely Freudian and sexual base.
Language	De-emphasized in some plays; intermingling of many stylistic forms.
Mood and Atmosphere	Varied; experimental theatre oriented to the serious and grotesquely humorous; commercial theatre oriented to comedy and music.
Pace and Tempo	Varied; experimental theatre unusually slow; commercial theatre unusually rapid.
Special Techniques	Analysis and application of intermix of characteristics; diversified grasp of contemporary experimental theatre.

NOTE: Because of the wide scope of contemporary Eclectic acting styles, the suggestions given in this list must be adapted individually according to the particular author, play, and role being acted.

Selective Readings

Bentley, Eric. *The Playwright as Thinker: A Study of Drama in Modern Times.* New York: Harcourt Brace Jovanovich, 1946.

————. *In Search of Theatre.* New York: Alfred A. Knopf, 1953.

Brockett, Oscar G. *Perspectives on Contemporary Theatre.* Baton Rouge, La.: Louisiana State University Press, 1971.

Brook, Peter. *The Empty Space.* New York: Atheneum Publishers, 1968.

Brustein, Robert. *The Third Theatre.* New York: Alfred A. Knopf, 1969.

Burton, Hal. *Acting in the '60's.* London: BBC, 1970.

————. *Great Acting.* New York: Hill and Wang, 1967.

Chaikin, Joseph. "The Open Theatre." *Tulane Drama Review,* Winter, 1964, pp. 191–97.

————. *The Presence of the Actor.* New York: Atheneum, 1972.

Cohn, Ruby. *Currents in Contemporary Drama.* Bloomington, Ind.: Indiana University Press, 1969.

Corrigan, Robert W. *The Theatre in Search of a Fix.* New York: Dell Publishing Co., Delta Books, 1974.

Croyden, Margaret. *Lunatics, Lovers, and Poets: The Contemporary Experimental Theatre.* New York: McGraw-Hill, Inc., 1974.

Dean, Joan F. *Tom Stoppard: Comedy as a Matrix.* Columbia: University of Missouri Press, 1981.

Drama Review, The. No. 71. September, 1976. (Acting in the 1970s.)

Elsom, John. *Post-War British Theatre.* London: Routledge & Kegan Paul, 1979.

Esslin, Martin. *Reflections: Essays in the Modern Theatre.* New York: Doubleday & Co., 1969.

———. *The Peopled Wound: The Work of Harold Pinter.* Garden City, N.Y.: Doubleday & Co., Inc., 1970.

Funke, Lewis, and Booth, John E. *Actors Talk About Acting.* New York: Avon, 1961.

Gardner, R. H. *The Splintered Stage.* New York: Macmillan Co., 1965.

Gassner, John. *Directions in Modern Theatre and Drama.* New York: Holt, Rinehart, and Winston, 1965.

———. *Form and Idea in the Modern Theatre.* New York: Holt, Rinehart, and Winston, 1956.

———. *Theatre at the Crossroads: Plays and Playwrights of Mid-Century American Stage.* New York: Holt, Rinehart, and Winston, 1960.

———. *The Theatre in Our Times: A Survey of the Men, Materials and Movements in the Modern Theatre.* New York: Crown Publishers, 1954.

Goldman, Michael. *The Actor's Freedom: Towards A New Theory of Drama.* New York: Viking, 1975.

Green, Stanley. *The World of Musical Comedy.* San Diego: A. S. Barnes & Co., 1980.

Grotowski, Jerzy. *Towards a Poor Theatre.* New York: Simon & Schuster, 1968.

———. "Holiday." *TDR The Drama Review,* June 1973.

———. "Interview" by Richard Schechner. *TDR The Drama Review,* Fall 1968.

Haues, William. *The Performer in Mass Media.* New York: Hastings House Pub., 1978.

Hayman, Ronald. *Contemporary Playwrights: Harold Pinter.* London: Heinemann Educational Books, 1968. In same series: Samuel Beckett and John Osborne.

Hinchcliffe, Arnold P. *Harold Pinter.* rev. ed. Boston: Twayne Publishers, 1981.

Homan, Sidney. *The Audience as Actor and Character.* Cranbury, N.J.: Bucknell University Press, 1988.

Houghton, Norris. *The Exploding Stage: An Introduction to Twentieth Century Drama.* New York: Weybright & Talley, 1971.

Jenkins, Anthony. *The Theatre of Tom Stoppard.* New York: Cambridge University Press, 1987.

Marranca, Bonnie, ed. *American Dreams: The Imagination of Sam Shepard.* New York: Performing Arts Journal Publications, 1981.

Ottemiller's Index to Plays in Collections. 1900–1985. 7th ed. Edited by Billie M. Connor and Helene Michedlover. Metuchen, N.J.: Scarecrow Press, 1988.

Schechner, Richard. *Performance Theory.* New York: Routledge, 1988.

Smith, Cecil and Glenn Litton. *Musical Comedy in America.* rev. ed. Theatre Arts Books, 1981.

Suggested Filmography

1. *All My Sons.* 1948. Universal. Playwright—Arthur Miller. Director—Irving Reis. With Edward G. Robinson, Burt Lancaster.
2. *All the King's Men.* 1962. Playwright—Robert Penn Warren. With Broderick Crawford.
3. *About Last Night.* 1966. Based on *Sexual Perversity in Chicago* by David Mamet. Director—Edward Zwick. With Rob Lowe, Jim Belushi, Demi Moore.
4. *Agnes of God.* 1985. Playwright—John Pielmeier. Director—Norman Jewison. With Jane Fonda, Anne Bancroft.
5. *Amadeus.* 1984. Playwright—Peter Shaffer. Director—Milos Forman. With F. Murray Abraham, Tom Hulce. Best Picture, Oscar, 1984.
6. *Anna Christie.* 1930. MGM. Playwright—O'Neill. Director—Clarence Brown. With Greta Garbo.
7. *The Birthday Party.* 1970. Playwright—Harold Pinter. Director—Wm. Friedkin. With Robert Shaw.
8. *Boom!* 1968. British. Based on Tennessee Williams's *The Milk Train Doesn't Stop Here Anymore.* Director—Joseph Losey.
9. *Born Yesterday.* 1950. Playwright—Garson Kanin. Director—George Cukor. With Judy Holliday, William Holden.
10. *Bus Stop.* 1956. 20th. Playwright—William Inge. Director—Joshua Logan. With Marilyn Monroe.
11. *The Caretaker.* 1963. Playwright—Pinter. Director—Clive Donner. With Robert Shaw, Alan Bates, Donald Pleasence.
12. *Cat on a Hot Tin Roof.* 1958. MGM. Playwright—Tennessee Williams. Director—Richard Brooks. With Elizabeth Taylor, Paul Newman.

13. *Country Girl.* 1954. Director—George Seaton. With Bing Crosby, Grace Kelly, William Holden.
14. *Crimes of the Heart.* 1987. Playwright—Beth Henley. Director—Bruce Beresford. With Jessica Lange, Sissy Spacek, Diane Keaton.
15. *Death of a Salesman.* 1952. Columbia. Playwright—Arthur Miller. Director—Laslo Benedek. With Fredric March.
16. *The Desperate Hours.* 1955. Paramount. Playwright—Joseph Hayes. Director—Wm. Wyler. With Humphrey Bogart, Fredric March.
17. *Detective Story.* 1951. Paramount. Playwright—Sidney Kingsley. Director—Wyler. With Kirk Douglas.
18. *Dracula.* 1979. Playwrights—Deane & Balderston. Director—John Badham. With Frank Langella, Laurence Olivier, Kate Nelligan.
19. *Equus.* 1977. British. Playwright—Peter Shaffer. Director—Sidney Lumet. With Richard Burton.
20. *Fool For Love.* 1985. Playwright—Sam Shepard. Director—Robert Altman. With Sam Shepard, Kim Basinger.
21. *The Fugitive Kind.* 1959. U.A. Playwright—T. Williams. Director—Sidney Lumet. (From *Orpheus Descending.*) With Marlon Brando, Anna Magnani, Joanne Woodward.
22. *Golden Boy.* 1939. Columbia. Playwright—Clifford Odets. Director—Rouben Mamoulian. With Wm. Holden.
23. *Great Catherine.* 1969. Shaw. Director—Gordon Flemyng. With Peter O'Toole, Zero Mostel, Jeanne Moreau.
24. *I Never Sang For My Father.* 1969. Columbia. Playwright—Robert Anderson. Director—Gilbert Cates. With Gene Hackman, Melvyn Douglas.
25. *The Importance of Being Earnest.* 1952. Universal. Playwright—Oscar Wilde. Director—Anthony Asquith. With Michael Redgrave, Edith Evans.
26. *The Lion in Winter.* 1968. British. Playwright—James Goldman. Director—Anthony Harvey. With Peter O'Toole, Katherine Hepburn.
27. *The Little Foxes.* 1941. RKO. Playwright—Lillian Hellman. Director—Wyler. With Bette Davis.
28. *Long Day's Journey Into Night.* 1962. Embassy. Playwright—O'Neill. Director—Lumet. With K. Hepburn, Ralph Richardson, Jason Robards, Dean Stockwell.
29. *Look Back in Anger.* 1959. Warners. Playwright—John Osborne. Director—Tony Richardson. With Richard Burton.
30. *My Fair Lady.* Based on Shaw's *Pygmalion.* 1964. Director—George Cukor. With Rex Harrison, Audrey Hepburn.
31. *Night of the Iguana.* 1964. Director—John Houston. With Richard Burton, Deborah Kerr, Ava Gardner.

32. *Loot.* 1970. British. Playwright—Joe Orton. Director—Silvio Narizzano. With Richard Attenborough, Lee Remick.
33. *Marat/Sade.* 1967. U.A. Playwright—Peter Weiss. Director—Peter Brook. With Glenda Jackson.
34. *Miss Firecracker.* 1989. Playwright—Beth Henley. Director—Thomas Schlamme. With Holly Hunter.
35. *'Night, Mother.* 1985. Playwright—Marsha Norman. Director—Tom Moore. With Sissy Spacek, Anne Bancroft.
36. *The Odd Couple.* 1968. Paramount. Playwright—Neil Simon. Director—Gene Saks. With Jack Lemmon, Walter Matthau.
37. *Our Town.* 1940. U.A. Playwright—Thornton Wilder. Director—Sam Wood. With William Holden.
38. *The Petrified Forest.* 1936. Warners. Playwright—Robert E. Sherwood. Director—Archie Mayo. With Bette Davis, Humphrey Bogart, Leslie Howard.
39. *The Philadelphia Story.* 1940. MGM. Playwright—Philip Barry. Director—George Cukor. With K. Hepburn, Cary Grant, James Stewart.
40. *Picnic.* 1955. Columbia. Playwright—Inge. Director—Logan. With William Holden, Kim Novak.
41. *Plenty.* 1985. British. Playwright—David Hare. Director—Fred Schepisi. With Meryl Streep, Sting.
42. *A Raisin in the Sun.* 1961. Columbia. Playwright—Lorraine Hansberry. Director—Daniel Petrie. With Sidney Poitier.
43. *Sabrina Fair.* 1955. Playwright—Samuel Taylor. With Audrey Hepburn, Humphrey Bogart, William Holden.
44. *Stalag 17.* Playwrights—Donald Bevan and Edmund Trzcinski. With William Holden. 1953.
45. *Strange Interlude.* 1932. MGM. Playwright—O'Neill. Director—Robert Z. Leonard. With Norma Shearer, Clark Gable.
46. *A Streetcar Named Desire.* 1951. Warners. Playwright—T. Williams. Director—Elia Kazan. With Marlon Brando, Viv Leigh.
47. *Torch Song Trilogy.* 1989. Playwright—Harvey Fierstein. With Matthew Broderick, Harvey Fierstein.
48. *Under Mikwood.* 1972. Director—Andrew Sinclair. With Richard Burton, Elizabeth Taylor, Peter O'Toole. Playwright—Dylan Thomas.
49. *A View From the Bridge.* 1961. Playwright—A. Miller. Director—Lumet. With Raf Vallone, Maureen Stapleton.
50. *The Visit.* 1961. Director—Bernhard Wicki. With Ingrid Bergman and Anthony Quinn. Playwright—Fredrick Durrenmatt.
51. *Watch on the Rhine.* 1943. Warners. Playwright—Hellman. Director—Herman Schumlin. With Bette Davis, Paul Lukas.

52. *Who's Afraid of Virginia Woolf?* 1966. Warners. Playwright—Edward Albee. Director—Mike Nichols. With Richard Burton, Elizabeth Taylor.
53. *Winterset.* 1936. RKO. Playwright—Maxwell Anderson. Director—Alfred Santell. With Burgess Meredith.
54. *You Can't Take It With You.* 1938. Columbia. Playwrights—George S. Kaufman and Moss Hart. Director—Frank Capra. With Jean Arthur, James Stewart.

Note

1. The original of this exercise is found in the kinesphere concepts of Rudolf Laban—the spatial area around the body in which one moves the whole body or part of it.

The contemporary approach to acting as described by Brecht, Artaud, Grotowski, Beck, Chaikin, and others does not ask the author to avoid illusion on the stage. Actors must recognize that *everything* in the theatre is illusion. They should be guided, provoked, stimulated, and occasionally even yielded to in order for them to realize a personalized performance. Actors must run the risk of penetrating the inner self. By using improvisation, actors must move away from lifelessness onstage and open themselves to creative impulses and thereby respond to truth instantly. Perhaps for the first time actors must realize that they have the vital responsibility to economize when creating a character. Actors must be capable of self-detachment and personal objectivity to discover the clichés and hollowness lurking in preconceived value systems. The concern of actors should be to live fully in mind and body, giving themselves over completely to really personalizing, not merely performing, through dexterity and expertness. Sincere, honest, dedicated art comes also from the unconscious state of the artist. Surface description makes for imitation and destroys spontaneity. Once you are in complete control of your mental, emotional, and physical faculties, you should be able to personalize onstage with confidence and with discipline. The late Lee Strasberg and many great actors and teachers of acting in this century personify just such personalization, confidence, and discipline in their art and in their instruction. Having discovered the ability to unmask yourself, you have found the means to interest an audience, lower its defenses, and provide it with awareness of the complex levels inherent in both existence and in art.

Personalizing and sustaining illusion are not paradoxical. Truth must lie beneath illusion, if not reality. Or as Plato stated it so many centuries ago:

> The mask which an actor wears
> is apt to become his face.

Separate your analysis into four major sections as follows. Effective play analysis must be written out. It is not merely mental activity. The acronym PASTO, used throughout these instructions, stands for preparation, attack, struggle, turn, and outcome.

Section One

In this section list the following important facts about the author of the play and its production.

1. Brief author information.
2. Brief information on the initial production of the play if known.
3. Brief information on any *vital* or *unusual* subsequent production if known.

Section Two

This is a specific discussion encompassing your overall analysis of the *form* of the play and its structural components, which you are to accomplish by completing twenty-three separate paragraphs, numbered 1 through 23, in the following sequence.

1. Identify and clarify the *Preparation* section of the play by specifying the pages and page numbers of your script used for this aspect of the PASTO.
2. Identify and clarify the *Point of Attack* in terms of the earliest incident in the play that exposes the basic conflict of the play. State the nature of the basic conflict—who is it between or what is it between, what it is, and page number of *Attack*.
3. Identify and clarify the *Major Dramatic Question*—MDQ—of the play.
4. Identify the *protagonist* of the play and give a brief justification for your identification.
5. Identify the chief *antagonist* of the play and state a brief justification for your identification.
6. Identify who or what resolves the conflict (i.e., the *Deciding Agent*) and state briefly how and where in the play the resolution occurs (give page number of the conflict resolution).
7. Identify and clarify the *Struggle* section of the play by specifying the pages and page numbers of your script used for this aspect of the PASTO. NOTE: You need to identify the key *Complications* of the play in paragraph 7 after you have clarified the pages and page numbers used for the *Struggle*. Simply list them in the order they occur: for example, p. 16, the protagonist's brother suddenly arrives from California; p. 27, the brother is discovered murdered in the library; and so forth. These complications should be numbered Complication No. 1, and so on.
8. Identify and clarify the major crisis or *Turn* of the play. Where and how does it take place? Give the page number of your script on which it occurs.
9. If a *Climax* can be distinguished from the major crisis, identify and clarify it. Where and how does it take place? Give the page number of your script on which it occurs.
10. Identify and clarify the denouement or *Outcome* section of the play by specifying the pages used for this aspect of the PASTO and by briefly clarifying what gets wrapped up in this section.
11. Identify and clarify the subject *Issues* of the play. List them as one-word subjects or as subject-and-issue questions or as both, as you prefer. List them in priority of importance (e.g., justice, revenge, and so on).

12. Identify and clarify the *key Drives* (nervosity) or character desires for all the characters in the play. List these in priority of importance for each character. Also list the characters in order of importance in the action of the play. Thus, Hamlet's *Drives* would be listed in order of their importance first; then Claudius's *Drives* would be listed in order of their importance; and so on.

13. Clearly state the *major Theme* or central idea of the play in one complete sentence. Then list any important subordinate themes in order of importance.

14. In one succinct paragraph comment on the quality of the author's skill with the *Plot* in the play (for example, is it strong with Suffering and Discovery, but weak with Reversal? How well is the story organized?).

15. Repeat number 14 relative to *Character*. For example, are the personalities clear and well distinguished from one another? Are they believable? Are they of full dimension? Do they possess emotion and thought?

16. Repeat number 14 relative to *Thought*. For example, comment on the overall intellectual content of the play: Is it shallow: Is it philosophical? Does it have a theme or themes?

17. Repeat number 14 relative to *Language, Diction, or Dialogue*. For example, does the play employ iambic pentameter verse? How good is it? Is it naturalistic American prose? How good is it? Is it good "heard" language?

18. Repeat number 14 relative to *Melody* and *Music*. For example, are the lines conductive to musical effect? Is there use of actual instrumentation? of singing? How good are all these effects?

19. Repeat number 14 relative to *Spectacle*. For example, are all the visual and aural effects theatrical? Are they handled well? evocative? static? What are their outstanding qualities? Do certain technical effects of spectacle tend to dominate the play? For example, is there constant use of drum sounds? Is lighting particularly vital to the play? If so, how? What do the costumes contribute? the scenery?

20. Clarify the meaning of the title of the play.

21. Categorize the *overall Mood* of the play. For example, does the overall mood of the play express the emotion and feeling of sexual heat or frustration? What are the dominant emotions and feelings that make up the overall mood of the play? Relate your discussion of mood to a few key specifics from the actual play.

22. Categorize the *overall Rhythm* of the play. For example, are the rhythmic surges of the play similar to a gathering thunderstorm? If so, explain how. Relate your brief discussion directly to major action incidents of the play that clarify your discussion of the rhythm. Categorize the overall *tempo* of the play (*speed*-of-movement factor). *Rhythm* evolves from a *combination* of tempo or speed, mood, and emotion.

23. As a categorizing label, state precisely what the *Style* (type or kind) and the *Form* of the play are, based on the foregoing twenty-two points of analysis (e.g., Classic Greek Tragedy; nineteenth-century Melodrama; Turn-of-the-Century Farce; Expressionistic Serious Drama; etc.). As needed for further clarification, elaborate upon the label: for example, an Expressionistic Farce in the French tradition, an Elizabethan tragedy in the Aristotelian sense influenced by the Roman plays of Seneca, and the like. (Remember that there are only two basic or pure *forms* of drama, namely, tragedy and comedy. All other forms are derivatives or amalgamations of those basic two, such as, farce, satire, melodrama, tragicomedy, and so on.)

Section Three

In this section you are to record the following important information on the script itself, in this manner.

1. Cut out the actual script and paste or mock it up on large sheets of paper with openings cut so that both sides of the script can be read. Standard-size acting scripts pasted on 8½-by-11-inch paper is the usual procedure.
2. Include on the script, written in the margins, both your *Literal* and *Metaphorical* analyses. Use separate Comment Sheets for lengthy comments and insert the sheets in proper order among the script pages.
3. On the script designate all *French Scenes* as they occur. Include both your *Literal* and *Metaphorical* titles for each French Scene.
4. On the script designate all major *Complications* as set down earlier in number 6, section 2.
5. On the script categorize the *Tempo* (rate of beat) for each French Scene (e.g., rapid to slow, etc.).
6. On the script identify the *Mood* of each French Scene (e.g., violence, anger, gentle love, etc.).

NOTE: In section 3, analysis of some items covered previously in section 2 (e.g., complications, major crisis, attack, MDQ, etc.) are usually repeated.

Section Four

Make the conclusion of your play analysis succinct. The conclusion should explicate the play's *Commanding Image* and should be stated in a clear, complete sentence that begins: The play is like. . . . Base your conclusion on the *Metaphorical Analysis* noted in the script margins as directed in section 3. For example: The play is like the eye of a hurricane.

NOTE: Your analysis should be the result of your *own* thinking. If you include the views of critics or scholars in any way, they must be properly acknowledged or footnoted. However, play analysis is *not* research. It should be individual, creative play analysis in preparation for acting or directing the play, and it should originate with you.

Comments Most Frequently Heard from Teachers, Coaches, and Directors

Good things *will* repeat. One must go back and work on it again and again. Like a dancer, musician, or athlete.

Don't move your head much when you speak.

Don't push or force for emotion and character. Be patient. Often let the lines do it—trust the playwright.

When in doubt, do less—even nothing.

Don't sermonize, posture, and play so much subtext you forget the text.

Don't frame every moment in emotion—it becomes pretentious and tedious. Don't show the art.

The key is to lean on yourself for that within you that wants to reach out to people. Doing this, you're less likely to act. However, once you tap yourself and use it, be it humor or pain, the thing must be crafted. *It* can't work *you*.

If you just let emotion pour out, it will use you up.

Risk yourself on stage. If *you* "hide," it will lead to mediocre acting.

In early rehearsals, explore *yourself*, not your role; dare to take risks. Later, learn craft. Mechanical actors and directors *begin* with craft. They allow no room for exploration and risk. The result is safe, mediocre, and boring theatre.

Be you for awhile; let the role come to you, be you.

Don't get with the role and lines too quickly (which is the initial risk!— avoiding that safety factor!). Don't run to "hide" too quickly in character and emotion.

"Not enough time" is always a "cop-out." Use well and use properly whatever time you have.

Faith begins with faith in self.

If you don't have the time to do something well, prepare it well, and strive for greatness, don't do it at all.

Working alone in a monologue should be more relaxed than working with someone else because one need worry only about oneself.

Never cry over criticism; only cry over failure to work purposefully and hard.

If you know it is not working in rehearsal, stop. Begin again.

Score a scene in terms of what your character *sees* and *hears*.

À la Stanislavski, do your homework and find the "why"—the past history—the motivation; *however*, it is even better to analyze the "what for"—the present *situation* and the future goal.

Subtext requires improvisation, not mere mental invention.

Never try to become an "actor"; try to become a fuller person. Keep your feet on earth, pavement, and wood.

Acting is serious business, but one can approach it too seriously and become grim.

Don't *feel* everything to the sacrifice of craft.

Too many actors are emotional rather than dramatic.

Don't "indicate." Don't move or speak as though saying, "Look! I'm moving! I'm speaking!"

Learn to *locate* as an actor. Know where you are—to whom you speak! And why! And what for!

Speak to me first as you, later as the character.

Let punctuation lead you to rhythm. Acting is all rhythm finally.

One can't act carrying self-criticism in one's head. Don't make clinical decisions. Just do.

Act one thing at a time—always use single intentions. Like a butcher, put one piece of meat on the wax paper at a time.

Use pauses, not holes.

Use opposite values.

You don't know the precise age of your character? Well, that's "spur-of-the-moment" acting for you.

Use of private moments is a risk actors must learn to take.

Don't be too dependent upon a director; respect him, but never be his slave or puppet. Most actors survive in spite of directors.

Good directors often listen to suggestions from actors; great directors even use the suggestions now and then.

Watch great actors over and over again. Watch Olivier, Tracy, Hepburn, Burstyn, Pacino, DeNiro.

Use real liquor in a drinking scene once in a rehearsal—never again.

You can't stand still on stage? Do the scene once with your back constantly against a wall.

The clearer and simpler the improv, the better it will be.

Don't suppress nervousness—channel it and use it.

Look—see—react. Brecht said that and so did Stanislavski.

Play clichés honestly—let the audience discover they are clichés. Don't lead them by indicating.

Don't fret about results. Leave it to directors and critics. Just act one intention at a time. When you get to the last one, there will be the results.

Never panic in the face of time and throw out necessary work to get to results.

If you scream and get hysterical, you'll get screaming, hysterical theatre.

Analysis, discussion, and exploration are more important than learning lines and blocking. The latter stuff will actually take care of itself. Of course, you'll never know that or believe that unless you try it.

To dwell on learning lines and blocking is to kid yourself; that isn't work. Technicians do that, not artists.

Musicians know what it takes to play a note—to execute. Why shouldn't actors?

Affective memory work (emotion memory) should be done at home, alone, if done at all. Homework should appear *in* the rehearsal, not *at* the rehearsal.

You have to be yourself before you can be any character. Acting is use of self.

Speak out. If you're angry, say so. Don't sulk and brood. Get rid of it. Then rehearse. Speaking out also builds confidence.

Drill cannot accomplish what improvisation can.

Don't show; do.

The supreme accomplishment is to get thinking and impulses to coincide. (Self coincides with character.)

Eventually get around to selecting and discarding. *Then* set it and polish it. What in hell is there to set and polish from the first week of a rehearsal devoted to line and blocking memorization?

Late in rehearsals, go ahead and repeat blocking and movement patterns. But never repeat inner reaction. Keep those fresh (especially if some fool director is "blocking" you).

If your director is a traffic cop, follow his law like any good citizen, but put essence (yourself) under it.

Don't imitate—re-create.

If a director says, "Drop the organic and Method crap and just do it—do what I tell you!" smile and do it, but do even more homework later by yourself.

Remember the lesson of the baseball hitter—every pitch is a bit different—you can't always hit the same way. React a bit differently—go with the pitch. The logic is the same—the territory—not the reaction/action.

Habit just leads to imitation. Add "Will" and "Adaptation."

Have only one intention at a time, even when you're doing many things at once. Instinct and craft must weld. You need both.

Don't act from the negative ("I will resist"). Use the positive ("I will triumph").

Some actors need "will" in their emotional flow to maintain control; others need no "will" and still have little emotion—the latter aren't really actors.

The other paradox: acting is indeed mental and the key approach to it is through the mind, but the actor cannot do a lot of thinking in the usual sense of that word while on stage performing. Instinct and some mystery are involved.

Trust cannot be bargained or requested—only earned via work.

An actor has to have a studio; a lab; a classroom—to just work in production and performance will make actors lazy and drive them insane.

You always have time for homework. No actor or director can do it all at rehearsal.

Prepare or get out.

Stop acting *before* you come on stage.

When you deny, you hide.

Don't do facile, easy things. If you rein everything in, you can't get "naked" up there. Think in physical terms, not emotional terms.

Stop coming to conclusions about your own work.

Don't let a director *force* you to do anything. You *find* a way to do it.

Don't be defensive about yourself or your character. Avoid personal negativism. Open up and let them at you.

Don't "pump up." Go to the toilet, then walk on and just say the lines. Stop having Dostoevsky seizures.

Note the weather you just left every time you come on.

Find some pleasure in yourself. It leads to confidence.

You have to be heard and understood.

Later in rehearsals, do you have the courage to face craft? *Then* accept direction, even commands?

A rare role will allow you to just personalize throughout. But no role will deny you starting with it.

Don't "glide" verbally. Speak.

Be patient—must you see the end of the journey at the start? Cool it and take it moment by moment.

Never play for laughs—it's not believable and it's undisciplined, exhausting, and unprofessional.

Artificial bellowing always leads to the same thing: losing your voice.

Goethe said an artist's career develops in public—but talent develops in private.

Let's struggle with your talent, but not applaud it yet.

Success often kills development. It's easy to get bought in this society. It's our profession's fatal trap. Why do you think most film and television actors feel guilty?

Be sure to bow beautifully in the face of your greatest calamities. The bow should say, "I did my best—for now."

Show me worlds within me I did not know existed.

The great actor has the emotion always *there*—but the greatness will not hold without continual practice and use.

A monologue must be done with an audience—even if unseen, it must be to someone. Thus, there is no such thing as a monologue. They are always to someone.

Always play action and situation; also, wait for your cue.

Learn to compress your preparation; tighten cues; establish a proper environment; nail down business specifically; use what you have, no matter the pain or discomfort.

With Pinter, don't worry about the mystery and menace and silence—all that stuff—just make your selections and do them. The Pinter stuff takes care of itself. If you play at his oddities, you'll drown in them. Just do solid, motivated acting. You don't have to understand all of it—search, think, select, and do.

Trust your playwright; remember, playwriting is not a collaborative process; production is, but not playwriting.

Good improvs should always be set up so that each actor is unaware of what all the other actors know.

Is there a great audience out there waiting and wanting art and artistry? Probably not. Most actors do it for each other and themselves. That's OK.

Most actors have to act; it is more real up there. That is what is meant by the power of acting. Do not fear it; most actors don't really act for money and fame and satisfaction. No, most hold to it for personal survival. No wonder George C. Scott says: "Don't." Nobody should be *encouraged* to be an actor.

Want to do a grim scene with depth? Then sing a happy song just before doing the scene. (Comb it the other way, in other words. That's what we often do in life— do something else to escape our pain and vulnerability. Naturally, then, the actor should do the same thing.)

If you are mechanical in movement patterns, play the scene once in the dark. Have someone put obstacles around. See what happens, but don't get hurt. (This is called, "Reacting honestly.")

Don't show your preparation *in* the scene. That's acting. Rather, use it *under* the scene or throw it away before entering.

To freshen an entrance, have at least four places to enter. In early rehearsals, never let the other actor know which one you'll use. (Fresh reactions!)

When acting poetry, learn first what you are doing physically—then add the poetry.

Never huff and puff a soliloquy.

Few can act well out of mere instinct and inspiration (George C. Scott— maybe). It leads to emotional posturing. Leave all that to the geniuses.

Act under the influence of the passion and in character, but don't act *in* a passion.

Try being deaf all morning; blind; without smell; without taste; without being able to touch.

Don't be a "Method Mutant"—an "Organic Ostrich." That is don't just use feeling. Eventually, get to the craft, too.

Don't just approach a scene through its language—go into it via intentions. What is the situation—what do you want to win? How do you win? And what for?

Don't anticipate.

Animal work is often good. A monkey is terrific for use.

With great acting, the "thing" is still there after it's done. It should never just be over. Try to act so you leave something behind.

Remember, a director is just an ideal audience of one. (Good ole Tyrone Guthrie! Or was it Arthur Hopkins?)

A director does not know everything, but should have authority whenever he tells the truth.

The best actors have a secret. Good directors get to know their actors well and allow those secrets to emerge.

Avoid the rap of opportunism as actors. Hold to your integrity as you do commercials and other such jobs. The times ahead will be morally dangerous for actors; no matter your work, can you also do it as a service to people? To better mankind?

Any one idea from an actor is worth more than four ideas from a director. Why? Because the actor is personally involved in a way no director can hope to match.

A good director will never tell you what to do, he will just tell you what not to do.

The hardest thing about acting is to not seem to know what is going to happen next. (Good ole Lee Strasberg!)

The key director's task is to discover what is unique about each of his actors.

"Blocking" an actor is the curse of actor creativity. So is forced line memorization.

A director must be careful of creative selfishness. Beware of the director who claims to have "a great idea or concept" about the play.

Good acting reveals a collision of values.

Your character's spine or super-objective or motivating force should plug into why the play was written.

Do not try to just "create a character"; just try to play action and situation. Let other characters "create" you through their response to your action.

Never play as direct to an audience as you play to another character. (This includes playing Brecht and soliloquies.)

As Zen said, begin with an empty cup. Fill it slowly and carefully and only to the rim. (Bottle is a good metaphor as well as cup.)

Some things cannot be acted; they can only be earned, as in life. Such a thing is dignity.

The best playwrights write for actors, not audiences.

A new play, one untried and unproven, is the most beneficial vehicle for actors to experience.

Ask the Charles Dickens question of your character: "Will he be the victim of his life or become the hero of it?"

No director that one might admire "blocks" a play. The ground plan takes care of that, as does actor instinct and the playwright. It is best to create a ground plan through director-actor collaboration; after that, the designer should enter the collaboration.

It was Chekhov who noted that the most important thing in acting is the placement of the furniture.

An actor must allow himself to be ambushed by his character's thoughts and, of course, by the thoughts of other characters and other actors. (Ambush = surprise!)

Good directors rarely use adjectives, adverbs, and directives *early* in rehearsal. To do this is to force actors to play qualities rather than action. Do not create barriers for actors by commanding them at the very start. This is the time barriers must come down. Trust them awhile and let them work on their own a bit.

The key to good directing is understanding people.

Good directors let actors evolve organically at their own pace toward some point *late* in rehearsals. *Then* the director steps in to command, edit, refine, polish, set, and clarify.

Pace and speed are two different things. Pace is the rate at which a good moment follows another good moment. A play can be performed and spoken at great speed and still be slow.

Pace cannot be a director's concern until *late* in rehearsals. Never tell an actor early in rehearsal to "speed up" or "pace it faster" or "move it more quickly." A good actor should only answer such commands with this question: "Faster with *what?*"

Always look to opposites. Always look for the tragic in the comic and the comic in the tragic. Shakespeare, Molière, and Chekhov, to name but three playwrights, always mixed opposites. (To do *The Miser,* first learn where Harpagon is *generous.*)

Style is mostly the mix of the tragic with the comic. Style does not imply that an actor has to do a lot of "performing." That is merely boring.

The key to directing is *through* actor work. First treat the actor as a person, then an artist. Finally, the actor will become more responsible for the play than the director and that is good.

Actors often save directors, rarely does a director save an actor.

"Block" a play, if you must, during the *final* two weeks of rehearsal.

The key is to free the actor early on, not rein him in like some wild thing. Line memorization is mere self-discipline. Leave it to the actor. Freedom does not mean anarchy. Free actors are profoundly disciplined.

To those who say we have no time to work organically, reply that the challenge is theirs to take up or reject. To resist is to repeat the same bad habits again and again. A class in directing should not create models of the director who is teaching the class.

If your theatre program is in too much of a hurry to work properly, try doing just one play a year well, not five or six poorly. Or do the five or six without quite finishing them in order to train actors better.

In America, especially in colleges and universities, we have tremendous facilities and better budgets than we care to admit. Yet we rarely free actors to create.

The readiness to respond to accidents and build on them is the key to good acting and directing.

Create chains of unbroken moments.

Authority belongs only to the teller of truth.

Create group ensembles; no one person is larger than the play, including the director.

Use passion; why am I doing this role and this play? Find out and be passionate about it.

Watch other actors.

Avoid a "production concept." Just stage the action.

Be certain your director works more than once with you alone, as an individual.

If you discover the style of the play, keep quiet about it.

Edit your own excessive ideas. Remember again that less is more.

Pascal said that "the sole cause of man's unhappiness is his inability to sit quietly in his room." Sit quietly in your room and in your rehearsals. Locate happiness through silence, observation, and listening.

Since Man often prefers the hunt to the capture, learn to prefer rehearsal to performance, art to success.

The Oracle claimed that "Our deepest Griefs may hold our brightest Hopes." Let every rejection and disappointment, every mistake and error, provide you with inspiration and knowledge to move forward. Move on.

And, once again, keep in mind that entering into acting is entering Purgatory. Good luck. "Break a leg."

And get on with it.

Above.   To be or go behind something or someone. The general area farther away from the audience.

Acoustics.   The qualities that govern the transmission of sound.

Action.   Any change of form or condition on the stage that forcibly affects the mind or senses of the spectator; physical movement; a lively series of stimulations causing a feeling of suspense; a rapid progression of arresting ideas. Action when conceived as the movement of sensory stimuli may be expressed by the voice of the actor as well as by his body.

Ad lib.   (from Latin *ad libitum*, "at pleasure"). To add, especially to improvise, words or gestures.

Affective memory (Emotion memory or recall; Sensory memory or recall).   Recollection of details and situations that have deeply moved an actor to assist him in achieving an inner justification that lets him enter into the character's experiences. Important to the Stanislavski system of acting (popularly called the Method in the United States).

Agon.   In Classical Greek drama, a dramatized debate or argument.

Alarum.   An offstage sound effect of trumpets, drums, and guns in Elizabethan drama.

Alienation effect.   (German, ver Fremdungseffekt). Theatrical devices in Brecht's Epic plays designed to estrange the audience from excessive emotional response; to "make strange" action in order to respond to it intellectually.

Antagonist.   The person, group, or force in opposition to the central character (hero or protagonist).

Antecedent events.   Part of *exposition* in a play; the important actions that have occurred *before* the play begins.

Apron.   The part of the stage extending beyond the proscenium curtain line toward the audience.

Arena.   A playing space for actors, which is surrounded by spectators; in England, a playing space with audience on three sides and a wall at the back of the players. In the United States, the latter is usually called *horseshoe* or even *thrust* staging.

Arras.   A curtain. A common term in Elizabethan drama.

Aside.   Dialogue intended for the audience with the accepted convention that other characters cannot hear it.

Attack.   *See* **Point of attack.**

Audience.   The viewers and hearers of a theatre performance.

Audition.   A demonstration of performance ability, usually competitive, usually prepared. Many directors distinguish an audition from a *tryout* by designating the latter as a reading without memorization or preparation.

Auditorium.   The theatre area usually designated for the audience; often called the *house.*

Auxesis.   A rhetorical device used on occasion in verse drama (especially Elizabethan drama) in which ideas are intensified via repetition.

Awareness.   A state of sensory alertness; a preparedness to respond to sight, sound, taste, touch, and odor. A sensitive recognition of other stage presences.

Backdrop or Backcloth.   A flat, screen, curtain, canvas, or scrim hanging behind the performers, usually painted with a sky or scene.

Backstage.   All of the theatre back of the stage proper including the wings, shop, dressing rooms, and so forth.

Balance.   The equalization of attention onstage (as between actors, between stage set properties, etc.).

Barnstorm.   To tour in a play performing in makeshift theatres.

Baroque. Usually associated with art and architecture, in theatre the term may be associated loosely with eighteenth-century drama, with its elaborate and ornate patterns of language. For example, the work of some of the English sentimentalists and even the work of Sir Richard B. Sheridan.

Batten. A wooden or metal stiffener used behind stage cloth or canvas or as a mount for lighting instruments.

Beats. A term employed by actors of the Stanislavski system meaning the distance from the beginning to the end of a character's intention, whether explicitly stated in the dialogue or not.

Below. To be or go in front of something or someone. The stage area closest to the audience in a proscenium theatre.

Blackout. A sudden extinguishing of all stage lighting; usually used for a theatrical effect at the end of a scene.

Blank verse. Any form of unrhymed verse with a regular metric pattern (usually associated with iambic pentameter).

Blocking. To work out all movement of actors.

Bombast. Ranting, loud, ornate dramatic speech.

Book. The nonmusical segments of musical plays.

Borderlights. *See* **Striplights.**

Bourgeois drama. Serious plays with middle-class characters, particularly popular in eighteenth and nineteenth centuries, as in George Lillo's *The London Merchant*, 1731.

Box. In some theatres an isolated seating area for four to six persons.

Box office. A place usually at the front of a theatre where tickets are sold.

Box set. Scenery representing an interior, usually realistic, with three walls, ceiling, doors, and windows.

Broadway. A famous avenue in the theatre district of New York City. By popular concept, the heart of commercial theatre.

Off-Broadway. The more artistic, less commercial *avant-garde* theatre performed in improvised theatres in New York City.

Off-Off Broadway. Usually considered the true standard-bearer of Off-Broadway drama since Off-Broadway has become very commercialized.

Build. The increase of emotion, tension, or energy directed toward a peak or climax.

Burla. Comic jokes, dialogue, and activity in commedia dell'arte.

Business. Minor physical action, often with the hands, by a performer (includes facial expression).

Cadence. The measure or beat of any rhythmic motion, as in verse, dance, and music.

Caesura. A pause or break in verse.

Call. (1) An announcement listing cast, rehearsals, and performances. (2) Readiness to do anything in the theatre.

Canon. The undisputed work of an author.

Cast. (1) Performers in a play. (2) To assign roles to actors.

Catharsis (Katharis). The purging of emotion and suspense that occurs at the end of a tragedy; experienced by the audience and, at times, by the characters as well.

Center (centering). Reflects a psychophysical condition whereby an actor finds emotional, mental, and physical freedom.

Center stage or stage center. A position approximately in the middle of the acting area.

Character. One of the dramatis personae; the personality of such a figure. The agent(s) of the plot. One of the six key elements of a drama according to Aristotle.

Character role. Normally an elderly or an eccentric character.

Cheat. To move or turn slightly to provide more space for other actors or to improve the compositional stage picture. To pretend you can see someone onstage as you speak to him when in reality you cannot. To project the voice more to the audience than to the character you are addressing.

Chorus. In Greek drama, a group of performers who play a role (in modern drama, the chorus is often supplanted by a narrator). In musical theatre, a group of dancers and/or singers.

Circle of Attention. Refers to an actor's selected focus on the stage. Circles of Attention are commonly divided into three groups: small, medium, and large. An actor's circle of attention is usually achieved with assistance from physical objects in the environment.

Classical. In ancient times, used to designate an author of the "first class." Today, term commonly means an author or work whose greatness is universally recognized.

Clean up. (1) To polish, work, or rehearse a scene to perfect it. (2) To move slightly to afford other actors space and provide a better compositional picture onstage.

Climax. The moment of highest interest in a play that leads to the answer to the MDQ and resolution of the conflict. The climax can be the *major crisis* or *turn*, or it can occur later. In *Hamlet* the *turn* occurs at the end of the play-within-a-play scene in act 3, and the *climax* occurs in the duel scene in act 5. In *Death of a Salesman* the *turn* and *climax* occur together after Biff cries in Willy's arms and Willy exits to commit suicide.

Close. To turn away from the audience.

Clown. A comic figure present in much drama. At times the clown merges with the *Fool*, a *jester* having unique wisdom.

Comedy. One of the two central forms of drama (tragedy is the other). Broadly, comedy is anything that amuses, movement from unhappiness to happiness, or action that excites mirth.

Communion. The connection between actors established primarily through eye contact, listening, touching, and reaction.

Community theatre. A theatre operated by and for the entertainment and edification of local people of a town or city.

Company. A group of actors who perform together. Also called a troupe.

Complication. An incident that alters the direction of a play's action line (turns the action in a new direction). For example, Hamlet's killing Polonius is a major complication.

Confidant. A character in whom a principal character confides (as Horatio to Hamlet).

Conflict. Forces of opposition, central to the action of most plays.

Constructivism. A scenic and staging movement associated with Meyerhold and Tairov in Russia in which painted realistic scenery was rejected in favor of ladders, platforms, and other constructed items.

Convention. An unrealistic device that the public agrees to tolerate or accept. (For example, it is a convention that one actor cannot hear another speak an aside.)

Counter. To shift position to compensate for the movement of another actor to maintain an effective compositional picture.

Couplet. In verse drama, a pair of poetic lines with end rhyme, usually providing a complete thought.

Cover. To hide from view of the audience, often deliberately, so as not to make obvious some necessary action of artifice.

Crisis (Major crisis). *See* **Turn.**

Cross. A movement onstage from one area to another.

Cue. A signal, usually a word or a gesture, to which an actor or member of the crew must respond.

Curtain. A drapery used to conceal part of the stage. Sometimes the term is used to denote the end of a scene or an act.

Curtain call. The appearance by the cast at the end of a play to receive applause. Generally considered a professional courtesy, it also provides the cast with the opportunity of acknowledging the audience. It is usually self-indulgent rudeness to forgo a curtain call.

Cyclorama, or Cyc. A shell-shaped structure at the rear of the stage, curved at the sides, usually made of cloth. Properly lighted, it gives the illusion of depth and of sky.

Deciding agent. The person or event in a play that resolves the conflict between the forces (between protagonist and antagonist). Often the deciding agent is a third person (such as a girl choosing between male rivals for her hand in marriage), or it is the will and decision of the protagonist (e.g., Hamlet is the deciding agent as well as the protagonist).

Denouement. Unknotting or resolution of the main plot. The end of a play; usually follows the climax.

Designer. One who makes the plans from which scenery, costumes, and the like are constructed.

Deus ex machina. In classical Greek plays, a god lowered in a machine or basket to provide an ending for the play. Today, an improbable device used to conclude a work.

Dialogue. Speech between characters; speech of a single character.

Diction. Choice of words or wording in a play. Language. Today, a performer's manner of speaking including pronunciation and phrasing. One of the six key elements of a drama according to Aristotle.

Directing. A process where the mind guides the body in a neuromuscular process to a more efficient pattern of self-use.

Director (Régisseur). The coordinator of all artists and technicians working on a theatre production.

Double. To play more than one role in a single production. In films, to stand in place of another performer, as for dangerous stunts.

Downstage. Toward the audience on a proscenium stage.

Dramatis personae. (Latin, "masks of the play"). The characters in a play.

Drame. A solemn but not tragic play; associated with eighteenth-century bourgeois drama.

Dress the stage. (1) To move slightly to provide more space for other actors and to improve the compositional stage picture. (2) To furnish props and items to hang on the scenery to improve the appearance of the stage.

Drive (Nervosity). The dramatic thrust of character desires in a play. The emotional hungers or nervosity of each character.

Dumb show. A scene having action without words; used frequently in Elizabethan drama.

Emotion. Feelings; impulses manifested outward from within (as grief, joy, anger, etc.).

Emotion memory or recall. *See* **Affective memory.**

Empathy. The projection of one's feelings into a perceived object. Distinguished from *sympathy:* we empathize if we feel *with* a character; we sympathize if we feel *for* a character.

Emphasis. Accent or special focus on an action, line, person, or word.

Ensemble acting. Presentation in which the performance of the group, rather than the individual, is stressed.

Entrance. (1) Act of entering the stage in view of the audience. (2) An opening in a set through which actors may enter.

Epic. The label given to Bertolt Brecht's plays whose aim was to arouse an audience's detached thought. Usually instructive episodic drama in the structural mode of Homer's Epic poems or narratives.

Epilogue. An appendix or concluding address in a play.

Exit. (1) Departure from a stage area. (2) An opening in a set through which actors may leave.

Exposition. The essential information provided the audience to begin the action of a play or given later to clarify action.

Extra (Supernumerary). One with so small a role in a play that he need have no training or talent (as a court guard who merely stands by the door in a trial scene).

Farce. A form of comedy that relies on artificial plot contrivance and slapstick or "low," physical activity, as opposed to wit and character depth, for its humor.

Flat. A light wooden or metal frame covered by canvas and used for scenery.

Flies. The area above the stage used for hanging scenery, lighting equipment, and so on.

Floodlight. A lensless lamp that provides broad illumination.

Floor plan (Ground plan). An outline drawing of a stage setting as it would look from above.

Fluff. A blunder or error onstage.

Focal point. The point of greatest interest onstage at any given moment.

Focus. An actor's selective attention to what he is doing, feeling, seeing, hearing, tasting, smelling, touching. The direction of attention to specific stimuli in the environment.

Foil. (1) A character who sets off another, as Laertes and Fortinbras set off Hamlet. (2) A piece of fencing equipment.

Folio. A book made of sheets folded once, each sheet providing two leaves or four pages. Shakespeare's plays were first published as a folio in 1623.

Fool. *See* **clown.**

Footlights. *See* **Striplights.**

Fop. A comic male character from Restoration drama, given to eccentricities and excesses of dress, vanity, and manner. (Such behavior is often played as mere femininity; this is a mistake and contrary to the key factor of *excess*.)

Form. *See* **Play form.**

French scene. That stage action contained between the entrance and exit of any character in a play.

Gallery. An area above and at the rear of theatres; called a balcony today.

Genre. Type or kind of play (such as revenge tragedy, Gothic melodrama, and so on).

Gestalt. The synthesis of separate elements of emotion, experience, and the like, to constitute an organic whole.

Give. To move a bit to provide space for another actor. To respond or offer emotion, energy, or activity onstage. To provide greater emphasis to someone else onstage.

Given circumstance. A Stanislavski term referring to any dramatic occurrence that affects an actor's playing of a scene.

Greasepaint. Stage makeup. Coloring matter mixed with grease in sticks or tubes used as base to help the features look natural under artificial illumination.

Greenroom. The traditional name for a theatre lounging room for performers and their guests. (From the actor tradition of waiting on the green or lawn.)

Grid. The framework of beams above the stage area in the flies.

Grotesque. A term in drama referring to the ludicrous or comic (associated with the work of Victor Hugo and Luigi Piradello, as examples).

Groundlings. The patrons who stand in front of a stage to see a play, particularly in an Elizabethan theatre.

Ground plan. *See* **Floor plan.**

Ground row. A flat or scenic piece with an irregular profile, usually used as a wall, mountain, hedge, or the like, often used to mask lighting instruments.

Ham. An incompetent performer who overacts.

Hamartia. A Greek-based word referring to the error in judgment of the hero in tragedy.

Heads up! A stage warning that something (usually scenery) is being lowered (or falling) onstage.

Heavens (Shadow). The canopy area over the stage in Elizabethan drama where an actor could hide from view from other characters or where musicians resided.

Heavy. A solemn major character, especially a villain.

Hero, or heroine. The central character or protagonist; the leading romantic character.

Hold. To stop or delay action onstage (usually because of laughter or applause).

Hubris. A Greek-based word for excess pride, the most common form of hamartia.

Humor. The quality of being amusing.

Humour. In ancient physiology, one of the four principal bodily fluids—blood, phlegm, choler (yellow bile), and melancholy (black bile). These humours were believed to influence health and temperament.

Iambic pentameter. A verse form consisting of ten syllables (five iambic feet) to the line. (See chapter 12.)

Iambic trimeter. A verse composed of three measures, consisting of three dipodies (six feet) in ancient or classical Greek dramatic poetry.

Imagination. The process of forming mental images. The reproduction of images from memory. The mental ability to create original and striking images and concepts. A key element in effective acting.

Imitation. (Greek, *mimesis*, "to imitate or imitative"). Not a pejorative term in the theatre. It implies "making" or "re-creating" or "representing" in the theatre.

Impersonate. To invest with personality; to personify; to assume or act the person or character.

Improvisation. Invention of lines and stage business by performers.

In. To the center of the stage.

Ingenue. (1) The role of a innocent young women. (2) The actress who plays such a role.

Intention. The major thing an actor determines that a character wants in a play or in a scene or in a single line of dialogue. According to Stanislavski, each character in a play has a psychological intention that often motivates physical and vocal action. The major intention for a character is called the *MF*, or Motivating Force, the *spine* of the role.

Interlude. Light entertainment, usually musical, while scenery is being shifted. In sixteenth-century England, a short farce play.

Intermission. A period between scenes or acts permitting audiences to go to the theatre lobby.

Intuition. Immediate comprehension or knowledge of something without the conscious use of reasoning.

Irony. A condition in plays in which the truth is the reverse of what the participants think. Irony is usually more fully understood by the audience than by the characters.

Jester. *See* **Clown.**

Jig. A short farce, sung and danced at the end of some Elizabethan plays.

Kill. To spoil by accident or deliberately cease any activity onstage.

Kinesics. The study of body motions as related to the nonverbal aspects of interpersonal communication.

Lazzi. Comic business in the commedia dell'arte.

Lead. A principal role.

Legitimate drama. In eighteenth-century England, a play performed in a *licensed* theatre. Today, a play, in contrast to a musical, vaudeville, film, and the like.

Libretto. The text or "book" of the dialogue and lyrics for a musical play.

Lighting. Illumination of the theatre, especially of the stage. Today, the province of artistic designers and technicians.

Limelight. (1) A stage lighting device of the nineteenth century that produced illumination by directing an oxyhydrogen flame against a piece of lime. (2) Today, to give special focus or attention.

Line. (1) A rope or wire used to hang scenery. (2) Dialogue in a play.

Living Newspaper. A cinematic dramatic form in the United States in the 1930s in which factual data and dramatic vignette were integrated. Part of the brief Federal Theatre Project headed by Hallie Flanagan Davis (1890–1969), the Living Newspaper produced such works as *Triple A Plowed Under* in 1936.

Lobby. The lounge area for spectators in a theatre, usually at the front of the building.

Major crisis. *See* **Turn.**

Major Dramatic Question (MDQ). The question upon which the action of a play focuses. Usually the MDQ is not presented as a direct question in the script but is recognized to be the key action factor by the audience. For example, the audience ponders whether Hamlet will revenge his father's murder and restore order to the Kingdom.

Make up. To disguise one's face by using cosmetics, false hair, nose putty, and the like.

Makeup. Materials applied to disguise the face.

Malapropism. The mistaken use of a word in place of another of similar sound. (See Mrs. Malaprop in Sir Richard Sheridan's *The Rivals*.) Example: *it will percussion the blow* for *it will cushion the blow.*

Marionette. A doll controlled from above or below by rods, wires, or strings.

Mask. A face covering worn by many actors, especially in Greek drama and commedia dell'arte.

Masque. An entertainment of the Renaissance using lavish scenery and costumes.

Matinee. (from French, *matin*, "morning"). An afternoon (and, rarely, a morning) performance.

MDQ. *See* **Major Dramatic Question.**

Mechanical Advantage. Refers to a condition reflecting effective use of the actor's instrument, in particular the relationship of the head, neck, and torso. A position whereby "maximum result is achieved with minimum effort."

Melodrama. A form of serious drama that uses artificial plot contrivances, stock characters, unexpected reversals, happy endings with "poetic justice," and sensational effects. (A valid and respectable form of drama although one type of it is "kidded" as comedy, such as *The Drunkard*. A higher form of it is a play such as *The Desperate Hours*.)

Melody, or Music. (1) Actual music in a play. (2) Any melodic element such as an arrangement of words. One of the six key elements of a drama according to Aristotle.

Method. An American adaptation of the Stanislavski system that focuses on inner motivation, whose chief exponent is an American school of acting, the New York Actor's Studio.

Mezzanine. The front or first balcony in a theatre.

Mime. An ancient dramatic entertainment in which acrobats, jugglers, singers, dancers, actors, and actresses perform. *See also* **Pantomime.**

Mise-en-scène. The stage setting including the scenery, lighting, and arrangement of actors.

Mono-Drama (Mono-Acting). (1) A piece for one actor. (2) One performer doing several roles.

Monologue. (1) A long speech delivered by one character. (2) A performance by a single actor.

Mood. The dominant atmosphere created by a production—usually a combination of tempo, imagery, rhythm, sound, lighting, scenery, costuming, acting, and so forth.

Motivating Force (MF; Spine; Super-Objective). The central emotional hunger or drive of a character; what the character wants above all, usually expressed relative to other characters. For example, the MF or spine of Willy Loman is that he wants to regain the love of his son, Biff; that is Willy's Super-Objective.

Motivation. Ground in character and situation that makes behavior plausible.

Multiple setting (Simultaneous setting). A stage that displays at one time several locales.

Musical comedy (Musical theatre). A piece in which songs and dances are integrated to form a story.

Narrator. One who tells a story rather than enacting it. (See the Stage Manager in Thornton Wilder's *Our Town*.)

Naturalism. A heightened style of realism. "A slice of life."

Neoclassicism. New or revived classicism. (As in the seventeenth-century French theatre and the late seventeenth-, early eighteenth-century English theatre.)

Neon acting. Overacting; performing everything with great emphasis. Usually very ineffective kind of performance unless varied.

Nervosity. *See* **Drive.**

Obligatory scene (Scène à faire). (1) A scene in a play that an audience foresees and desires and whose absence it may, with reason, resent. (2) The necessary and most dramatic confrontation between two characters.

Observation. (1) The act of studying something closely. (2) The act of learning by observing (in acting, for the purpose of imitation). A key element in effective acting.

Off-Broadway. *See* **Broadway.**

Off-Off Broadway. *See* **Broadway.**

Offstage. The part of the stage out of view of the audience.

Onstage. The acting area of a stage in view of the audience.

Open. To turn more toward the audience.

Organic. Acting made up of systematically interrelated parts; theatre work that promotes actor creativity; working from within a group with a common goal; guided acting rather than commanded.

Out. A direction away from the center of the stage, often toward the audience.

Out front. Refers to the auditorium, house, or audience.

Overlap. To move or speak slightly ahead of cue.

Overplay. To act with more exaggeration than is needed.

Oxymoron. A thing is described in terms of its opposite. ("A wise fool.") A favorite device of Shakespeare.

Pace (Pacing; Tempo). The speed with which a play or actor moves.

Pantomime. An ancient dramatic performance featuring a solo performer who gestures and dances without using dialogue. *See also* **Mime.**

Parallel movement. When two or more actors move in the same direction at the same time.

Pathos. A quality that evokes pity.

Peripeteia. (from Greek for "reversal"). A plot indicating a sudden change in conditions, usually in tragedy.

Personalization. A process whereby the actor discovers and explores in himself characteristics, qualities, and attributes that are legitimate dimensions of the role he is creating.

Pickup. To increase the playing pace or to shorten the interval between cues.

Pin. *See* **Rail.**

Pit. An area at the front of the stage where the orchestra sits.

Pity and fear. The chief emotions inspired by tragedy (according to Aristotle).

Places! A command for actors to get in position to begin a rehearsal or performance.

Plant. A device to call attention to something that will have special significance later in a play.

Play. (1) A story communicated by impersonators. (2) To act.

Play doctor. One called in to patch up a play's weaknesses by rewriting, cutting, and adding.

Play form. The characteristic nature of play such as tragedy, comedy, farce, melodrama, and the like (as opposed to play type, which refers to the stylistic mode of the play, e.g., Realism, Expressionism).

Playhouse. A theatre.

Play type. The stylistic mode of a play such as realistic, expressionistic, and the like (as opposed to play form such as tragedy, comedy, farce, melodrama, etc.).

Play up (Plug). To emphasize a key moment.

Play-within-a-play. A representation of a drama within the drama itself (as in *Hamlet,* act 3, scene 2).

Plot. Story organization. The most important ingredient in a play according to Aristotle—*the* key element in the six elements of a play.

Plug. *See* **Play up.**

Poetic drama. A play whose language is metrical.

Poetic justice. A term denoting reward of the virtuous and punishment of the vicious, coined by Thomas Rymer in 1678.

Point of attack. The earliest incident in a play that arouses strong audience interest and exposes the basic conflict of the play; the point at which an author chooses to begin the story.

Practical. A functioning prop or piece of scenery that can actually be *used* by the actor and is not merely decorative or ornamental (as a window that can actually be opened).

Precast. To select actors for roles prior to auditions or tryouts. A very unpopular and infrequent practice, particularly in educational and amateur theatre.

Preface. A statement by the dramatist that serves as an introduction to the play.

Premiere.   The first public performance of a work.

Presentational.   The style of performance that is openly theatrical and delivered directly to the audience. (A nonrealistic device.)

Preview.   A tryout before an audience of a play previous to the performance considered "the opening."

Producer.   In England and Ireland, the director, but in the United States, the entrepreneur chiefly concerned with raising money. The person who often hires the artistic staff.

Production.   (1) A dramatic entertainment onstage. (2) The process of getting the work onstage.

Prologue.   A preface or introduction.

Prompter.   One who reminds forgetful actors of their lines. Often the assistant director-assistant stage manager.

Property, or prop.   An object or article used in a play and called for in the script.
>   **Hand props.**   Props used by the characters in a play.
>   **Set props.**   Furniture and other standing props; often unused by the characters in a play.
>   **Trim or dress props.**   Objects hanging on the walls of a set.

Proscenium arch stage.   A playing area framed in the front and thus separated from the audience.

Protagonist (from Greek for "first contender").   The chief figure in a play.

Public Solitude.   An experiential condition in the actor allowing him to behave publicly (in front of an audience) with the same freedom, spontaneity, and naturalness he experiences while alone.

Pun.   A play on words; one word suggests another that is pronounced similarly but with different meaning. (Hair; hare.)

Puppet.   A doll that can be manipulated. The operator places his hand into the body of a puppet to manipulate it.

Quarto.   A book made of sheets folded twice, each sheet supplying four leaves or eight pages. (Shakespeare's plays were issued in quartos before they were collected in a folio.)

Quibble.   An elaborate pun (*see* Pun). Especially popular with Elizabethan playwrights.

Rail (Pin; Tie-Off; Trim).   Part of the flies and grid system used to hang scenery in a theatre; related to sandbag and counterweight flying systems.

Raillery.   Witty banter and repartee.

Raisonneur.   A character in a chorus; any character who serves as a "mouthpiece" for the author.

Raked stage.   A playing area that slopes upward toward the rear wall. In present-day theatre, the rake is usually under the spectator area, rather than under the acting area.

Ramp.   A sloping platform used in the manner of a step unit.

Rant.   Wild, violent language.

Realism.   A style like life; carefully selected or crafted to represent life believably.

Régisseur.   In Germany and Russia, the director of a play.

Rehearsal.   A practice performance of a dramatic work or part of the work. Rehearsals: reading, line check, blocking, working, polishing, technical, run-through, dress and costume.

Repartee.   Witty remarks and cleaver, unexpected answers, usually in rapid delivery.

Repertory (Repertoire).   The body of dramatic works a company is trained to perform in turn or frequently. A *Repertory Company* performs a number of plays daily, weekly, or monthly rather than a single play for an extended run.

Representational. The style of performance that is illusory and represents life with fidelity; delivered only between characters who ignore the audience whom they pretend is nonexistent (or hiding behind an imaginary "fourth wall").

Response (Respond). A player's manifest reaction to another presence on the stage. Especially, a particular reaction called forth by a particular act.

Return. A flat set parallel to the audience at the downstage edge of the set jutting into the wings just above the tormentor. Any similar flat attached to a larger piece of scenery.

Reversal. *See* **Peripeteia.**

Revival. A production of a play usually long unperformed.

Revue. A loose collection of musical numbers, skits, comic bits, and the like.

Rhythm. The combination of tempo, emotion, mood, imagery, stress, beat, sound, accent, motion, and so forth, that creates a pattern of activity. A play has a rhythm; a production has a rhythm; an actor and his role have a rhythm.

Ritual. A ceremonial act.

Routine. Specially rehearsed stage actions, lines, songs, and dances.

Run. (1) The period during which a company performs a play. (2) To run through a scene or act without interruption from the director.

Satire. A work ridiculing aspects of human behavior, usually socially corrective in nature and intended to provoke both laughter and thought.

Scansion. Determining the meter of verse by analysis of metric feet, syllables, and accents.

Scenario. A detailed outline of a dramatic entertainment.

Scene. A subunit of an act or a play.

Scène à faire. *See* **Obligatory scene.**

Score. To determine character activity, business, and pantomimic dramatization. To score a role.

Scrim. (1) A loosely woven gauzelike fabric. (2) A theatre drop. When lighted from the front, a scrim becomes visible, almost opaque, and when lighted from the back it becomes semitransparent, nearly disappearing. A scrim with a scene painted on it is called *transparency.*

Script. The text of a dramatic work.

Sensory memory or recall. *See* **Affective memory.**

Set speech. A device where a long speech accomplishes many points without another character interrupting.

Shadow. *See* **Heavens.**

Share. Equal attention for two or more actors.

Show. A theatrical entertainment.

Side. A sheet containing an actor's lines, cues, stage directions, and so forth.

Sight line. The line of vision from any seat in the spectators' area to the stage.

Simultaneous setting. *See* **Multiple setting.**

Sketch (Skit). A short comic entertainment.

Slapstick. A board used by comics in classical plays to strike other characters in buffoonery. Broad, physical farce action.

Soap opera. Domestic melodrama on radio and television.

Soliloquy. A speech wherein a character utters thoughts aloud while alone; usually delivered directly to an audience and less frequently as self-meditation given aloud.

Sonnet. A form of lyric poetry (see the work of Shakespeare). A regularized form of fourteen lines with a set rhyme scheme.

Soubrette. (1) A minor young female role, usually a maid. (2) An actress who plays such a role.

Sound effect. An imitative sound, often performed offstage. Can be produced "live," on record, on tape, and by machinery.

Spectacle. *All* that is seen or heard onstage, including the actors. Today, that which appeals to the eye, such as lavish scenery. One of the six key elements of drama according to Aristotle.

Speech tag. The name of the speaker in a play, or the stage directions.

Spine (Super-Objective). *See* **Motivating force (MF).**

Stage business. *See* **Business.**

Stage center. *See* **Center stage.**

Stage left. Left of stage center; on the actor's left facing the audience.

Stage manager. The person who coordinates the efforts of the producer, director, playwright, actors, technicians, and the like. He (she) "runs" the production during performances.

Stage right. Right of stage center; on the actor's right facing the audience.

Stage time. The running time of a play. (Dramatic time is the fictional time covered by the action of the play.)

Star. A leading performer whose appeal is so great that his or her name may precede the title of the play.

Static. Little or no movement; a slow pace.

Steal. When one actor draws attention to himself at the expense of other actors (a practice greatly frowned upon when not called for in the script).

Stichomythia. In classical tragedy, individual lines of verse dialogue assigned to alternate speakers.

Stock character. Any traditional, stereotypical character (such as Harlequin).

Stock company. A repertory group attached to a theatre that commonly changes plays weekly, as in summer stock (the straw-hat circuit).

Straight role. A role without marked characterization; not very particularized or eccentric (normally a young man or young woman).

Straw-hat circuit. *See* **Stock company.**

Striplights. A lighting unit consisting of a row of lamps. When on the floor at the front of the stage called *footlights*. When suspended on iron pipes overhead called *borderlights*.

Strong. High attention value.

Struggle. The major action line of complication in a play. The longest segment of a play (its body).

Style. (1) The mode of expression. (2) The essence or truth of particular reality. (3) The total work of art: its material, its language, its historical era, its customs, and the like. (See Introduction to Part II of this book for a full discussion of style.)

Subject issues. The basic subject matter and questions raised by a play, usually expressed by a single word such as incest, murder, or justice.

Subordinate. To restrict focus or emphasis.

Subtext. A term common to both the Stanislavski system and the Method. Refers to the meaning underlying dialogue and stage directions.

Subtitle. The second or alternate title used for some plays.

Suffering. *Any* emotion felt by a character. Part of plot, according to Aristotle.

Supernumerary. *See* **Extra.**

Surrealism. A literary, dreamlike style in theatre promulgated as a reaction against realism. (See the plays of Alred Jarry.)

Symbolism. A late nineteenth-century antirealistic movement in theatre focused on the spiritual, symbolic, and mystical. (See the work of Maurice Maeterlinck.)

Synopsis. A summary of a play's action.

Tableau. A picture presented on stage by motionless actors.

Tag line. The final line before an exit, before the end of a scene, act, or play, or at the end of a joke.

Take stage. To achieve prominent emphasis or to command a scene or situation.

Teaser. Scenic mask (a drop) at the top of the stage.

Telescope. To overlap the reading of lines or execution of business.

Tempo. *See* **Pace.**

Tetralogy. A group of four plays, each complete, but which tell a larger story. (Such as Shakespeare's *Richard II, Henry IV, Part I, Henry IV, Part II* and *Henry V*.)

Text. The dialogue and stage directions of a play without reference to the underlying meaning.

Theatre, or Theater. (1) A seeing place; a hearing place. (2) A playhouse. (3) A body of plays.

Theme. The intellectual content in a play. Generally considered to be that idea basic to the thought of the play; the author's central idea. Usually the theme is expressed in one full sentence using an active verb: Pride taken to excess causes destruction. *See also* **Thought, or Idea.**

Thesis play. A play in which the dramatist argues a point of view, such as Ibsen's *A Doll's House.*

Thought, or Idea. The intellectual content of a play including its theme or central idea. One of the six key elements of a drama according to Aristotle.

Three unities. Unity of time, place, and action; a prescriptive theory of drama and play action constructed by Renaissance Italian and French critics; often *mistakenly* attributed to Aristotle.

Throw away. To deliberately underplay a line or business. Often used to place greater emphasis elsewhere.

Thrust stage. *See* **Arena.**

Tie-Off. *See* **Rail.**

Timing. The art of delivering words or performing movement at the effective instant.

Tirade. A long declamatory speech.

Top. To emphasize a line or an action to make it more emphatic than the preceding dialogue.

Tormentor. Scenic mask at the sides of the stage.

Tragedy. One of the two major forms of drama (the other is comedy). It involves suffering and frequently death and contains universal truths. For Aristotle, a tragedy was a dramatic imitation of action of high and serious importance.

Tragicomedy. A play that mixes tragic and comic material to a suitable balance, or that emphasizes tragedy but ends happily.

Tragic flaw. *See* **Hamartia.**

Transparency. A gauze theatre drop with a scene painted on it. *See also* **Scrim.**

Trap. Door or opening cut into the floor of the stage for access to the cellar or area below.

Trilogy. A unit of three works, for example, *Oresteia* by Aeschylus.

Trim. *See* **Rail.**

Tryout. *See* **Audition.**

Turn (Crisis, or Major crisis). The high point of suspense when a decision or action occurs that turns the rising action of a play toward an immediate or eventual climax and denouement (ending). The key turning point of a play.

Type. *See* **Play type.**

Type casting. A theatre practice in which performers are cast according to their age and physical and personality characteristics.

Underplay.   To deliberately restrict or de-emphasize emotion when acting. To de-emphasize delivery and stage action.

Understudy.   One who prepares a role normally performed by another in order to substitute in the role when necessary.

Upstage.   Away from the audience in a proscenium theatre.

Use.   The organization of the actor's instrument. Specifically the relationship of the head, neck, and torso with respect to alignment. "Good Use" reflects a position of mechanical advantage. *See* **Mechanical Advantage.**

Vaudeville.   (1) A stage entertainment of song, dance, acrobatics, skits, trained animal acts, and the like. (2) A series of specialty acts. (3) A short comic play or skit.

Vehicle.   A play especially suited to exhibit the acting skills of a performer or company.

Villain.   A type of character predisposed to evil or doing harm. (The villain is featured as a figure of evil in melodrama.)

Walk-on.   A small role without lines. *See* **Extra.**

Wardrobe mistress.   The person who collects, cares for, and stores costumes.

Weak.   Low attention value or weak position onstage.

Well-made play.   A play with suspense that relies on a tight, cleverly constructed plot, as in the plays of Scribe, Sardou, and Ibsen.

Willing suspension of disbelief.   Samuel Coleridge's phrase to identify the basis upon which "poetic faith" is operated in the theatre. An audience usually does this to appreciate and "believe" the play being enacted before it.

Wing.   The space offstage right or left of the acting area.

Wit.   (1) Knowledge, sagacity, good sense. (2) The sudden ingenious association of ideas and words, often amusing.

Zanni.   Comic characters (usually servants) in commedia dell'arte.

Ian Anderson
Bernhard and Williams
Photographers, Inc.
Robert Clayton
Susan Cook
Chris Davies
Steve Droes
Gerry Goodstein
Diane Gorodnitzki
Ken Howard
Louisa Johnson
Hank Kranzler
Beth Odle
Ruth Pearson
Alan Magayne-Roshak
Boyd D. Redington
David Rees
Dave Robbins
Martha Swope
Randy Tunnel
Andrew Tsubaki
Sandy Underwood
Terry Zinn/Zinn Unlimited